the
Living
Christ

the

Living
Christ

The Extraordinary Lives of
Today's Spiritual Heroes

Harold Fickett

Doubleday

New York   London   Toronto   Sydney   Auckland

PUBLISHED BY DOUBLEDAY
a division of Random House, Inc.
1540 Broadway, New York, New York 10036

DOUBLEDAY and the portrayal of an anchor with a dolphin are
trademarks of Doubleday, a division of Random House, Inc.

Book design by Donna Sinisgalli

Library of Congress Cataloging-in-Publication Data

Fickett, Harold.
The living Christ : the extraordinary lives of today's spiritual
heroes / by Harold Fickett.—1st ed.
p. cm.
Includes bibliographical references.
1. Christian biography. I. Title.

BR1700.3 .F53 2002
270.8'3'0922—dc21
[B]
2001042318

ISBN 0-385-49586-2
PRINTED IN THE UNITED STATES OF AMERICA

April 2002

Scripture quotations have been taken from the
following translations:
The Holy Bible, New International Version, copyright © 1973,
1978, 1984 by International Bible Society.
King James Version.
New Jerusalem Bible, copyright © 1985 by Dartman, Longman
& Todd, Ltd., and Doubleday & Company, Inc.
New American Bible, copyright © 1970 by the Confraternity of
Christian Doctrine, Washington, D.C.
New Revised Standard Version of the Bible, copyright © 1989 by
the Division of Christian Education of the National Council
of Churches.

First Edition
1   3   5   7   9   10   8   6   4   2

to

Luci, Philip, and Tim

Author's Note

This book is composed of many types of stories, all of which, I believe, are truthful. The profiles of Christian workers that take center stage in each chapter are based on personal interviews and public records, and I have drawn them as accurately as possible without infringing on others' privacy. The subsidiary stories about those involved in the various ministries often combine and conflate accounts from my principal subjects and information from my own research. Names, details, and elements of the secondary stories' dramatic actions have been changed to protect people's privacy and any and all confidences. The same is true with private individuals involved in the life histories of my profile candidates. Any resemblance to persons living or dead is entirely coincidental and unintentional in these instances. I have done this to be fair and for the sake of truths that are best understood by the reasoning imagination.

Contents

Introduction

A journalist often gains a close-up and even privileged view, whether that means ringside seats or access to famous people. It's a great job for anyone interested in expanding his own experience of the world. My work as a reporter on religious subjects—and in particular Christian ones—has introduced me to everything from a little old lady who spends her days charitably corresponding with violent criminals to a ballroom full of Hollywood celebrities raising their hands and shouting out in ecstatic prayer. I've had to ask the inevitable question—what's going on here?

Skepticism toward Christianity usually dominates in our culture. When a Christian shows up in a film, for example, mayhem or mendacity often ensues. This tendency may have reached its apotheosis in Martin Scorsese's remake of *Cape Fear* (1991). Before the nemesis, Max Cady (played by Robert De Niro), attempts the rape of Leigh Bowden (played by Jessica Lange), he shouts, "Ready to be born again, Mrs. Bowden?" The arts reflect the West's increasing secularization. Each Sunday more people attend Christian churches in China than in all of Western Europe.[1]

Occasionally, though, exemplars of the Christian faith enchant the public imagination. Beginning in 1971 with Malcolm Muggeridge's *Something Beautiful for God*, the whole world became fascinated with a tiny, stoop-shouldered woman in a white-and-blue habit named Mother Teresa. Similarly, when John Paul II visits a country—even if querulous articles have appeared beforehand—news organizations soon join the love-in. The preeminent evangelical Billy Graham has much the same effect, and the briefest mention of South Africa's Bishop Tutu always brings a smile.

What's at stake in this battle of image versus image?

As both a Christian believer and a reporter, I've found myself unable to address that question, although its presence lurked in the background of many assignments. It's a big question, of course, and the usual formats of writing and modes of discussion tend to skip off its surface.

Christianity does have a working theory about the question, one articulated first by Jesus himself and then by Saint Paul.

According to this theory, in the battle of image versus image the truth of Christianity itself is at stake; it rests in Jesus' claim to being the Messiah, the Christ. Everything comes down to Jesus' true identity.

The image-versus-image question turns into *Who was (and possibly still is) Jesus?* While scholars from skeptical Jesus Seminar members like Marcus Borg and John Dominic Crossan to champions of tradition like N. T. Wright pursue a "third quest" for the historical Jesus, microscopically examining the generative texts and traditions, there's a completely different strategy available for examining Jesus' character and claims. We can, as novelist Walker Percy once advised, "take a look around the neighborhood." We can examine the contemporary scene to see Jesus. "I will be with you always," he said to his disciples, "even to the end of the world."

Jesus' prophecy of continuing to abide among his followers meant far more than the usual elegiac memorializing. He didn't simply predict that his followers would remember him, and so he'd gain immortality. He gave us reason to believe that his very personhood—who he is—would invest itself in those who choose to follow

Jesus' way. His earthly life would continue *on this earth*, even after his death. He would be truly present in his followers.

In the rhapsodic post–Last Supper discourse in Saint John's gospel, Jesus says, referring first to his disciples and then to those who will come after them:

> My prayer is not for them alone. I pray also for those who will believe in me through their message, that all of them may be one, Father, just as you are in me and I am in you. May they also be in us so that the world may believe that you have sent me. I have given them the glory that you gave me, that they may be one as we are one: I in them and you in me. (John 17:20–23)

This passage serves, along with others like it, as the foundation of Christianity's belief in the Mystical Body of Christ. Jesus promises to abide with his followers, according to this teaching, to be present to them as God was present to Jesus, even to bestow on his followers God's own glory—which is called the *divinization* of humankind.

Of course, it's difficult to know everything this means. But it does lead to a working theory as to the importance of the Christian church's behavior. It should manifest the personhood of Christ and display his glory—his holiness, or perfect love. If the church fails to do this, if the church is not a true witness to the continuing life of its Christ, then the world has genuine reason to doubt not just the veracity but even the sanity of a man who would pray such a prayer.

Saint Paul, while admonishing one of the early Christian communities about poor behavior, reminds the community, "You are the Body of Christ." As Christ is present in each believer, so all believers taken together are united in the one Mystical Body. The essential identity of every Christian and of all Christians taken together is Christ himself—the *living* Christ.

The stakes of the image-versus-image question turn out to be, at least for the Christian, *ultimate*. "If Christ be not raised from the dead," Saint Paul writes, "we are of all people the most miserable." Jesus' resurrection in all its aspects, including his promise to invest himself in the lives of his followers, has to be real. The good apostle wanted no truck with a sham, and why would anyone?

The early Christians evidently thought they had good reason to believe that Christ was continuing to dwell with them: "I in them and you [Father] in me." Saint Paul also writes, "I am crucified with Christ, nevertheless I live, yet not I, but Christ lives in me." Paul declares that what Jesus promised can be an experienced reality.

Along the same lines, theologians have speculated that the reason Saint Luke divides his work on Christianity into two parts—first his gospel and then the Acts of the Apostles—is that he was aiming at a two-part biography: first a portrait of Jesus' earthly life and then an account of Jesus' resurrected life as seen in his followers. Certainly, the greatest evidence for the resurrection itself must be the extraordinary lives Jesus' handful of disciples went on to live after their Lord's death. After the gloom of the crucifixion, their lives were certainly reenergized by something, and they went to willing deaths professing that that something was a someone: the risen Christ.

The early church also claimed that Christ's continuing presence with them was no mere wispy remnant of his earthly life. The church's experience of Christ was his "fullness," in Saint Paul's view. The way in which Christ lives in every Christian, as he lived in Paul, keeps filling out our understanding of Christ's identity. This is why the lives of the saints have always played a role in Christianity. Their experience opens up, renews, and comments on who the living Christ is and how Christ works. For the Christian faith is not essentially a set of teachings—it wasn't that to the Jesus we meet with in the gospels. He teaches to explain what he's *doing*. Jesus' ministry is a divine action of reconciliation—bringing God to humankind—that begins with his earthly life and continues through the Mystical Body. "I came that you might have life and have it more abundantly," Jesus says. "I am the way, the truth, and the life. No one comes to the Father but by me."

These ideas, so foundational to my faith, have insinuated their presence in situation after situation I've dealt with as a writer, begging to be more fully addressed. I've longed to do exactly what I've launched out into here: take Christianity's working theory about the living Christ and put it to the test. Is it possible to see Christ in the world today? Would it even be possible to draw a portrait of the living Christ through contemporary stories of his followers?

With this idea came tremendous excitement. My past experience indicated there was an untold host of stories about people doing Christ's work in the world in the most varied, dramatic, and intriguing circumstances. I guessed these people and their stories could show me the living Christ as I had never seen him before.

I began doing spadework, thinking through what I knew of the various aspects of Jesus' personality as we see him in the gospels. I became convinced that the most illuminating way of looking at Jesus centered in the roles he played in the lives of those who met him, whether followers or opponents. If Jesus came not so much to deliver a teaching as to inaugurate the final reconciliation of humankind to God, then he might best be understood through his different behaviors toward that one unifying end. I began thinking of Jesus in these various roles: Jesus the wayfarer; Jesus the healer; Jesus the man of prayer, and so forth. I thought of contemporary people and stories and situations where the living Christ might be playing these same roles—the Lord of the Dance kicking up his heels. I started contacting people about whose stories deserved to be told, and then the people themselves.

I also thought, of course, about the difficulties this inquiry would inevitably present. The preeminent one quickly came to mind: the way even the best people have their foibles and weaknesses, whether out in the open or secretly.

The already redeemed and yet still sinful character of the believer is at the core of the Christian tradition. No one believed more strongly in Christ's indwelling presence than Saint Paul, who nonetheless confesses, "The good I want to do, I do not." He teaches that the believer, while in the process of being conformed into the image of Christ, remains, in himself or herself, a fallen creature. "In Christ we are a new creation," he affirms, but in our "old nature," our broken humanity, we are often scallywags or worse.

The people I contacted were candid about their frailties as well. One quickly wrote back to remind me, "We are all very wounded healers," and, "As Cardinal Newman says, in the spiritual life 'we fall to rise.' " My subjects were conscious—sometimes overly conscious—of how their own debilities might come through far more clearly than any reflection of Christ's character.

The saints have always understood that the presence of Christ in their lives accounts for the work they accomplish in Christ's name. It's the love of God within us that returns God's love through the redemptive action we take. Saint Augustine writes:

> Indeed we also work, but we are only collaborating with God who works, for his mercy has gone before us. It has gone before us so that we may be healed, and follows us so that we may be called, and follows us so that we may be glorified; it goes before us so that we may live devoutly, and follows us so that we may always live with God: *for without him we can do nothing* [my emphasis].[2]

In the same spirit, St. Thérèse of Lisieux prays:

> In the evening of this life, I shall appear before you with empty hands, for I do not ask you, Lord, to count my works. All our justice is blemished in your eyes. I wish, then, to be clothed in your own justice and to receive from your love the eternal possession of yourself.[3]

I assured my subjects—as I assure the reader—that I wasn't looking for perfect people. Whatever holiness exists in this world belongs to Christ, Christians believe. The lives of those who open themselves to his holiness may sometimes become so transparent, though, that they allow us a glimpse of their inspiration.

So I began traveling far and wide—from South Carolina to Mexico City to the California coast, Thailand, Rome, and elsewhere—interviewing people and researching situations where Jesus might be at work. I found numbers of extraordinary people engaged in Christlike work, and quickly became aware that the recipients of this work were a big part of the story. I ended up with profiles of remarkable contemporary believers in the context of their work with other people. To tell these stories I have used fictional techniques, reportage, and other narrative devices, attempting in each instance to render the world of the story as well as its action. The stories I found opened up the gospels anew for me and caused me to reflect, as I do here after each major narrative, about what we see of Jesus in the scriptures. A portrait of the living Christ began emerging.

In South Carolina
The Wayfarer

Throughout his public ministry, Jesus was a wayfarer, a traveler by foot. Across the Galilean hills to Cana and Nazareth, down through Samaria, and along the banks of the Jordan to the holy mountain of Jerusalem, Jesus and the disciples lived out their picaresque, if tragic, adventure.

So I thought I would look for Jesus first where he was most often to be found—on the road.

I've always wondered about the life of long-haul truckers. I suspect that the romance of the trucking life, expressed in such country-and-western songs as "Six Days on the Road" and "Convoy," draws its inspiration from the obscure depths of our collective memory—all the way down to our nomadic wanderings, the time when the patriarch Abraham departed into a far country. The trucking life, like joining the merchant marine, provides a working-class means of participating in a nearly universal longing: whether by running away to join the circus or hitching up with a rock 'n' roll tour or sailing the seven seas, the vagabond in all of us wants *to go.* As William Carlos Williams remarked, "Americans believe in the green light."

I started investigating the various Christian ministries that work with truck drivers and eventually found a truckers' chaplain in South Carolina, Ted Keller, who opened up the truckers' world and taught me about the specific character of Jesus' wayfaring.

Chaplain Ted told me the following story about two people he had recently encountered, and then something of his own life.

✤

Troy could hear every cylinder ping in the old rigs before onboard computers, for the sake of fuel economy, put a stop to black exhaust between gearshifts and double-clutching gave way to automatics smoother than a Chevrolet. That was before the DOT (Department of Transportation) came along with its thicker-than-a-Bible operating manual and urine tests, which turned his own rolling twenty-year party into hard labor. No time off for good behavior, much less fun. Oh no! Once he had been king of the road and its pleasures. "Hey, babe, got to keep moving. It's my job." (His CB handle is Poon Dog.) The life kept him free, even with a wife and kids. Now that's all gone, including the wife and kids, who, all grown up, find him embarrassing. Except maybe for Angela.

He is driving one of the new Peterbilts owned by a small company in his hometown, Bellevue, Washington, hauling eighty thousand pounds of machine equipment from Gary down to Columbia, South Carolina, on a short December day, when a squalling storm is coating the overpass approaches with black ice. (A driver can slip and slide on that stuff right into his coffin.) The dormant grasses on the rolling hills outside of Knoxville are stiff with tracings of snow, the bare tree limbs the color of ash, and the evergreens sagging and stunted as the sandier soil of South Carolina draws nearer. Spinouts litter Interstate 75. Everyone on the radio yammers about the oil truck he passed about ten miles back, jackknifed into a culvert. He should have stopped, but he has five clear hours left in his logbook and he doesn't make any money playing the Samaritan.

He is back to being a mileage slave after once owner-operating. Twenty-seven cents a mile to starve; twenty-eight to eat; twenty-nine and above to flourish or something like it. Thirty-five years of haz-mat,* tankers, low-boys†—name it. All to yearn for twenty-nine cents a mile and a bit more to feed the video poker machines.

Those refrigerated loads of beef had to be about the worst. They swung the box around behind him like he was a gnat the cow meant to switch. He remembers loading up close to the slaughtering yards in bone-dry western Kansas, heading to Denver and across the continental divide on I-80, all the while dreading those one-lane snaking curves before Aspen. He drove those runs in his own Freightliner, smaller and more compact than this rig, but all guts and heart. The Freightliner's big solenoid starter, the size of a seawater fishing plug, always fired her right up, while the Peterbilt is so rocket-scientist wired he never turns it off.

The Peterbilt does have a double cab, which he needs now that he is all the way back to living out of the truck. Everywhere to go and nowhere. His married daughter in Bellevue, Angela, still pretends to be glad to see him, although he has to bear her born-again husband, Dan, and his innuendo about how his daughter needs God so much because of her lousy upbringing. Angela is much like her great-grandmother (the one who tried to shove religion down his own throat): the praying, the sitting down to meals, the polite talking, even to their kids, like they are training them for the diplomatic corps. (How he hated all that when he was a kid.) Within minutes he wants to vamoose and start eating concrete again.

He knows the road will have to lead back somewhere—or to the end of driving, at least. At fifty-nine he has only a few years left, ten max. He'll have to save the whole time to put himself in a trailer on a piece of country property, where social security and odd jobs can sustain him. Fat chance of saving anything. His last pipe dream—to live in an aluminum box.

He is in one of those moods today when a skull-cleaving headache is so close it's already fitting itself to his head like Darth

---

* Hazardous Materials
† low-lying trailers, used especially for moving wide loads.

Vader's mask. He doesn't want to listen to music or yak on the CB; he doesn't want to care about the lousy weather or the people being stranded. He can't even bring himself to do the isometric exercises that might loosen up the wrenching pain in his lower back.

He hates when he gets this way and can't let go of everything and just drive—feel a little bit of the old road magic. There isn't any of that today. Only the years and what they have led to. What's zero plus zero? his son, Freddie, once asked. Who says education isn't relevant?

He's almost rooting for the black ice. A quick meeting with an overpass stanchion would blow the cab clean apart and turn the machine equipment behind him into shrapnel. Shove the accelerator down and let it ride. What did it matter? There are all kinds of temptations in life, he's found, although he never thought death would look sexy.

Chaplain Ted Keller and Jimmy B. are talking over an early dinner of catfish and hush puppies. The tall cook, Nelson, his chef's hat pinned to his cornrows, busies himself behind the bin-filled serving counter, and there isn't anyone else in the blank, white-walled restaurant side of the truck stop to hear them.

"I need to find that boom box if I can, Jimmy B.," Chaplain Ted says.

"Steve did it. I'm sure he the one. He was talking so loud," Jimmy B. says, "shouting about how you all is racists and that terrible white people music you play. He hate that music. He can't sleep in his truck. Not with that Enoch music."

" 'Enoch'?"

"Sound like."

" 'Eunuch'?"

"Maybe. He mean to get you back. Do something terrible. That's what he say."

"Last week?"

Jimmy B. nods yes.

Chaplain Ted stares across at Jimmy B.'s round, shallow, amber eyes, trying to judge how much the afflicted young man, in his open-mouthed excitement, is exaggerating. Most robberies are committed by people close at hand, though. It makes sense.

"But you haven't seen him with the boom box, Jimmy B.?"

"Not that one. He has one, though. A big, big one."

"Don't say anything about this, okay, Jimmy B.?"

"Steve probably sell that other one."

"You won't say anything until I find out?"

"Everyone in here talking about it, Chaplain Ted. They all heard it. Steve standing in the middle of the store, shouting stuff."

"Don't tell Steve you talked to me, Jimmy B. I don't want you to get hurt."

At this, Jimmy B.'s head turtles back into his shoulders, his soft jowls balloon, and his narrow-spaced eyes pinch so close together they look crossed.

"Steve's not violent," Chaplain Ted says, "not really. Just don't get yourself into any trouble you don't need to."

Jimmy B. looks suspiciously toward the door and forms his lips like a goldfish sucking water.

"Are you coming to the service tomorrow?"

"If I be there," Jimmy B. says.

"Can't argue with that. You take care of yourself whatever you do, hear?"

After saying good-bye and paying the tab, Chaplain Ted crosses the parking lot from the United Truck Stop building to the Whispering Hope Chapel, an aluminum trailer permanently set up where the truck stop's property fronts the road. The chapel has a wooden front porch, a red-lettered sign with *John 3:16* at one end, and a neon outlined cross, which Chaplain Ted switches on, the late afternoon being so dark. The cross buzzes for a few seconds before snapping into a steady glow. Beside the John 3:16 sign sits Steve's van, his home when he's not driving. To the left of the van, a seasonal fireworks stand flanks the chapel, cracker exploding lettering arcing over its boarded windows.

"It must have been Steve," Chaplain Ted says to his assistant,

Harlan, and one of his best volunteers, Libby, as he comes through the door. "I was over there talking to Jimmy B. Steve was shouting about how we're all racists and he hates our music." Ted looks down and his usual tricornered grin shrivels into a sour pucker. "I guess he really meant the part about the music."

"He parks his van there because of us!" Harlan exclaims, a grandfatherly croak in his voice.

"Are you going to contact the police?" Libby asks.

"No, I think we're going to take him out to breakfast. You know what I mean, Harlan?"

The two men look at each other and nod. Ted's eyes glint, catching the chapel's hard fluorescent light.

"Out to breakfast?" Libby asks, her dark-haired head forward, her eyes popping.

Chaplain Ted gets a look on his face like a bullfrog that's already snapped up its next meal without having swallowed yet. "Sure. We'll take him to breakfast. Tell him a story about our boom box getting stolen. Ask him if he knows anything about it."

"Let him know that we know," Harlan says, his voice thumping the bass line.

"And what we could do if we wanted," Ted says. "He'll probably bring it back that way."

"I'm not sure I like the idea of someone that close who is messing with us," Libby says.

"The man's under spiritual conviction," Chaplain Ted says. "You don't park your home right next to a chapel and start stealing stuff unless the Lord and the devil are fighting over you big time. Let's give the Lord a chance to work."

Libby still looks like a reproving mother.

"In the meantime, Harlan, we'd better go buy another boom box. You want to come with me?"

Harlan nods.

"You know what he called our music?" Chaplain Ted asks. " 'Enoch music'—that's what Jimmy reported. I think he meant 'eunuch.' Why would he call it that?"

"Enoch walked with God," Harlan says.

"And the Lord took him," Libby finishes.

After dropping the machine parts at a dock outside Columbia, Troy huddles in a driver's booth at the Columbia 20 Truck Stop's restaurant. He has calls in to a dozen dispatchers. It's Friday night. He'll probably be here for the weekend. But with the weather, there's an outside chance a hot load will need to be rescued. Anyway, he wants to make sure he's gone first thing Monday morning.

After half an hour, the phone rings. "I've got a great run for you," the dispatcher says. "You'll be going to Cincinnati. You know how easy the turnarounds are in that area."

"How much?"

"A dime. Ten K."

"Okay, I'll run the numbers and call you back."

"I've got another driver . . ."

"Yeah, I know, there's always another driver. Just give me five minutes, okay?"

Troy takes out his calculator. So much for fuel costs, state fees, road taxes, the owner's share—all straight off the top. His take works out to twenty-four cents per mile. There's no way he can do that.

He calls back the dispatcher and tells him he'll need substantially more. "With this weather, I'm one of the few drivers . . ."

"Sorry, can't negotiate on this one." The dispatcher hangs up before Troy can get another word out.

He's had this happen before, of course, many times. Sometimes the dispatchers can negotiate, as often not. It's always like romancing a hooker, coy eagerness followed by purse-snapping departures. Wham, bam. There's a hot load for you, but who's doing the delivering?

The waitress appears with her coffeepot. "You lose your best friend, hon?" she asks.

"A load that's leaving without me," he says.

"Same-old same old, huh?" She's almost a blonde and has terrific legs. The truck stop Bettys often have decks and look appealingly snug, if a little ample, in their jeans—but they are the kind who are attracted to beefy guys and usually have a complementary heft, especially south of the equator. Legs like hers, tapered ankles, teardrop-toned calves with an elegant bevel along the shin leading into strong, narrow thighs, that's rare. She fills his coffee cup again.

"Yeah, it's always the same," he says. "I was just thinking how dispatchers are like hookers."

She gives him a look and starts to turn away.

"I mean, they're not really interested in your problems."

"There's a lot of that," she says. She doesn't walk off.

"I guess I'll be here all weekend. You're going to get sick of me."

"You look like you've learned how to spend your time. How long have you been driving?"

"Oh, I'm a youngster," he says.

"As old as you feel, Mister Buddy?"

"Depends on what you're feeling."

"Yeah," she says slowly, and pushes out her cheek. "Stay out of trouble, then." She begins walking away.

"Hey, Miss . . . Diane," he says, making use of her name tag.

She looks back, up from under her eyebrows, warning him.

"I might want a piece of pie later," he said.

"I'll check back with you. Make your other calls. You'll feel better."

Troy places a few more calls. He watches his fellow truckers come in. After driving so long, he'll often see people he's met. No one this evening, though.

Soon enough he wants that pie, if only to stave off the boredom, and he watches Diane walk to the pick-up station for an order, deliver it, write out a check, turn to another customer. When she looks up from taking the new order, he waves at her. She goes back to the pick-up station to put in the order first, as if she hasn't seen him. When she turns back to the U-shaped counter from the station, he waves and mouths "Diane," the name projecting as a whisper.

She comes over to his booth. "You want that pie now?"

"What kind do you have?"

She takes a breath, winding up for the list.

"I bet you have rhubarb," he says.

"No, we don't," she says.

"Right," he says. "Rhubarb is a summer thing, isn't it? But this is the South, so I'll bet you've got chocolate. Chocolate pie grows year round in the South." He gives her his best look, waiting, expectant, cheerful, patient, and dead-on interested.

"You know, you're acting sweet, but I bet you aren't all that."

"Oh, I'm a sugar daddy."

"Yeah, well they give me cavities."

"Not my kind."

"Don't go getting carried away with yourself now, Mister Buddy."

Is that a blush he sees? "I'd carry you anywhere you'd want to go. That's what they say in the South, isn't it? 'Carry' for taking someone somewhere."

"Yeah, like on a real ride, I'll bet. Listen, I've got someone who already carries me fine."

"Someone?"

"A serious someone."

"Is he around?"

"Is he *around*?"

"On Friday night, that can count for a lot."

"Whoa, sugar. It don't count for that much. Not nearly. You'll be lucky if I bring you back that pie." She turns away, then swivels back around. "Take the hint now. I'm working a double shift and you'll starve otherwise. Got it?"

He throws up his hands in surrender.

A little after 6 P.M., Chaplain Ted and his assistant, Harlan, are looking at the boom boxes in the Gold Plate Pawn Shop. Ted notices one, a Sony, that's been cleaned up but still shows chalky markings near the volume control. Ted spilled Wite-Out on their stolen boom box at the same spot. He reaches around to the back and gives the electrical cord a tug. It's firmly attached. He looks at the cord closely and notices it's new white-and-black braid.

Chaplain Ted turns around to Jetu Sangaree, the shop's owner, who is behind the counter, a fleshy Indian in his thirties whose square head is topped by thinning jet black hair that pops up like quills from a low hairline. "Jetu," Chaplain Ted calls, "you replace this electrical cord on the Sony?"

"Oh, I put a lot of work into that one. It's shipshape now. Totally reconditioned."

"Had an old black cord when it came in that wouldn't stay connected half the time, didn't it?" Chaplain Ted asks.

"I had it out for a few days like that. But now it's A-one. Topnotch."

"I haven't been in here looking at these before, Jetu," Chaplain Ted says, walking over to the counter. "I know because it's the chapel's boom box. We had it stolen out of there."

The owner stares at Ted and Ted's look holds steady.

The next moment, the owner throws up his hands, hangs his head. "People selling stolen goods. The great, great evil of a pawnshop. I warn them. I do what I can. You never know what these people are selling you."

"You remember who brought it in?"

His reply doesn't miss a beat. "Oh, I could not remember. Always people coming in. Sometimes I am here, sometimes the boy."

"A black guy, African-American, usually wears a dashiki on his shaved head and kind of pulls his right leg along after him a bit? His complexion's like coffee with cream in it, and he has rheumy eyes, all yellowed like—too much drinking."

The Indian looks quickly back and forth from Ted to Harlan and back again.

"His name's Steve. Talks a lot about being a Moslem. Despite the drinking."

"I know many such men. He may come in here, yes. But I could not say about the Sony. I don't have a loan tag on it. An outright sale. Maybe the boy took it in. I could not say."

"Don't you think you should give it back to us?" Harlan asks. "Given the circumstances." Harlan is standing up straight and tall and thin. He looks more like a retired bird colonel than a preacher, even in a farmer's dungarees.

"How could I charge you? If this is yours. You are sure it's yours, then? You are sure?"

"Sure enough," Chaplain Ted says, and grins and tilts his head and holds still in that attitude for a long moment with such a fanciful air that he looks like a musical actor hitting the song cue, waiting for the band.

"Oh, I would not charge you. I would not think of it," the pawn-shop owner says. "But the new cord. The cleanup." He extends his hands, palms up. "You see how much work I have put in. We have both been taken advantage of. This is not good situation. Not good. Not good at all."

"What about us paying you for the reconditioning?" Ted asks. "We could do that."

"It's only that I have done so much work. Spent my time. This place has so much work connected with it. You'd be very much surprised."

"We'd be pleased to do that. You did a nice job on that cord, Jetu. A real nice job." Chaplain Ted looks to Harlan, whose expression curdles along the jaw as he looks away from another instance of the ever-enthusiastic Ted dispensing grace with both hands.

A little after ten o'clock, Troy makes a few last calls and O-fers, blanks. Nothing to do now but wait here through the weekend. Everyone has his beeper number. He can only hope a call comes through that will see him off Monday.

Troy walks from the restaurant into the trucker's lounge for a dose of TV noise. A young girl's huddled in the front row of the theater seats, a blanket around her, a canvas bag by her feet. He edges closer, no more than five feet off, where he can see across her left shoulder. She's asleep or pretending to be. She has honey blond hair that swarms in curling strands. Fair complexioned, she wears lots of (smudged) black eyeliner and what looks like the remnants of apple green lipstick, outlined with a plum color. Her left ear, nose, and bottom lip are studded, the ear so many times along its tender rim that it looks brightly barnacled. Sunny blond freckles swim under her makeup, which is slowly receding off her cheeks, leaving lines like high-water marks on a beach's shingle.

Baby driver, what brought you here? Most likely she's a drop-off, a kid who hitched a ride—maybe running away from Mom—and now finds herself nowhere. She's the age of Angela's daughter Melinda, sixteen or seventeen going on criminal. "So much like her grandfather," his pious son-in-law never fails to add. God, he hates that weasel, even if he's right about Melinda, who does have her grandfather's desire to go and his carelessness about how. There's something magnificent about that girl, really. By far the best of the Callahans at prayer.

He's stayed hovering too long, because the drop-off looks up at him, her speckled hazel eyes crystalline bright. "Hi, mister. How're you?"

He nods at her, blows out a long breath—oh boy.

She shakes her swarming curls and smoothes her hair back as the web of sleep drops away. All innocence, she looks back up at him and asks, "You want a date?"

Does he want a date? She's seventeen max! "Are you hooking?" he asks, too shocked to deny his curiosity.

"Well, I'll be your girlfriend if you're going toward Florida. Or most anywhere. I'm going to have to get out of here soon enough."

There's Georgia in her voice and a terrible hopefulness. Here I am, Miss Peach Pie. Kindness à la mode, no extra charge.

"*My* girlfriend?"

"You look all right. Wiry. Muscles like Popeye under that warm-up jacket, I imagine. You probably still roll the sleeves of your T-shirts in the summertime."

It makes him uneasy that she's taken in his body.

"See, mister, I'm from Meeks, Georgia." Her voice goes up as if it's a question, and plunges from there into her whole story. "I woke

up one morning inside this café, because I had gone out the night before with one of my boyfriend's buyers and he must have . . ."

He starts shaking his head and backing way. No part of that.
Sorry, little schoolgirl. No way. But even as he's excusing himself, he
notices how her sea foam green car coat falls away from her sweater-
straining breasts and he's swallowing his spit as he weaves through
the TV lounge toward the outside air. Do you want a date?

He goes outside to smoke a cigarette. He's into his second when
he looks around and sees through the plate glass window that Miss
Peach Pie is sneaking looks his way, giggling to herself, as she fingers the Christmas cards in a standing rack. Does she take him for
harmless? That could be the only attraction. The back of his neck
starts to burn. Maybe she's only amusing herself now, giving the old
geezer a hard time. *You're acting sweet but I bet you're not all that.*
And how could she be, Troy thinks, having taken to prostitution at
her age? She has enough of a rough edge to survive, probably. He can
stop worrying—and thinking—about her.

When he glances toward the card rack again, she's gone.

It's cold out here in the December air, and his breath plumes
white. Lots of trucks are still grinding in, both here and across the
street, where there's another truck stop, United, that black drivers
mostly frequent. He notices a neon red cross against the cloud-low-
ered night sky. He guesses there must be one of those little truck stop
chapels there, usually a box that's been set up permanently. Once
around Milton, Pennsylvania, he heard shouting busting out of a
chapel like that. At first he thought there must a fire in there and
people were burning alive or something. Then he figured out it was
only Pentecostals, speaking in tongues. His grandmother did some of
that too. But he hadn't heard it himself, and it scared the heck out of
him, at first.

As he's finishing his second smoke, two young white guys in
watch caps and baggy prison-style pants approach. The gas pumps
are straight out from him, but Troy cannot remember a car driving
up or anyone parking just then. The two come straight toward him
and don't veer.

"Hey, Pops," says the shorter one, "you got the time?"

"Almost eleven."

"Pretty cold out here."

They don't move along but stand right in front of him, meaning to have a talk.

"What's on your mind?" Even if they think he's carrying a ton of cash, would they mug him right in front of the truck stop?

"We've got some candy," the short one says, touching his nose. Despite the prison rags, he's pure preppy: almost white hair up under his watch cap, sky blue eyes, baby skin. "Wondered if you wanted any. A lot of drivers have a sweet tooth."

"With the urine tests? All the candy these days is for middle-class punks like you."

"Must be tough not to party," says the taller. He's got thick rusty brows, a long horse nose with large, black nostrils, and moles scattered over his face. He looks like a Middle Eastern kid ready for a ji-had. The preppy's muscle.

Troy glares at them.

"Okay, Pops, but you know, you got a bag, even the young chicks will come around."

They go right into the truck stop then, and he thinks about the young chick who is already around. Made for each other?

Not knowing what to do, where to go, he lights another cigarette, although he doesn't want one. *Booze is legal.* The thought finally comes to him like a revelation. Sure, he's fought against going into the bag for years, but right now he only wants to be where booze takes him—straight out of his mind. Young hookers and punks selling coke—all on top of this skull-cleaving day. Why *didn't* the black ice get him?

He keeps a bottle of scotch in the truck, just in case. So well hidden in the paneling around his cot that he rarely thinks of it. He heads off to the back of the lot double-time for warmth.

He unlocks the Peterbilt, grasps the steering wheel, and hauls himself up and around the driver's seat. He steps back to his cab bower, a poster of Marilyn with her white skirt billowing up from *The Seven Year Itch* on the back wall.

Would you like a martini? the movie's lead, Tom Ewell, asks her.

Oh yes, a nice big tall one, Marilyn coos.

He sits on the cot and takes out the bottle from its hiding place. He's more than ready for *a nice big tall one.* He pours the scotch into a clean coffee mug and takes a big swallow. Those AA people are crazy, he thinks; that's the best stuff that's ever been invented. He's on to the next drink before the burn from the first one cools.

He could watch TV, a fourteen-incher that's mounted on the cab's right-hand wall. But he'd rather check his favorite porn site, Pussy Galore. As his laptop dials up, he wonders if this is going to lead to 900-number phone calls on his cell phone—a vice that runs his credit card through the roof. But all bets are off now. It's been so long since he's gotten drunk and had a good time! What with the urine tests and AIDS and his getting older, getting into a decent amount of trouble has become virtually an achievement. He's not going to be stupid. He's just going to get wasted in his cab and in- dulge his fantasies. He'll pay for it all with his credit card and a headache, and the universe and he will call it even.

His laptop browser finds the site. He enters his log-in number, and he's welcomed by a black background home page with red hy- perlinks. He likes the James Bond setups for the kinky stuff, espe- cially the pictures found at the links *I came back to my room, and there in my bed* and *Shaken not stirred.* He keeps drinking and click- ing through the photos. Why is it that as good as one picture may be, he's always impatient to get to the next?

As he's navigating, a pop-up blooms with a phone sex ad. There's a blond girl in profile, her lips parted. She's a dead ringer for the girl in the lounge, swarming curls and all. Could she be the same kid? "Talk to me," she begs.

He shuts the pop-up down and takes a drink. Did the dealers find Miss Peach Pie? he wonders. He suddenly feels protective of her. And he can't quite forget her car coat sliding back from her breasts. He looks back at the porn site. He sees the familiar link to the *Teen Girls Galore!* section. Video streaming there, the works.

He shuts down the site. Maybe he should talk to her, find out what her story is. He puts the bottle back in its place, and as he's stumbling around the cab, he realizes he hasn't taken off his Seattle Mariners warm-up jacket. He's all ready to go.

Troy gets down out of the truck again, locks it, and starts walking back toward the truck stop building. He's surprised to see that the two young punks who were selling coke are still hanging out in front of the restaurant. Now that he's loggy with drink, a little blow seems like a much better idea. The second revelation of the night comes to him: he'll buy the crank and give the girl a ride. She didn't think he was so bad—why should *he*? His heart's racing. An adrenaline rush hits him as if he's already had a snort. She approached him, after all. Who's ever going to know? As he walks, his options seem to open up with such interior force that the world around him stretches weirdly wider, and the familiar truck stop appears new.

He's about to gesture toward the kids with the coke when Diane, the waitress, walks out the restaurant door. He looks at her and instead of glancing away, she grasps the lapels of her leopard-collar white coat and stops.

"Hey," she says.

Troy stops and then catches himself from lurching forward as the momentum of where he was going runs up his back.

"You okay? You look poleaxed."

"What?"

"I didn't mean to treat you *that* bad."

"Oh,"

"*Oh?* What's with you, Mister Buddy?"

"You didn't. You didn't treat me that bad."

"Catch up in the conversation. What's going on with you?"

"Nothing."

"Nothing?"

Troy stops and breathes in the cold December air that ignites the scotch vapors still lying deep in his throat. He looks up and sees a gauze of cloud hiding the moon. The crazy adrenaline is leaving him, for which he's grateful. "I enjoyed that chocolate pie," he says, hearing himself talk like a normal person.

"Listen," Diane says, "when someone tells you she's another man's girl, sometimes she means that. That's what you've got to understand."

What's he stirred in her? He hears a big truck pulling in with a grinding of low gears and a spitting explosion of brakes and looks off to the left to see whether, as it sounds to him, it's a Freightliner. His eyes once again catch on the neon red cross across the street. He wonders if they are singing and hollering like in Pennsylvania.

"What are you looking at?"

"You know about that chapel over there?"

"Sure. Good people."

"They are?"

"They're open all night most weekends." She looks around her. "Your interests always change this fast?"

"What?"

"I'll catch you on the next trip. Be good, Mister Buddy."

Should he go over there? Better there than where he was headed, he supposes, and he needs to shake what he was about to do while he has a chance. A stiff antidote, but he needs the strongest thing he can find.

He walks the three hundred yards across from Columbia 20 to the United Truck Stop and he's moving in another dream now. One he understands even less. He sees that the lights are on in the aluminum-trailer chapel. Through the chapel's windows he can see the head of a sandy-haired middle-aged man with gray-colored glasses and a taller, older, more rawboned gentleman. Troy walks up the carpeted ramp and enters.

"Hey there, fellow? Are you a driver?"

He nods.

"I'm Chaplain Ted and this is Harlan. Sit down. What can we do for you?"

He makes so little of these two and this whole scene that he's willing to say just about anything. He blurts out his condition as simply as can be. "I'm lonely."

"How long you been driving?" Chaplain Ted asks.

"Twenty-five years and more."

"Well, that can make for a lot of loneliness."

"Yeah, I'm so lonely, I'm willing to talk to you." He looks up at where he is. "No offense."

Ted and Harlan exchange a keen look. "Would you believe me," Ted asks, "if I told you I had an answer to your problem?"

"To loneliness?"

"Yes, an answer to loneliness."

"You mean going to church and all that?"

"No, not exactly. The answer to loneliness is *hope*."

This surprises Troy so much that he sits calmly for the next thirty minutes while Chaplain Ted and Harlan take turns explaining the Christian faith.

Jesus traveled the countryside when he lived, too, Chaplain Ted and Harlan tell him. Jesus was misunderstood and abandoned by his friends, but he was never lonely, except maybe once, when even God deserted him. But Jesus was willing to suffer the worst rejection of all so we'd always have his companionship. And now that we've got it, we've got *hope*.

An hour after Troy leaves the chapel, he's back with the young prostitute, Miss Peach Pie, in tow. When he approached her the second time, she opened her speckled hazel eyes and asked, just as brightly, "You ready for that date now?"

He told her he had something better for her, put his hand under her elbow, and escorted her out of the lounge. He kept talking about how he didn't mean to hurt her, how he was going to take her to people who could really help her, how he'd give her money for nothing if she needed that, rambling on all the way over to the chapel so she wouldn't bolt.

Once inside, he said simply, "She needs what I just got. Tell her. Tell her about hope."

"What's your story now, miss?" Chaplain Ted asked.

This would be good.

She had been busting to tell it, and now she got her chance. "Well, I got dropped off here by a trucker"—again, with the rise of a question. "I was like his girlfriend for about a week, after I was another one's. That one lasted about a week, too. Maybe a little longer—I don't know, my days started getting mixed up. Anyway, the whole thing started when I woke up in an all-night café, just an old coffee shop, really, in downtown Meeks, Georgia. I was out on this date the night before, because my boyfriend asked me to accompany a customer. He's not bad, really, you know, but he sells *drugs*, and this time he wanted me to go with this man. Anyway, I guess I fell asleep in the café, and I didn't want to go home, because Momma didn't know where I'd been or how much school I'd been missing, and I didn't want to go back to my boyfriend, because I was still holding the drugs—the ones I was supposed to be delivering the night before. I guess I didn't explain that. So, anyway, a trucker came along and asked me, did I want a ride to Florida? And I thought that might be fine, because Jennifer Fulton, a girl I'd been friends with since we were little, just moved there, and maybe if I went there, I could call Momma and she'd want me to come back so much, she wouldn't be too mad. You see? I didn't want to go back to Momma right away, so I thought I'd take this ride to Florida, and then, I don't know, things just happened." She looked down and squeezed her black-eyeliner-smudged eyes tight. "I've been sleeping with a good number of men."

"Miss?"

"I'm sure you think that's bad, don't you?"

"Miss, what's your name?"

"Chrissy."

"Well, Chrissy, I bet your momma would like us to give her a call."

"She might, but she might be awful mad, too."

"How's this for a plan? Let's call Momma and let you talk to her, and then we'll talk to you about the *hope* Troy mentioned. Harlan will get you a hotel room while we're talking. One you can use all by yourself. Would you like that? Then we'll see about getting you back to Momma in Meeks, Georgia. Would you like that?"

"I sure would. I been meaning to get back to her all the time. I really have. But things happened, as I said. The problem is, I don't have any money. And I don't know what Momma's going to say about all this."

"We have a fund for emergencies like yours, Chrissy. Let's go make that call now."

Mom is glad to hear from Chrissy, and she is soon home, her interests so much changed that she helps her mother out with a Sunday school class.

Troy leaves Columbia on Tuesday, after a long weekend of talking about his newfound faith with Chaplain Ted and Harlan and Chaplain Ted's wife, Tammy, and Jim and Dixie and Dan and Annette and Libby and the whole pack of them attached to that place. Heading up I-75, on his way to Ohio with a load of furniture, he has all these stupid gospel tunes that his grandmother taught him going through his head and he doesn't care; in fact, he *likes* it. How in the world has he found Angela's God?

The first thing all these people told him was that the devil would come and tell him that saying a "little old prayer in a trailer chapel" couldn't mean much—couldn't change his life. But he knows his life has been changed. The moment he prayed the prayer—to accept Christ, become a genuine, believing Christian—something hit him that at first made him think he was having a heart attack; then it became this unbelievable feeling of peace and love, like he was sunbathing on God's own personal beach. Floating on his back in the Jordan River, maybe—not a care. He could say that for sure, *not a care.*

If he can't get a quick load for the Pacific Northwest in Ohio, Troy thinks, he'll deadhead back home, because he wants to see Angela and even her holier-than-thou husband. He wants to tell her it's real—he knows it now, too. And he wants to tell the husband to cut it out. The Jordan River isn't embalming fluid.

Troy feels alive now, really alive for the first time in years. He still knows his days on the road are coming to an end. He suspects his journey will end in a little trailer someplace in the country outside of Bellevue, where he'll grow increasingly crotchety, lose his teeth and very likely his memory—given the family's history. He'll have to depend on Angela to stick him in a nursing home and then a box when the time comes.

Still, he's capable of a few things now—he's sure of it—that he once thought beyond him. He feels he has the power to save for that trailer, for one. Give up his porn subscription for another. And he can show Angela, and maybe even her brother, Freddie, and sister, Dana, that he loves them. Because he does. He loves them. He always has, of course. What he carries in his heart flows from that same Jordan River, the rush of those waters, but only now that they are carrying him forward willingly does he recognize their source.

❖

When I met with Chaplain Ted Keller and his coworkers in Columbia, South Carolina, in the early winter of 1999, I asked him Troy's question: What do you say to people who are lonely?

"Hope is the antidote for loneliness," he said quickly, matter-of-fact, with genuine authority.

His answer surprised and delighted me. Despite hope's being one of the three great Christian virtues, along with faith and charity, I had never thought much about its function. Hope seemed only a cheerfulness that haloed the other two virtues, nothing specific in itself.

How did Chaplain Ted know this? By losing his own hope, as it turned out, then being given a "hope beyond hope."

Ted was born in Columbia in 1948. His parents owned four modest restaurants, making a good living from hard work over long

hours. Ted's interest in ministry came about through his grandfather
Henry S. Mosser, who was a circuit-riding Wesleyan minister, pas-
toring a number of scattered country churches. Grandpa Henry had
a bullhorn mounted on his old '55 Pontiac and would gather crowds
for impromptu evangelism by broadcasting George Beverly Shea
records. Roaming the countryside with his grandfather, Ted found
out he could sing, accompanying George Beverly Shea on "It Is No
Secret What God Can Do" and "How Great Thou Art." Then he'd
stand on the car's roof and preach about Lazarus—how Jesus had
raised him from the dead.

After Charleston Southern College, where Ted studied music,
specializing in voice, Ted began serving as music director for summer revivals. He worked alongside such preachers as Wayne Lovett,
Bruce Newby, James Watterson, Stewart Harding, and Frank Shiv-
ies. People streamed down the aisles as Ted sang the invitation
hymn: "The Savior is waiting to enter your heart / Why don't you
let him come in?" He became adept at revivalism, using "The Savior Is Waiting" and other songs to extract more and more emotion
from the crowds. People praised him for his musical gifts and he began to attract notoriety. More than a few pretty young South Car-
olinians wanted to date the minister of music.

Ted resisted the common temptations of revivalists; he never
made off with bags of cash or bedded those sweet young belles.

He did fall to one temptation, though—the most insidious
known to the ministry. He fell victim to pride; his vocation became
his idol. The revivals became all about the greater glory of Ted
Keller. Ministers have been known to spend lifetimes in that snare,
but Ted soon tired of his own pretensions.

His interest in the ministry waned, until, by the early 1980s, he
had stopped singing in churches, stopped conducting choirs, stopped
ministering in revivals or anywhere else. Ted describes this time as a
period when he "ran away from God." His journey became a meta-
physical hiding out.

One Friday afternoon in 1988, Ted and his father were talking in his dad's garage. They were looking through a magazine about RVs together as they waited for Ted's girlfriend, Tammy, to arrive from Fort Sumter to spend the weekend with the family. Ted had met Tammy through his sister Margaret, a dedicated Christian who worked for a parachurch organization called Child Evangelism. Tammy was a good deal younger than Ted. She wore her chestnut hair over her shoulders with hot-iron-crimped bangs. Her soft pink skin was dewy and fresh. Ted found it difficult to keep his mind on what his father was saying about RVs. He couldn't wait for Tammy to arrive.

In the midst of this casual conversation, Ted's heart stopped. It just quit. Ted went into full cardiac arrest; he flat-lined. Describing the incident, Ted says simply, "I dropped dead."

His father administered CPR. The emergency services were summoned. His dad's aid and the paramedics' brought Ted back to life.

In the local hospital for two weeks being stabilized, Ted considered whether his life would have meant much if he had succumbed to his heart condition. He had to recognize what had led to his withdrawal from ministry: the ugliness of using holy things to his own glory.

Ted felt God wanted to know whether he would begin to serve him once more, this time completely and absolutely, on whatever conditions God specified. After derailing his life's journey and hiding from God, Ted was now, by virtue of his illness, "alone with the Alone," in Cardinal Newman's phrase.

Ted began saying yes to God, but without understanding, as yet, how pointed his illness would make God's question.

He was transferred to Duke University Medical Center for further testing and treatment. Since being examined for the draft, Ted had known he had Wolff-Parkinson-White syndrome, a congenital condition of the heart's electrical circuitry. The testing at Duke revealed that Ted's heart had at least four redundant circuits and these needed to be disengaged so that the signals reaching Ted's heart weren't confused, triggering deadly arrhythmias. Bypass surgery has become common enough, but rewiring the heart's electrical circuits is far more difficult. Ted's surgeons could make no promises about his ability to survive. Surgery was his only choice, though.

The night before the surgery, he asked his mother and father and other family members to leave him alone for a moment with Tammy. Ted said, "I know this isn't fair. But would you spend the rest of your life with me, if I have a life?"

She said yes.

Whether Ted would survive the surgery remained unknown well after post-op. He went into a coma that lasted for days, then weeks.

Unknown to those who visited him during this time, Ted was aware of who was in the room and their activities. He had that experience of near death which has frequently been reported; he felt as if he were hovering above the room, suspended between life and eternity. God's question to him remained crucial: Would he serve God? He felt no fear. He wasn't being threatened with damnation if he refused. He felt only peace tinged with a small sadness, for he could see his parents beside his bed, grieving for their son. He told God once again that he would serve him, totally and absolutely; that he wanted the second chance he was being offered.

While Ted remained in a coma, his family played his favorite music, everything from praise choruses to his old mentor George Beverly Shea. He also heard strange reports of the outside world. His mother told him, "Bush got the nomination, and he chose Dan Quayle!"

Who was Dan Quayle? Ted wondered.

After more than five weeks in a coma, Ted came back to consciousness one morning, looking up at a stunned, white-hatted nurse, who ran immediately for the doctors. When they gathered around, Ted's first words were, "Do you think I could have a Coca-Cola?"

When he finally returned home, Ted found to his dismay that he had lost his precious baritone voice. The tubes in his throat over so many days had damaged his larynx. His doctor told him that the damage might well be permanent.

"Will you serve," God seemed to be asking once more, "even if you no longer have your gifted voice?"

God was demanding obedience beyond any expectation on Ted's part of what it would mean to obey, how he would serve.

"Yes," he said. He would do the most menial of tasks, if that was what God wanted.

Ted could not keep himself from bargaining, though. "Lord, I'll sing in rest homes and funeral parlors and anywhere at all, if you'll only give me back my voice."

Happily, Ted's voice did come back within the year, which he learned all at once while visiting his aunt Sula in a rest home. She asked him to sing for her friends in the rest home's parlor. Without being sure he could croak out a note, he launched into "How Great Thou Art." He could sing again.

Ted never went back into revivalism, though. He eventually found his place to serve God—completely and absolutely—through Tammy.

Tammy's father, Bill, was a lifelong trucker. Because of her father's absences, heavy drinking, and macho behavior, Tammy's early home life was so troubled that she was raised mostly by her grandmother.

After the couple married, Tammy and Ted began praying for her father and a closer relationship of father and daughter—and maybe even son-in-law. Their prayers coincided with them becoming aware of the trucker chaplain ministry through a friend, Gene Nipper. As an extension of their concern for Tammy's father, they began volunteering at the local truck stop chapel run by the national ministry Transport For Christ.

When Dave Friddle, the chaplain in Columbia at the time (who now serves as the ministry's regional director), became ill, Ted stepped in.

Not without reservations, though. Despite his triple affirmation that he would serve Christ absolutely, he wasn't eager to take over the trucker chaplaincy. There would be too many day-to-day problems for him to cope with, he thought, with finances to worry over and an army of volunteers to supervise in order to keep the chapel open twenty-four hours every day. Still, he said yes. He began working at Whispering Hope Chapel on July 13, 1994.

Not quite four years later, in March 1998, during a special commissioning service for Ted as a member of the Southern Baptist denomination's North American Mission Board, Tammy's father attended church for the first time in twenty-seven years. When Ted led the congregation in "The Savior Is Waiting," Tammy's father walked down the aisle and came to the faith in which his family had instructed him long, long ago. "It's time I stopped running," he said.

Since then, Bill has stopped drinking, and his relationship with Tammy, after a lifetime of alienation, has been healed.

In the previous section, as Troy drives his rig to Bellevue, Washington, he's hopeful that he can be reconciled with his family. Ted can cite an instance close at hand that fully justifies Troy's hopefulness. Reconciliation and renewal are possible, getting "back on the road" an option, because faith, hope, and love are, we might say, meant for one another.

Jesus' own wayfaring is filled with a hope that—like the hope Ted eventually found—transcends circumstances and even his personal fate. Jesus' hope centers in his mission and, beyond that mission, God's will. "I seek to do not my own will but the will of him [the Father] who sent me" (John 5:30).

Jesus' wayfaring has a consistent purpose that's not self-invented—he is "sent," commissioned, as the anointed one, the Messiah, the Christ. Early on in his public ministry, according to the gospel of Luke, Jesus makes this emphatically clear by commenting on a messianic passage from Isaiah 61. He attends the synagogue in his hometown of Nazareth and reads out this passage:

> *The Spirit of the Lord is on me,*
> *because he has anointed me*
> *to preach good news to the poor.*

He has sent me to proclaim freedom for the prisoners
and recovery of sight for the blind,
to release the oppressed,
to proclaim the year of the Lord's favor.

He sits down and gives the scroll back to the attendant. Then, with the eyes of everyone in the synagogue on him, he delivers a one-sentence sermon—the shortest and most memorable in history: "Today this scripture is fulfilled in your hearing." (See Luke 4:16–21.) I am fulfilling Isaiah's messianic prophecy, he says. This is who I am and what I'm about.

Jesus' mission, his calling, it's important to note, has an *immediate* purpose, one that goes well beyond the delivery of his teachings. The theologian Romano Guardini in his classic *The Lord* insists that we consider as real the possibility that Jesus' public ministry might have succeeded in its own terms.[1] Although God foreknew the outcome of Jesus' ministry, as reflected in such messianic passages as Isaiah 53, God did not impose this outcome on Jesus' contemporaries. Guardini reminds us that it was possible that Jesus could have been believed and accepted in his day as the Messiah.

Jesus may also have been working more strenuously and even organizationally to that end than we imagine. The scholar N. T. Wright argues strongly that Jesus' sending out of the twelve and the seventy-two shows Jesus beginning to organize his church, in the midst of his public ministry, as an alternative to Temple Judaism.[2]

What would have happened if Israel had collectively recognized Jesus as the Messiah and turned to him? We cannot know how the story would have played itself out, of course—whether the true messianic era would have commenced or the Romans in their turn would have stopped Jesus' movement. We can say that nothing dictated that the religious authorities would reject Jesus, with the high priest, Caiaphas, declaring, with infinite irony, "It is better . . . that one man die for the people than that the whole nation perish" (John 11:50).

Jesus' triumphal entry into Jerusalem a week before his crucifixion always tantalizes us with images of what the true fulfillment of his earthly mission might have looked like. "Hosanna in the highest!" the crowds cry. "Blessed is he who comes in the name of the Lord!" If Jesus had been received as the living Christ at that time— Israel, the Romans, and other cultures turning to God's hope in the man Jesus—what truly new world order would have resulted?

It would be wrong to assume that Jesus didn't hope for this. His mentoring of the disciples, his sending out of the twelve and the seventy-two, and his own itinerant ministry should be seen, I think, as the inauguration of a new, messianic Judaism that could have changed all of human history.

We can tell that he longed for his movement to be embraced by his anguish at its rejection. "Woe to you, Korazin!" Jesus cries. "Woe to you, Bethsaida! If the miracles that were performed in you had been performed in Tyre and Sidon, they would have repented long ago in sackcloth and ashes. But I tell you, it will be more bearable for Tyre and Sidon on the day of judgment than for you" (Matthew 11:21–22). Jesus' warnings spring from a profound grief. "O Jerusalem, Jerusalem, you who kill the prophets and stone those sent to you, how often I have longed to gather your children together, as a hen gathers her chicks under her wings, but you were not willing" (Matthew 23:37).

So Jesus hoped, just as we all hope, for his work in this world to succeed. He was trying to change the world, right then, on his own terms. This was his work, what he had been sent to accomplish.

Jesus' mission and his longing for its success are probably the easiest aspects of his hope for us to identify with. Many of us feel called to a particular vocation and desire that the purposes of our vocation be fulfilled in the here and now. Like Ted Keller, we have our dreams and grieve when these dreams die. Often, the end of our immediate plans brings with it alienation from God.

The greatness of Jesus' hope lay in his trust in the Father's will in the midst of failure. Jesus understood that the Father could use any and all human circumstances—even what was shaping up as the utter defeat of Jesus' movement—to the Father's own glory. Understanding that his mission had a transcendent dimension not subject to human limitation, Jesus embraced the temporal failure of his public ministry as the means God would use to redeem humanity. Sent by the Father, Jesus trusts his Father's providential rule over all things merely human.

Jesus begins to explain to his disciples that he must suffer and die, and most strangely, rise again. The most striking instance of this follows Peter's declaration that Jesus is the Christ, the Son of the living God. Immediately afterward, Jesus begins to explain that he must go to Jerusalem and be killed, and "on the third day be raised to life."

> Peter took him aside and began to rebuke him. "Never, Lord!" he said. "This shall never happen to you!"
>
> Jesus turned and said to Peter, "Get behind me, Satan! You are a stumbling block to me; you do not have in mind the things of God, but the things of men." (Matthew 16:22–23)

How hard this must have been on Jesus. His merely human hope must have wanted to side with Peter, and in rebuking Peter, Jesus was also reaffirming his own commitment to the Father's will.[3] Jesus could not let his own thoughts rebel against rejection and its consequences. He knew that only a "hope beyond hope"—an absolute trust in his heavenly Father's ultimate victory—could sustain him, or any of us.

In Mexico City

The Healer

Not long after I started working on this project, I began to wonder whether I could find a miracle worker whose healings would prove beyond a doubt that Jesus is alive and working among us. I found this prospect particularly exciting because God's way of dealing with me has been almost exclusively through hints and guesses. If miracles were performed right before my eyes, my difficulties would be vanquished forever—or so I thought.

A charming and wise Camaldolese monk named Father Bernard steered me toward Father Peter Rookey, O.S.M.—a man Father Bernard truly believed had the gift of healing. When I called Father Rookey's office, which is located outside of Chicago, I found that he would soon be celebrating healing masses in Mexico City, and we arranged for me to meet him there.

✤

In a hillside neighborhood, Colonia Cruz del Farol, along the Carretera Panorámica (scenic highway) to Ajusco, with mountain-ringed Mexico City and its vast mosaic of barrios below, the people come streaming through narrow side streets to a poor church,

Sagrado Corazón y San Charbel Makhluf (Sacred Heart and Saint Charbel Makhlouf).

At first glance, the church and its grounds look more like a private residence hosting a garden party on this bright, sunny day. A wrought-iron fence surrounds the property. Beyond the gates lies a courtyard where a portable altar has been set up under a white awning decorated by blue stars. The linen-covered altar table stands on a raised dais with metal folding chairs for the priests behind. A midmorning breeze snaps the starred awning, as well as the huge yellow-and-blue tarpaulin that lies directly beyond, covering the church's lower grounds. The church itself stands to the left of the courtyard and is little more than a three-sided cinder-block garage with a corrugated metal roof. A bold mural on the far wall depicts two superimposed images of Christ: the king, holding his gold crown in one hand, rises above the cross-bearing servant. Today, July 23, 2000, the church is being used like a side chapel for the open-air healing Mass. Its already-crowded pews have been turned around from the altar toward the patio.

On the patio, to the right of the portable altar, stand two statues: the Virgin and a lean, black-cassocked, white-bearded Saint Charbel Makhlouf, the late-nineteenth-century Lebanese mystic, one of the Church's "incorruptibles." His statue holds out hands that are draped with yellow, white, blue, and pink ribbons, signs of thanksgiving for the *milagros*—miracles—obtained by the saint's intercession.

Opposite the two statues, a choir of teenage girls and boys in white shirts and black pants begins singing, "*A-le-lu-ya, a-le-lu-ya, a-le-e-lu-ya, a-le-lu-ya!*"

Those who have been brought to the Mass in wheelchairs are in front, two rows deep. Behind and around them in every available space sit others, who arrived hours in advance. The crowd pulls apart as blue-smocked ushers help carry in a woman on a litter. She is placed behind the altar, where an attendant holds up her IV bag. A white cloth covers her head and a flowered topsheet rests just below her chin.

The first among the overflow crowd are allowed to enter the wrought-iron gates and directed to the church's lower grounds. Hundreds, and then two or three thousand more, soon accumulate outside the church's gates, as the narrow streets fill and umbrellas sprout against the bright sun. Street vendors sell small dishes of cantaloupe and fried pepper cakes.

The people who have come this Sunday to Sagrado Corazón y San Charbel Makhluf differ from most church crowds. There's little practiced reverence; the spirit of the gathering is more like an army massing for action. What will happen? What are the possibilities and their demands? Those in wheelchairs, as well as the ten-year-old boy with chemotherapy's bald head, the blind, mercury-eyed Indian woman, and the thin-shouldered young man cowering from his own ghosts—all have come today to the *Santa Misa y Oración de Sanación* (the healing Mass) to present themselves and their needs to God. There is little chitchat. People's faces are set, quietly determined; they bite their lips, rub their hands. They are going to ask, but will they receive?

The Mass will be celebrated by Father Peter Rookey, O.S.M., whose healing ministry keeps the eighty-three-year-old priest on the transcontinental road full-time. This is the tenth straight year he has visited Mexico. Before the day is out—and the service will take most of it, as the eleven-thirty Mass will not end until well past six in the evening—as many as four or five thousand will be blessed with oil and prayed for individually by Father Rookey.

Among the blue-smocked ushers, the team of people helping Father Rookey, most have stories to tell about the impact of Father Rookey on their lives. Led by Alexandra Altamirano—who will serve as Father Rookey's translator today—the ushers are composed both of Mexico City residents and of a troupe of people who have come from the States. Strictly volunteer workers, many give up vacation time to support the Masses through prayer and by handling logistics.

When Father Rookey, in the company of two of Sagrado Corazón's own priests, processes to the altar, what the crowd sees is a broad-shouldered man with white hair combed back from a middle part and a full white beard. As he greets the people, *"En el nombre del Padre, y del Hijo, y del Espíritu Santo"* (In the name of the Father, and of the Son, and of the Holy Spirit), his voice has a crackle to it—the grain of his Midwestern upbringing in Wisconsin—while the lights in his eyes still dance to the Irish jig of his ancestry. There is something unusually youthful about him—more than a vestige of an almost teenage handsomeness. (Young surfers, one remembers, often wear their hair that way.) Only the volume of his stage whispers and the crotchety way he can occasionally issue directions suggest his hard-of-hearing age. Otherwise, there's a lightheartedness about his presence that's truly reminiscent of a youth's.

When he begins his homily, he jokes about being a Superior (Wisconsin) man, or maybe only an *hombre in-fe-ri-orr* from *Su-pe-ri-orr.* He says not to mind it when he makes bad jokes, because as a priest he's only a Rookey! Later, in the midst of a peroration about the name God calls himself, " 'I AM,' meaning the God who was and is and ever shall be," he cannot resist declining into a description of man as "the one who is and always will be—but wasn't once." It's not Svengali behind the altar or an infinitely composed hermit but the class clown. Is this truly the internationally celebrated healer?

Father Rookey's homily at Sagrado Corazón y San Charbel Makhluf turns serious with accounts of recent miracles. They build up to the ultimate—a contemporary Lazarus. One of Father Rookey's correspondents, a Detroit, Michigan, physician, tells of how he was brought to a hospital and declared dead. Nevertheless, the man's family continued to pray, using Father Rookey's "Miracle Prayer." "I just want you to know," the man writes Father Rookey, "that I came back to life and now I feel fine!"

When he leads the congregation in the Miracle Prayer, Father Rookey's composition turns out to be essentially a prayer of conversion. "Lord Jesus, I come before you just as I am ... I repent of my sins ... Lord Jesus, I accept you as my Lord, God, and Savior. Heal me, change me, strengthen me in body, soul, and spirit."

"Like John Paul II," Father Rookey says, concluding the homily, "we should all adopt the motto *Totus Tuus,* 'Totally Yours,' in order to see God's power in our lives. The disciples waited in the upper room praying, giving themselves utterly to God, after which the Holy Spirit came upon them. Let's do the same here today in order for the Spirit's power to come upon us."

Once the Eucharistic liturgy ends, Father Rookey asks everyone to pray together as he begins anointing people. "Because if they get to talking," he tells his translator, issuing one of his brusque directions, "the Spirit won't be able to work. They have to keep praying with us!"

He remembers the woman on the litter and goes to her first talking with the woman's attendants, especially the man holding up her IV bag. The priest looks into the woman's eyes and nearly shouts at her to see if there's any response. He wants to know if the woman understands what is happening and can participate in praying for her recovery. He folds her hands around his silver cross. Then he anoints her and says a prayer for her healing. When he is finished, he puts his hand on her chief attendant's shoulder in a brotherly way and then summons the ushers to help the man take the woman home. There is no outward sign her condition has changed in any way.

After his first prayers, with the litter-borne woman, Father Rookey moves quickly to the two rows of people in wheelchairs. Besides his silver cross reliquary, he holds a little gold case with a jellied anointing compound and begins working the line, as another priest in a white cassock stands by him with the Eucharist in a gold monstrance. Talking quickly to each person in a wheelchair, he finds out something about the person's condition, then anoints them and prays, after which he inquires whether they'd like to take a step or two out of the chair. A few risk it.

One of these brave people, a middle-aged woman, actually begins a stumbling walk forward, holding on to Father Rookey's hands. An usher turns her chair around, and she clasps on to its handles. The person who has brought her is invited to sit in the chair, and then, astonishingly, she begins pushing the wheelchair back toward the iron gates through the crowd. People applaud and call, *"Gloria a Dios!"* This happens twice more, as another woman rises from her wheelchair, and then an older man.

Father Rookey begins blessing the rest of the people. The ushers place a group of a dozen or so in line, and "catchers" position themselves behind each person. If the person "rests in the Spirit"—receives what most describe as a jolt of refreshing peace—he or she will fall backward into a catcher's waiting arms, or simply fall like an elevator, going straight down, with the catcher struggling to rest the person's head gently and straighten out the legs.

Father Rookey begins making the sign of the cross with his compound-anointed right thumb and pressing his reliquary-holding hand against people's foreheads. Nothing seems to happen at first, and then suddenly five or six people are lying on the ground, so much at peace, it seems, that others walking close to their heads are no disturbance. More than a few topple backward as soon as Father Rookey reaches out toward them. Often the blessing seems to extend itself in waves.

I've been sitting through the Mass by a woman holding a three-year-old boy on her lap. He is dark haired, with eyebrows so rich they are dewy with highlights. His look is both distracted from his immediate surroundings and concentrated by pain. His back flexes awkwardly and his legs shoot out stiffly, never folding at the knees. A crippled three-year-old with congenital scoliosis or cerebral palsy, I'm guessing. I pray for him throughout the Mass as his mother's fervent whispers rise up, and wait expectantly for his blessing by Father Rookey.

Father Rookey eventually greets him, pats his cheek, and tries his best to engage him—to distract him from his pain. After carefully anointing and blessing him, Father Rookey then sets his feet on the ground, urging him to walk into his arms.

The child finds all of these ministrations vexing and painful and he cries out in protest. Father Rookey prays over the boy another moment or two, but the child only twists and turns away as he cries ever louder. His mother finally sweeps the child back up in her arms and carries him away. She looks back over her shoulder at Father Rookey, murmuring her thanks. The priest has at least tried to help.

Why wasn't that child healed? I wonder. I had so much hoped he would be and I find myself grieving for the woman and her son. Then I begin questioning whether the people who pushed their wheelchairs away have truly experienced a miracle. The sick use wheelchairs for different reasons, after all; they can simply be weak, not paralyzed or lame. Have any of those in wheelchairs truly been restored, or have they only been temporarily energized?

What about all the people who are resting in the Spirit, then? Isn't seeing believing?

What sense can be made of such contradictory evidence?

The questions we all ask about divine healing and a few surprising corollaries inform Father Peter Rookey's life story. As I talked with Father Rookey during the week I spent in Mexico City, I came to understand how he had been chosen for this work and purified in its crucible, a process from beginning to end of pure fire.

When Father Rookey closes his eyes to pray, the close observer notes the unusual smoothness of his eyelids and the small flarelike scars shooting outward from the sockets. The first burning was literal.

In 1925, the day after the Fourth of July celebrations in Superior, Wisconsin, eight-year-old Peter Rookey and his brother Bernard were walking through town, looking for fireworks that hadn't been exploded. They found a prize—a skyrocket that looked perfectly intact, its only flaw a dangling fuse. Peter and Bernard carried the rocket home to their ramshackle three-story house and set its stickholder in the ground in their backyard. They lighted the fuse, ran away, and waited. It failed to go off. When they dared come close again, they saw that the fuse had stopped burning halfway up. They lit it again, only to see it die. Exasperated, Peter leaned down and blew on the smoldering wick to see it if would reignite. The rocket exploded in his face.

When he awoke, three days later, he was in the hospital, with bandages covering his eyes. His mother, Johanna, told him he was blind. Dr. Barnsdahl had done all he could, but the damage to his eyes had been severe.

The doctor was certain Peter's blindness would be permanent. But the child was born into an Irish-Catholic family that put no limits on God's generosity, either to the gift of children—Peter was one of thirteen brothers and sisters—or to the graces needed to raise them. While the church's theologians were becoming ever more rationalistic in their apologetics, Peter's family still practiced a Catholicism of simple devotion: a faith of novenas, Marian shrines, holy cards,[1] and above all the rosary—a faith that embraced the miraculous. On the way home from the hospital his mother told Peter that the family's nightly rosary would be offered up with the special intention that Peter see once again. The family began praying, long and hard.

In May of the following year the family was still praying. Johanna set up a special altar in the attic, and the family intensified its Marian devotions, all for the sake of Peter's healing.

Peter himself made a deal with God. If he were healed, he would become a priest. But he couldn't be one as a blind man, could he? God must understand the logic in that. Terrified and confused by the darkness that had suddenly engulfed him, Peter waited for God to act.

Astonishingly, over a period of eighteen months following the post–Fourth of July explosion, Peter Rookey regained his sight. At first he saw only moving shadows, and then, like the man in the gospels, confused images—"men like trees walking." One eye, the left, lagged behind the other and was still nearly useless when Peter, at age thirteen, kept his bargain with the Almighty: he entered a Servite seminary, Mater Dolorosa, in the Chicago suburb Hillside. The Servites are an order, founded in Florence in the thirteenth century, devoted to Marian spirituality and compassion for the poor.

Despite the gradual nature of this healing, Peter never doubted its divine inspiration—the doctor had been too adamant about the permanency of his condition and had no explanation for its reversal. The first miracle Peter Rookey ever experienced happened to him.

Peter's healing saw him through long teenage years of homesickness and struggles with his studies—as a scholar he was not particularly gifted. The suburb of Hillside was best known for its massive cemeteries, where many of Chicago's most famous gangsters, including Al Capone, were buried. Mishearing what Peter had said, people would ask, "So you're up at the cemetery?" and sometimes the young seminarian felt like that. The gigantic cemeteries with their ornate headstones actually became places of retreat, where Peter would take walks, praying for the souls of gangsters as he went. Peter and his peers also blew off steam by throwing a dummy down from the seminary's upper stories, delighting in the horrified reactions of passersby.

Peter kept his bargain to the end, though, and was one of seven from his entering class of twenty-nine who became a priest. He received a diploma from Saint Philip Benizi Servite High School, obtained his bachelor of arts degree from Loyola University, Chicago, and finished his advanced philosophy and theology courses back at Mater Dolorosa. He was ordained a priest on May 17, 1941.

During his time in seminary, Peter came under the influence of the seminary master, Father James Mary Keane, a charismatic figure who initiated the Perpetual Novena to Our Sorrowful Mother at the Servite basilica in Chicago. The devotion became a phenomenon as seventy thousand Chicagoans poured through Our Lady of Sorrows on Fridays during the late 1930s, 1940s, and 1950s. The Chicago Transit Authority had to put on "Novena Specials" to handle the traffic.

In terms of his own spirituality, the young Father Rookey was particularly attracted to the life of prayer. He wanted to offer himself for the lifting up of the Servite Order and the life of the whole church, and he thought he might do this best in continual prayer. His attraction to the life of prayer would endure through the various posts of his early ministry. At one point Father Rookey spoke with the general of the Servite Order about going to live at Monte Senario, the retreat house of the Service Order's *laudesi*, the thirteenth-century "praisers" of Christ through Mary who founded the order. All through his early years of religious life his prayers, as it turned out, were disposing him toward another way of offering himself up—of loving God and humankind—that he could not yet imagine.

Peter Rookey's seminary training, his intellectual formation in latter-day scholasticism (reading Aristotle, Thomas, Bonaventure, Suarez, and their many interpreters), persuaded him against what began to seem his family's superstitious piety. He now jokingly refers to this time as the period "when I used to be an intellectual." Johanna Rookey had no qualms about praying for her son's miraculous healing, but Father Peter learned to think of miraculous healings as theoretically possible but functionally out of bounds. After the days of the early church, miracles had been used by God—the church was teaching then—mostly as a verification of an individual's heroic sanctity, a means of validating saints. The average priest could not pretend to be Saint Francis, and therefore any prayers for miraculous healing on young Father Rookey's part could only be presumptuous. He was no saint.

Besides, the whole world of novenas and bleeding statues and miraculous springs belonged to a pre-Enlightenment spirituality that the modern world had largely discredited. The rosary itself, as young Father Rookey informed people, was a low-water substitute for recitation of the psalms.

In 1948, however, Father Peter had an experience that forced him to reconsider whether miracles were performed only at the behest of saints. One of his nephews, Mark, a sixteen-year-old, was dying of cancer. The family called Peter to Mark's home, in Anoka, Minnesota, to administer last rites. Recounting this incident, Father Rookey jokes, "I've seen stiffs look better than he did." Mark had been a child of great promise and now wore cancer's stretched-skin death mask. His breathing was already shallow and rapid, his pulse racing—all his vital signs deteriorating. Grief stricken, Father Peter administered last rites and happened to bless the young man with a relic of Saint Peregrine—a Servite who experienced a miraculous healing from cancer himself.

After the ceremony, the family went downstairs to have a cup of coffee together. Returning to the room for a last good-bye, they discovered the color had come back into Mark's face. Before Father Rookey left that day, his nephew was up out of bed and walking around. In a matter of days, he was out of the house—healed.

His uncle's joy was tempered by questions Father Rookey did not know how to answer. What had he done? He almost felt like protesting that he had healed young Mark through no fault of his own. He wasn't a saint. This wasn't supposed to happen.

Almost immediately thereafter, in August of 1948, Father Rookey went with his seminary master, Father James Mary Keane, to found the first Servite house in Ireland: a seminary college in Country Tyrone, Northern Ireland.

Through Father Keane's unflagging efforts, the Servites purchased an old manor house—Bruce's Mansion—that commanded the northern side of the village. From its second- and third-story windows, the Servites looked across sparkling green pastures to the Blackwater River and Wingfield's Bawn, an ancient castle perched on a limestone cliff. The river ran fast over waterfalls and salmon jumps and through weirs that controlled its flow, and the friars did some fishing for their dinners. The manor's grounds included an old clock tower, greenhouses, and gardens where Father Keane imagined building a Rosarium—a walkway with fifteen mammoth rose beds, one for each mystery of the rosary.

The newborn priory became a place for priesthood candidates to do their training in philosophy before being passed on to seminaries either in the United States or in Rome. The Servites converted the manor's ballroom into a chapel and opened their doors to the villagers on Sunday mornings. The presence of a Servite chapel in the middle of Protestant County Tyrone—the territory of fiercely protective Orangemen—brought many of the district's Catholics to

Mass. Who were these new friars? Why had they come to Northern Ireland?

As Catholics often used to do, members of the congregation asked for Father Peter's blessing after services. Without knowing that several of those who asked to be blessed were seriously ill, Father Rookey made the sign of the cross and prayed for God's blessing. As a result, a prominent local man and his wife reported that they had both been healed of cancer.

The word quickly spread throughout Ireland that Father Rookey was a healer. Once again, Father Rookey could only wonder at why such healings were being reported. What was God doing? For if the people's reports were true—and he found no reason to doubt them—these phenomena could only be God's work. He was certainly under no illusion that they were his own. In fact, he almost felt victimized by such blessings. Why him?

Within the first year after the Servites came to Northern Ireland, their converted-ballroom chapel could not contain the crowds. Soon busloads of pilgrims began to arrive from Derry and other towns.

Father Keane went off to establish another Servite foundation and Father Rookey became prior of Benburb. While the notoriety of Father Rookey's healing blessings continued to grow by word of mouth, his own efforts went into making the Servite Order known through running the college, preaching missions, writing articles, and making up devotional materials like holy cards. His appointed task was to acquaint people with the order and its needs.

What the people wanted, though—and "mercilessly," as Father Rookey describes it—was to bring to him *their own* needs. He was always receiving a telephone call, a batch of letters, someone stopping by, an inquiry through one of his students about a relative. The crowds at the Masses grew ever larger.

Eventually, Father Rookey responded to the many requests for healing blessings by conducting open-air services in the pastures attached to the priory—not Masses, at this point, but talks about faith followed by anointing people with oil. Great seas of people, huddled in overcoats against the rainy weather, spread out over the priory's grounds. Father Rookey made sure to bless the people with relics of Servite saints, which he began having placed in silver cross reliquaries. If anything miraculous happened, Father Rookey reasoned, he could always blame it on the saints.

One of the most notable and well-documented healings came about in the life of a child, Patricia Magee. She was born blind, with detached retinas in both eyes that were inoperable. Her father, Patrick, and his wife, May, brought the toddler Patricia to one of the early healing services, along with little Patricia's grandmother. Because they had made an appointment, the family was directed through the thronging crowd to the front. Father Rookey laid his hands on Patricia's head, then blessed her with his cross and prayed for her. He told her parents they should invoke the prayers of Our Lady and Saint Philip Benizi several times a day, especially while praying the rosary. "Your child will see," he predicted.

On the way home from the service, Patrick and May began praying the rosary. Patricia, who was seated on her grandmother's knee, suddenly reached for the window blind, quickly, without fumbling. Her grandmother turned her around and looked into her now-attentive eyes. She could see! The child had been healed at that moment and her healing was permanent. Almost forty years later she would greet Father Rookey in the community center beside Saint Agnes Parish Church in Belfast to thank him.

Run off his feet during this time in Benburb, Father Rookey stopped troubling himself about why miraculous healings should result from his ministry. He wanted to be glad and thankful.

He found that his reading of the New Testament changed dramatically. Even the Old Testament. He saw how the scriptures were filled with miraculous healings—virtually on every page.

Jesus promised his disciples that they would do greater works than Jesus' own miracles after the Holy Spirit's advent. The disciples were deeply flawed men, and yet God chose to work through them. Perhaps the Lord's miraculous work should still be considered central to the priestly vocation? Again, it wasn't any special sanctity on his part, Father Rookey knew, that provoked the recent healings. His own unworthiness made these events all-the-greater testimonies to God's love and care.

Without any self-promotion and almost against his will, Father Peter Rookey, the prior of Benburb, became a sensation in the early 1950s. His activities attracted unprecedented newspaper, radio, and television coverage. Nothing like this had broken out in Ireland, commentators said, since Saint Patrick.

The healings taking place through Father Rookey's ministry struck some as suspect, perhaps even demonic. Was this the fire of God's love that was falling, or something hellish? In so many words, the doubters repeated the Pharisees' accusation against Jesus: "It is by Beelzebub that he does these things." The criticism came not only from doubters but from Father Rookey's colleagues, the local clergy.

Cardinal D'Alton, primate of all Ireland, called Father Rookey into his office, clearly worried. Was this true? Were people being healed? Might the people's ordinary faith be damaged by this fever for the sensational? What of those who were not healed and their disappointment? There had been angry inquiries. Clergy were complaining that their own ministries were being disrupted.

Father Peter simply replied that he couldn't deny what was happening. Why didn't the other priests just offer to anoint people for healing as well?

There the matter stood until 1953, when the Servite Order conducted its general chapter, its governing meeting. As a result of the general chapter's deliberations, Father Rookey received a new job. *Promoveatur*, as the Latin tag goes, *ut amoveatur:* to move him out of Ireland, they promoted him. The prior of Benburb was made Consultor to the Father General of the order in Rome. The healer was ordered to become a bureaucrat.

His superiors also asked Father Rookey not to heal anyone anymore, and for thirty-three years—a working lifetime—he didn't.

Father Rookey did just about everything else, and all under obedience to his superiors: from the first administrative post, in Rome, to academic jobs in Germany, Belgium, and the Middle East, to a final circuit-riding pastorate of mission churches in the Ozarks.

Father Rookey resists all urgings to recount the interior drama of his three-decade hiatus—what it cost him.

We do know that while stationed in Rome Father Rookey sought the advice of the famous stigmatic Padre Pio, a Capuchin friar who spent his life in the town of San Giovanni Rotondo. Padre Pio may prove the most famous mystic of the twentieth century. His own gifts caused such disruption that the Holy See barred him, at one point, from all priestly activities except the private celebration of Mass. So when Padre Pio advised Father Rookey to do "everything under obedience," he listened.[2]

Finally, in 1986, Father Rookey's newly elected superior, a younger priest who had once been his student, called Father Rookey back into the healing ministry. Without ever having made the request, Father Rookey received the long-desired phone call. He began praying for people to be healed again in the Chicago Servite basilica, Our Lady of Sorrows, where he had been ordained more than forty years before.

The thirty-three-year hiatus in Father Rookey's healing ministry cries out for explanation. Why would Father Rookey need a further period of preparation? Why did the gift itself need to be renounced in order to prepare for its late flowering? Even as I asked these questions, I recognized a familiar pattern: gifts always seem to cause trouble, and their proper use, renunciation. As Father Rookey reminded me, *Gift* in German means "poison." The doubt anyone brings to the idea of divine healing has an equally powerful flip side: the wildest possible hope.

When extreme responses both of hope and of doubt come into play, the conventional spiritual crucible becomes white-hot. So corollary questions of how the healing minister will withstand such pressures are critical.

Almost all the clergy, missionaries, and other Christian leaders I have ever met suffer to a degree from a star mentality. Their gifts inevitably bring them disciples; they become the center of every activity around them. All of this encourages pride, and often results (as news reports frequently make clear) in the infamous few indulging their darker appetites. What's more, if any spiritual gift presents temptations for abuse, healing must be the worst. I cannot describe the extreme vulnerability of the thousands I saw approach Father Rookey during our short week together. His coworkers enjoyed trading Father Rookey stories, speculating on whether he could bilocate—be in two places at once—or perform other such wonders as Padre Pio was said to. Obviously, Father Rookey could exploit such hero worship in a second.

But Peter Rookey is the most direct man I have ever met, to the point of forswearing unhelpful personal reflection. He's interested in what God is doing in the here and now and not much else. He truly has almost no interest in his own personal drama.

His constant joking is a sign of this. While many use humor to hide from their misgivings, Father Rookey simply longs for the world to open up to delight (one of God's mini miracles), and he's always willing to risk personal embarrassment to produce a moment of fun, truly not caring how all this might reflect on him. He just wants the world to laugh.

The temptation to pride for the healing minister has an even more sinister weapon at its command than self-indulgence or simple egoism, though. As Cardinal D'Alton admonished the young prior of Benburb, the angry and the disappointed are also part of the story, as are lame children like the little boy I sat by at Mass. The temptation to pride carries despair as its most fiery dart. The person who prays for divine healing and occasionally sees God work such wonders must also witness the massive human suffering that God does not choose to address immediately.

I asked Father Rookey whether he wasn't overwhelmed by the needs of people who are *not* healed. He said no. Since he's not responsible for the healings, he's not responsible for those who are not healed. God's mercies are indeed a mystery. Father Rookey's job is to be faithful and to leave whatever healings take place to God. After all, the great healing, as he says, is to be transformed into the likeness of Christ, and God knows best how to accomplish this within each soul. Father Rookey's Miracle Prayer, the emblem of his ministry, emphasizes the great miracle—*conversion*—because God's other mercies, such as divine healing, are signs of God's power to save us eternally.

To remain grounded in this reality, though—to suffer the little children and not see all of them healed—requires Father Rookey's long baptism in God's fire. The proper frame to miracle stories must always be God's will, both the loving intent that Christ proclaims and the unknowable means—God's ways are not are our ways—by which God accomplishes his love within us. Father Rookey has received the grace to operate strictly within this greater mystery, neither presuming nor despairing.

That grace must be renewed every single day, of course. His lifelong devotion to prayer keeps centering his startling ministry in God. Father Rookey has grown into ascetical habits that he believes are necessary to his participation in God's work. He spends three hours every morning in prayer, using the universal prayer of the church: the Divine Office, or breviary. As he recites the familiar psalms, he also performs his daily calisthenics, doing *hundreds* of push-ups and sit-ups. (He must be in the best shape of any octogenarian I've ever met.) After Morning Prayer, he meditates on the gospel text of the day, praying the lines. Then he adds certain traditional prayers that he particularly likes, such as the Consecration to Our Lord of Saint Louis de Montfort, the seventeenth-century Catholic French divine. He prays the *Angelus* and the Chaplet of Divine Mercy, and the distinctive scriptural rosary of the Servite Order (in which the scriptural text of each mystery threads through the ten Hail Marys of each decade). He prays the *Stabat Mater* and concentrates on the prayers of thanksgiving that he will be reciting after celebrating daily Mass.

About his experience of prayer, what it's like for him to be in communion with the Lord, he won't say much, and like many old and wise religious I've met, Father Rookey tends to wave off questions about remarkable experiences. He will confess his gratitude for the "gift of flowers"—a sudden effusion of the scent of rose—that he often experiences. (The first time he had this experience, he was helping Padre Pio in the sacristy after Mass, when he returned to the bare altar and was enveloped in the scent.) He often sees an image of Jesus in the consecrated host as well. He's willing to talk about these things only because he believes them *common* experiences of the people attending the healing Masses. About contemplative union, he will say only that he tries to keep his concentration directly on God while reciting the rosary.

His prayers sustain him, anyone would have to say, becoming for Father Rookey—as his prayers were for Christ—the bread the disciples "know not of." In fact, Father Rookey fasts all day, every day, until he's celebrated Mass and blessed each and every person who requests it. The day of the Mass at the Mexico City hillside church Sagrado Corazón y San Charbel Makhluf, I watched him celebrate and then pray with people tirelessly for more than seven hours without a break, without sitting down, without pause. Father Rookey kept a similar schedule throughout the rest of the week—a schedule that he follows for all but a few days each month. This may not be a miracle, but for an eighty-three-year-old man, it's close.

I traveled to Mexico City, I have to admit, partly out of curiosity and even bad faith—or the desire to avoid faith's demands. I did experience many remarkable events in Mexico City, and meeting Father Rookey will always be one of my life's treasures. At the same time, I have a much greater appreciation for how people in the gospels could witness the miracles of Jesus and not know what to make of these wonders and the person who performed them. There's no getting away from the necessity of faith, because even what we see with our own eyes demands interpretation. Miracles simply do not make sense unless the facts of the case accumulate into a larger meaning, and that meaning can be recognized only with what Jesus described as "eyes to see."

As I reflected on my experiences in Mexico City with Father Rookey and looked into the gospels, I became uncomfortably aware how little time Jesus had for people like me—the merely curious and those seeking to avoid the demands of faith.

Alongside the miracles of Jesus, the gospels record occasions when Jesus either refused to perform any of his mighty deeds or was blocked from doing so by the people's attitudes. One of these "antimiracle" stories takes place in Jesus' hometown. Very early in his public ministry, after an initial tour through Galilee, Jesus arrives back in Nazareth and announces to his local synagogue (as we saw in the previous chapter) that he is Isaiah's Messiah.

Jesus then voices the synagogue crowd's doubts about him and their desire for a miraculous sign: " 'Do here in your native place the things that we heard were done in Capernaum' " (Luke 4:23). After declaring that no prophet is accepted in his native land, he cites instances from the Old Testament when the prophets worked miracles for alien peoples instead of Israel. "There were many lepers in Israel during the time of Elisha the prophet; yet not one of them was cleansed, but only Naaman the Syrian" (4:27). The broad implication that his neighbors are unworthy of God's mercies makes them so angry that they try to throw him off a cliff. "But he passed through them and went away," Luke tells us, recording Jesus' ironically miraculous exit (4:30).

Jesus repeatedly turns down direct requests for a sign that will vanquish the religious authorities' doubts. The Pharisees and the Sadducees come to Jesus and ask him to show them a sign from heaven; they are ill at ease with his invitation to faith and want Jesus to prove his identity and mission beyond doubting. Jesus gives them a peremptory response: "A wicked and adulterous generation looks for a miraculous sign, but none will be given it except the sign of Jonah" (Matthew 16:4). With that, Jesus turns and walks away.

The question then becomes, why did Jesus perform miraculous

healings and other wonders, such as walking on the water? A moment's reflection tells us that Jesus did not simply wave his hand and cure all those who were suffering in Israel at the time. He responded only to specific people and circumstances. So we are compelled to ask why, and for what purposes.

We noted that contemporary miracle stories have little significance unless the facts accumulate into larger meanings. Father Rookey's own healing as a boy, for example, prepared the way for his ministry as an adult. In a similar way the miraculous healings Jesus performs are intended by Jesus as signs of a greater reality.

The miracles of Jesus—like the hope that impels him forward—can be understood only in the context of his mission, which Jesus characterizes as a great task, a mighty work. Saint Paul explains the mission of Jesus as the defeat of death itself. "For since death came through a human being, the resurrection of the dead came also through a human being. For just as in Adam all die, so too in Christ shall all be brought to life. . . . For he must reign until he has put all his enemies under his feet. The last enemy to be destroyed is death" (1 Corinthians 15:21–22, 25–26).

Jesus' mission—his work—is to extend his own supernatural existence to humankind, and that can happen only on what we would all recognize as a miraculous plane.

All four gospel writers understand Jesus' miracles as signs of Jesus' greater work in reclaiming God's creation and restoring humankind to God's eternal fellowship, and they dwell on those miracles that best serve the purpose. They present the panoramic sweep of Jesus' healing ministry, too, of course, telling us how "wherever he went—into villages, towns or countryside—they placed the sick in the marketplaces. They begged him to let them touch even the edge of his cloak, and all who touched him were healed" (Mark 6:56), with the inevitable effect that "those with diseases were pushing forward to touch him" (Mark 3:10). (After witnessing Father Rookey's ministry, I can read this line only as the most polite of understatements.)

The miracles of Jesus first show us God's love and care for his creation—the essentially loving nature of the divine will. To do this, Jesus initiates healings without being asked and even without requiring faith. When Jesus sees a lame man by the pool of Bethesda and learns that the poor man has been an invalid for thirty-eight years, Jesus goes up to him and asks, "Do you want to get well?" (John 5:6). He then promptly heals the man, even though it's the sabbath and Jesus knows this will cause controversy.

When the formerly lame man identifies Jesus as his healer to the authorities and they question his healing on the sabbath, Jesus replies, "My Father is always at his work to this very day, and I, too, am working" (John 5:17).

Jesus uses healing miracles as a means of verifying his divine authority to engage in this work. This is especially clear in the healing of the paralytic. The paralytic's friends show both faith and perseverance in taking their litter-borne neighbor up onto the roof of the house where Jesus is teaching and lowering him into the Lord's presence. Jesus first responds to the faith of the sick man's friends. They believe that God is still at work and Jesus is his instrument. "When Jesus saw their faith, he said to the paralytic, 'Son, your sins are forgiven' " (Mark 2:5).

The teachers of the law sitting in the crowd ask themselves the obvious question, "Who can forgive sins but God alone?" Jesus knows their thoughts. He asks them, " 'Which is easier: to say to the paralytic, "Your sins are forgiven," or to say, "Get up, take your mat and walk"? But that you may know that the Son of Man has authority on earth to forgive sins . . .' He said to the paralytic, 'I tell you, get up, take your mat and go home' " (Mark 2:7–11). The paralytic is immediately healed and his friends rejoice.

By forgiving the man's sins, Jesus first addresses the alienation of God and humankind—the problem of sin and evil. The healing of the paralytic, in response to his friends' faith, is a sign of Jesus' authority to reestablish God's kingdom on this earth through reconciling God and humanity. It's a miniature of Jesus' redemptive offer to everyone.

Jesus' most memorable deed, the raising of Lazarus, anticipates the miracle of the redemption itself.

Although Jesus purposely delays his arrival in Bethany until two days after Lazarus's death, nothing can keep him from responding to Mary and Martha's request to help their brother, not even the threat of death. The authorities are known to be looking for Jesus and the disciples; they may be walking into a trap. When they finally depart for Bethany, Thomas urges his fellow disciples on—"that we may die with him" (John 11:16).

The short journey occurs without incident, though. On arrival, Jesus meets the always busy Martha first. She cries out that if he had been there, her brother would not have died. Jesus quickly predicts that Lazarus will live. Martha responds with a conventional piety about the resurrection of the last day.

But Jesus says, "I am the resurrection and the life. He who believes in me will live, even though he dies; and whoever lives and believes in me will never die" (John 11:25–26).

This provokes the one response Jesus truly seeks. Martha confesses that Jesus is the Messiah. At that point Jesus' personal closeness to the family must have come rushing in, for when Mary makes the same complaint, Jesus responds in a completely different way. He weeps.

On his way to Lazarus's grave he walks amid people complaining that surely this man who heals the blind could have prevented Lazarus's death. He's deeply troubled. His own grief over his friend's death merges with his frustration at not being believed and perhaps anger at being scolded.

Then Jesus faces the grave—not only his ultimate opponent but his personal future. Yet if the gospels are to be believed, Jesus can already look past the grave. He means to use the raising of Lazarus as a sign of the life within him that death cannot conquer.

When Jesus prays for the miracle, he speaks aloud: "Father, I thank you that you have heard me. I knew that you always hear me, but I said this for the benefit of the people standing here, that they may believe that you sent me." Then in a loud voice Jesus calls: "Lazarus, come out!" (11:41–43).

The gospels report that many came to believe in Jesus as the result of Lazarus's healing. They also tell us that the religious authorities' conspiracy to bring Jesus down became deadly earnest. Soon, Jesus would provide a "wicked and adulterous generation"—and all those after it who long to avoid the demands of faith—with the sign of Jonah, a resurrection after three days in the belly of the earth.

Still, many will not believe, as Jesus knows. Jesus laments aloud, "Even though you do not believe me, believe the miracles, that you may know and understand that the Father is in me, and I in the Father" (John 10:38).

It's strange, though: it's almost impossible to believe in miracles unless we come to know and believe in the one who performs them. We all sense this, and with Jesus, it was much of the point.

On the California Coast
The Man of Prayer

Prayer is clearly the source of Jesus' dynamism. "I do nothing on my own," Jesus says, "but speak just what the Father has taught me. The one who sent me is with me; he has not left me alone, for I always do what pleases him" (John 8:28–29). These characterizations of Jesus' ministry as a response to God's leading are reiterated throughout the gospel of John, until they are expressed in complete identification: "I and the Father are one" (John 10:30).

As I thought about Jesus as a man of prayer, I wondered how I could possibly find someone whose story would render visible the intimate, purely spiritual negotiations of prayer. If we believe Jesus to be the Son of God, then the type of communication Jesus must have enjoyed with his Father quickly becomes unimaginable.

Yet I found great encouragement in Saint Paul to understand something of Jesus' prayer through a contemporary believer. "I am crucified with Christ," Paul writes, "nevertheless I live; yet not I, but Christ liveth in me" (Galatians 2:20). In this cherished apothegm Saint Paul establishes the principle of identification through which all Christian spirituality (our personal understanding of God) proceeds. Paul's identification with Jesus is so complete that Paul's life has been transformed into Christ's own.

This indwelling of Jesus through the Holy Spirit is something promised to every believer, as we recall from our foundational passage in John 17:22–23: "I have given them the glory that you gave me, that they may be one as we are one: I in them and you in me." Through Christ, then, every Christian experiences something of Jesus' union with his Father. We participate in the same identification that Paul speaks of with Christ, and through our identification with Christ we have communion with the Father.

Again, though, how might this invisible reality be seen? Of course, the saints often recount experiences of being drawn more directly into God's presence, of experiencing a preview of heaven in which we will know as we are known (1 Corinthians 13:12). Paul himself speaks of someone he knows being caught up into the third heaven, which is usually interpreted as an autobiographical reference to his own prayerful ecstasy (2 Corinthians 12:2). Saint Augustine and his mother, Monica, looking over their garden in Ostia, experience being drawn so close to Christ that the master rhetorician Augustine can only allude to the experience, finding its reality unspeakable.[1]

In reference to ecstatic visions, I thought of the two great sources of mystical theology Saint Teresa of Avila and Saint John of the Cross. Both experienced the direct presence of God as a dark, consuming fire and were transformed. But are there any Saint Teresas among us today?

That question eventually led me to Barbara Matthias.

✣

Off the main drag through Santa Maria, California, in a McDonald's fronted by a playland of loopy, smiling plastic trees, a worker takes her mop and wringer-equipped pail into the bathroom alcove. She posts her yellow warning cone, *Cuidado Piso Mojado* (Caution: Wet Floor), and with her pail props open the women's bathroom door. She walks back to an adjacent work closet and finds the bristly toilet scrubber and a disinfectant. The toilets are first, and then the floors.

In her uniform's striped shirt, blue visor, and straight blue pants, the worker looks like a child on an amusement park holiday. She stands only four feet eight inches tall, with the body of an eleven-year-old who's about to sprout into adolescence. But the worker is no child, although her thinning brown hair is cropped boyishly short. It would be difficult to guess at her age, but certainly beyond thirty. Each ear is muffed with a large earphone and she hums to herself as she begins scouring a toilet.

When she turns to go out for the mop, her eyes appear bright and quick and her face has a determined, even enthusiastic cast, as if in the midst of scrubbing toilets she's enjoying herself. Her smooth complexion, so responsible for her cheerful look, appears almost untouched by care. There's a straight-ahead, pointed character to everything she does—a happy intention.

When a man goes in the opposite door, she startles him with a greeting. "How are you today?"

Taking no notice of his gruff reply, she's back at the floor, putting everything she has into it. Two groovelike indentations ray out from the corners of her lips, and the roots of her neck muscles grow taut. Her mop working feverishly, she scurries from one corner of the room to another. That visor might as well be Mickey's ears on this quick, friendly mouse. Who is she? What's she about? Another poor, simple soul, or something else?

After the worker finishes with the women's and men's bathrooms, she goes into the employee lounge for lunch and takes out the sandwich and apple she's brought along.

Three coworkers are taking their lunch break as well. A tall, buzz-cut, athletic Anglo stands over by a built-in counter with its stainless steel napkin dispensers. He's so big-boned his clavicles look like I beams beneath his nylon shirt. A wavy-haired Chicano, sitting on the edge of the lunch table, his feet on a chair, spins his visor around one finger while teasing the ripe, liquid-eyed Chicana across the table. There's a rough dignity to her face—an Incan gravity to her ridged nose and sharp-planed cheeks—but her head-nodding manner says she can take the banter as casually as the boys.

"I heard you embarrassed even Umberto, you were so ripped," the Chicano says.

She wags her face at him, as if nothing like this could ever be of any account to her. "I wasn't there with Umberto. I was just there to party."

"Oh little sister, you are a bad girl."

"The baddest," she says, and smiles to herself.

"There's a party at Glen's tonight," the Anglo says. "Everybody's going to get bad."

The two Latinos look at the Anglo. What's he up to? "Everyone" meaning the white sports and the star athlete Latinos they keep around as salsa?

The Anglo retreats by picking on the other outsider. "You like to get bad, don't you, Barbara?" he asks.

She fingers a crucifix in her pocket and says, "You don't have to 'get bad.' That's the way everyone is. Getting good—that's the hard part."

"Yeah," the Chicana says, "it's hard for Barbara to be good. She's too down with her three amigos. You still see them every day? I hear you partied for like six hours once."

The Anglo boy laughs, but the Chicano looks around as if someone might have heard.

Barbara's face falls and the grooves ray out from her lips so markedly that she looks constrained by a mask of torture. She puts the unfinished sandwich back in her brown bag and pockets her apple close by the crucifix.

"Hey, Barbara," the Chicano boy, Vicente, says, "finish your lunch. Rosa is just a *puta*. Everyone knows that."

"Yeah, and everyone knows you're a *puta*'s rag, Vicente," Rosa says bitterly.

Barbara pushes her chair back and stands up. She holds the top of her brown bag in two blanching hands. "I think you are such beautiful young people. I wish you could understand how much God loves you."

A long moment, and then the firecracker goes off. "The priest was always trying to show me how much God loves me, Barbara," Vicente says, his eyes lasering at her. "You know what I mean?" He grabs his crotch.

Barbara hurries to her half locker in the lounge's entryway. Her face burns with shame. She cannot think what her lock combination is—what to do next. Finally, she asks, "Am I on the grill this afternoon?"

"The grill?" the three look at one another and smirk.

"Well, what?"

"I think you're on fries. Ask Jeff."

When she hurries out front, she hears the three young people laughing—but their whoops are not exactly carefree. Vicente has been almost a friend. He must have been telling the truth about the priest.

At three-thirty, when her shift ends, Barbara walks out quickly to meet Jerrie Castro in the parking lot. Her friend—the head of Mission West Communications—is driving her to a local hotel where they are hosting a special group for today's apparition. Thirty-five women are coming from Saint Jean Vianney Parish in Yorba Linda.

They arrive at the Santa Maria Inn, whose six-story tower looks like a wedding cake, its beige stories layered and topped with chocolate brown. Barbara has a change of clothes in a shopping bag and walks directly to the public bathroom to change.

Jerrie stands in the long foyer next to the dinner music piano, greeting the women. They are middle-class Catholics, dressed so simply they might almost be nuns in secular attire, dress or pants suits in single colors. They wear their hair short and curled and, if they are daring, frosted.

Their eyes dance around, excited; their pleasant expressions are also tight with apprehension—they might be going into a doctor's office. One already has a rosary draped over her hand and is fumbling with it as if sorting through a ring of keys for the one to the exit.

Jerrie shepherds everyone into a windowless meeting room

down the hall, where in front of ordered rows stands a lone chair before a wood table. The Holy Family, in plaster of paris statuettes,
adorns the table, along with an urn full of red roses.

The focal-point table and lone chair look somehow incomplete
or too formal or simply incongruous with the Rotarian surroundings.
There are no other attempts at creating atmosphere. The fluorescent
lights are bright and unrelenting.

The group fills the chairs and their chitchat dies away.

Jerrie says, "It's almost four-thirty and Barbara will be here in a
few moments. Let me tell you something about what we'll be doing.

"When Barbara comes in she'll sit in this chair up front. We'll
pray the rosary together and when Barbara makes the sign of the
cross—usually about the second decade—the apparition will have
begun. The Virgin Mary always appears to her in the middle, with
Saint Joseph on the Virgin's right and Jesus on the left.

"You'll see Barbara reach out to the Holy Family. The Blessed
Mother draws Barbara's hand to touch her feet or her heart or causes
her to lift both arms in order to be embraced. She draws Barbara's
hands to Saint Joseph and Jesus, too.

"Sometimes during her ecstasy Barbara will motion for someone
to join her. I can usually tell who she wants. I'll let you know if you
are to join her. You can sit or kneel, whatever feels comfortable. Let
Barbara guide your hands . . . Oh, here she is."

Barbara has changed into a simple but feminine white blouse
and a pair of dark green slacks. She greets everyone on the outside
rows individually on her way to her chair.

"Do I have time?" Jerrie begins to ask.

Barbara settles in her chair. She looks back at the group of
women with a welcoming but hurried expression. It's clear that she
feels she has her own appointment to keep. "I will pray for each of
you today," she says, "and for your families—that you will be
brought closer to the Holy Family. Particularly that there will be
conversions in your family, where that's needed. It's always needed
in our own lives too, of course." Barbara faces forward again and her

small, shuffling feet grow still. Her right foot, which is resting on its side, will remain in exactly that position for the next two hours.

"All right," Jerrie says, "I can see that Barbara is ready. Let's begin the prayers. I'll lead the first decade. Cathy," she says to the group's leader, "if you'd do the second? As it's Friday, we're on the Sorrowful Mysteries, of course."

Jerrie makes the sign of the cross and leads the group through the Apostles' Creed, the Our Father, three Hail Marys, and "Glory be to the Father, and to the Son, and to the Holy Spirit, as it was in the beginning, is now, and ever shall be, world without end. Amen."

"The first Sorrowful Mystery, the Agony in the Garden."

"Hail Mary, full of grace . . . ," the women begin. "Holy Mary, Mother of God . . ."

By the time they reach the second bead of the first decade, Barbara makes the sign of the cross herself and the apparition has begun. For the next two hours, Barbara Matthias will be, by her account, in the presence of Jesus, Mary, and Joseph. She'll see them as one person sees another, and converse with them personally.

This is the essential shape of Barbara Matthias's fascinating life: a McDonald's worker who also happens to have, if her experiences are authentic, the most spectacular prayer life imaginable—at least as far as an outside observer can know. For the past ten years, since March 24, 1990, Barbara Matthias claims the Holy Family have been appearing to her every day between 4:20 and 4:40 P.M. They remain with her for an hour and a half to two hours, communicating messages that she writes down as soon as the apparitions end. Barbara also claims, as do the people associated with her, that many healings and conversions have resulted from people attending Barbara's apparitions.

To Catherine Labouré of the Miraculous Medal, Saint Bernadette of Lourdes, and Saint Faustina Kowalska of the Divine Mercy devotion, add Barbara Matthias?

That the Holy Family appears to a handicapped woman in Santa

Maria, California, every day like clockwork strains, if not sunders, credibility. Who could ever believe such a thing? And why? What purpose would it serve? Why should I be telling such a story? Even the Roman Catholic Church, which has often been host to such visionaries, finds their existence problematic and goes to great lengths to examine such phenomena so that people will not be scandalized. Worse, especially for our ecumenical purposes, the history of apparitions has been bound up with the promulgation of the Marian doctrines that divide Protestants and the Orthodox from Catholics. Many suspect that more than a few Marian apparitions, if not all, are demonic in origin. Everyone, Roman Catholics included, would acknowledge that visionaries, strictly speaking, add nothing to our understanding of the Christian faith. In fact, their messages, when authentic, tend to be boring: a long series of religious admonitions that we've already heard a million times. Why, then, should God inspire such people, and why should we pay attention?

Yet somehow visionaries are like politics in a novel: while being in very bad taste, they are irresistible.

Barbara Matthias currently lives in a ground-floor bungalow apartment, its small space divided into a one-person kitchen, a living room, and a bedroom. The walls are adorned with a few simple holy pictures, the Sacred Heart, the Holy Family, and a print of da Vinci's *Last Supper*. From her kitchen, the visitor sees her couch, one easy chair, her TV with an aluminum-wrapped coil serving as rabbit ears, and up against the back wall, her bed with its turtle green slipcover. When I visited in the winter of 2000, she showed me a recent gift: a plastic sunflower whose secret button revealed a smiley face as the toy began playing, in music box fashion, "When Irish Eyes Are Smiling."

While her visions these past ten years have brought her a modest notoriety, they have not brought her wealth or even material comfort. About her job at McDonald's cleaning toilets, she states, "I have to work," with an urgency that declares need.

In 1991, Barbara went through a rigorous set of medical tests at the University of California–San Francisco Medical Center with a team of experts headed by Dr. Linda Davenport. A final battery of tests was performed in 1992 under the direction of neurologist Dr. Philippe Loron. Many of these tests, including EEGs, were administered while Barbara experienced ecstasy.

The physicians shone lights into her eyes, poked needles into her nostrils, and pressed rolled, pointed tissues directly against her naked eyes. While in ecstasy, Barbara did not react to these stimuli. She flinched quite normally at all other times.

What science knows about her visions is that they are not caused by hysteria, hallucinations, catalepsy, epilepsy, sleep and dream states, self-hypnosis or autosuggestion, schizophrenia, psychosis, neurosis, multiple personality disorder, or any other pathological or psychological disease. They are also entirely unrelated to her basic handicap: Turner's syndrome, a genetic abnormality that accounts for her small stature.

The doctors' MRIs and EEGs revealed that Barbara experiences a profound meditative state in which the beta waves of the brain are minimized and the alpha waves augmented. It appears that her cerebral cortex dissociates from the lower brain functions—which is why she does not respond to common stimuli. At the same time the activity in her cerebral cortex can send signals outward to direct her voluntary muscles—allowing her, for example, to guide other people's hands toward the figures in her visions. Science has demonstrated that Barbara is—at the very least—an instance of a genuine human phenomenon.

Father René Laurentin, a renowned theologian and a Marian specialist, concludes, "The clinical tests and observations, achieved with more sophisticated scientific equipment than at Medjugorje or Kibeho ... reveal a very profound ecstasy ... [her] disconnection with the ambient world conditions a coherent contact with the other world that she witnesses."[2]

Still, the questions remain: Why Barbara? And why, period?

Barbara's story is one of personal simplicity vexed by contemporary confusion. In many ways her life answers the question, what would happen to Saint Bernadette if she were born today?

That question has a recoil like an elephant rifle. We'd have to admit, I think, that the teasing of Barbara's coworkers expresses our own skepticism, if we wouldn't want to be cruel about it. We can even see why the importance of her claims, if pressed, might provoke a much greater violence from otherwise levelheaded people. The most disbelieving among us know what it is to long for immortality, and Barbara's experiences bring the transcendent so close, give us such reason to hope for an eternal destiny, that any fraud on her part would be unforgivable. That's why this one small woman in her McDonald's uniform is a spiritual atomic bomb. She may be more of a problem to the faithful than the unbelieving because, like all enthusiasts, she threatens our comfortable notions about who God is and the way God works.

The earliest part of Barbara's life resembles many saints', especially in its early religious focus. She was born in Rio de Janeiro, Brazil, in 1947 of a Brooklyn-born father, Paul Matthias, and a Guyanese mother, née Mary Adelaide Ferreira, and lived in a high-rise apartment a few minutes walk from Copacabana Beach. Her father worked for Pepsi-Cola, establishing distribution in South America. Her mother suffered severely from rheumatoid arthritis and Barbara depended on Pat, her half brother, twelve years older, to carry her and change her diapers. Her rambunctious middle brother, Brian, was her first teasing tormentor, but she understood even as a toddler that he was only growing up. She knew that he loved her.

In Rio, the famous statue of Christ on Corcovado Mountain opens wide its arms over a distinctly Catholic, if often hedonistic, culture. Barbara's Catholic mother explained the Christian faith to Barbara, read her children's book about baby Jesus, his mother, Mary, and the saints, and taught her traditional prayers. Barbara's earliest memories find her lying in bed, having what she calls "conversations from the heart" with God. She talked to him during her struggles to fall asleep and had a palpable sense of God's watchful care. She understood that God had "special friends" and she wanted to be one. Soon she began pleading to be baptized as a Catholic, but her mother explained that her father, an Episcopalian, thought she should wait.

When Barbara was five and a half, in 1953, her parents decided to move back to the United States. Her father, Paul, built the family a home in a suburb close to Asbury Park, New Jersey, and began commuting into New York. Although the family's church attendance was infrequent, the Episcopalian Paul would sometimes take his Roman Catholic wife, Mary, into the city on weekends to attend Mass at Saint Patrick's Cathedral. Barbara began attending a parochial school, Holy Spirit.

Soon after the family's arrival in the United States, with her mother's easy-access cabinets and shelving still smelling of paint, Barbara's father was fired by Pepsi-Cola. The company wanted a younger man. The move from Brazil, where Paul's position had been secure, had come at Mary's urging, and yet as far as Barbara knows, her father did not blame Mary for this turn in the family's fortunes. He began worrying constantly, though, as to how he would support his family of five and pay for his wife's always high medical expenses.

One day Barbara was home, sick with the flu, resting on the couch in the living room. She watched her father tidying up the painters' job around the windows, scraping off smudges on the glass and applying a more careful finishing coat of latex. As she watched him, God spoke to her. She experienced what Catholics call an "inner locution": Her father was going to die the next day of a heart attack. God loved her very much and he wanted her to be prepared.

The next day, her father and mother were still at work on the windows when Paul decided to make another run to the paint store. He thought he'd take a friend along for company, the visiting brother of his next-door neighbor. "I'm going over to Wes's house to see if Greg wants to come along," he told Mary. "I love you."

A little later Greg rushed into Barbara's house and whispered a fevered message to her mother. Mary burst into tears, snatched up a blanket, and ordered Barbara not to move from the couch; she was going next door.

When her red-eyed mother returned, she sat on the side of the couch. "Your father got sick, honey," she said.

"I know, Mom. He died, didn't he?"

"How . . . how did you know?"

"God told me. It's going to be okay, Mom. It's going to be okay." The five-year-old child hugged her mother and tried not to cry.

After the initial shock, Barbara's grief naturally emerged. She felt too sad to go to school for the next two weeks. The day of the funeral, she asked to sleep in "Daddy's bed."

After her father's death, Barbara began pleading once more to be baptized. The six-year-old girl assured her mother she knew what she was doing—she would be a Catholic the rest of her life, she absolutely promised. Her mother granted her wish, and the morning of her First Communion, Barbara could hardly restrain her excitement.

In another year, the family moved to Colton, California, a brown-baked town close to San Bernardino, where Mary's sister and family lived. Pat, at seventeen, had already married, and remained on the East Coast. At ten years of age Brian became the man of the family. With the proceeds from the New Jersey house, funds from Paul's years at Pepsi-Cola, and her own disability payments, Mary managed to buy a small house in Colton and raise her two growing children.

In 1955 Barbara went to Immaculate Conception School, run by the Immaculate Heart sisters, and began manifesting such an extreme piety that it worried even the nuns. Why didn't this little mite of a girl go out to play with the other children? She was always reading a holy book or praying during recess.

Barbara explained that she feared the other girls would get her into trouble. Nonetheless, her mother ordered her out to play, and Barbara became more social as she began running with her five nieces and two nephews and made friends at school.

Even so, her mother once asked her, in ironic exasperation: "Why is it always yes? When I tell you to get up or go to bed or eat or pick up your room, it's always yes."

"Because God wants me to obey you."

As early as ten years of age, Barbara began to express her desire to become a nun. When her great-aunt Divina, a Dominican sister, visited, she asked whether Barbara might return with her, a prospect Barbara embraced. Her mother said she still needed her, though. Barbara went through preliminary vocational screening during junior high. She was promised a place with the Immaculate Heart sisters once she finished high school.

For her first year of high school, she went to Saint Bernardine's. At this stage Barbara was not so holy that she didn't recognize who the attractive boys were, and the nuns enjoyed teasing her about her crushes. Unfortunately, family finances dictated that Barbara leave Saint Bernardine's after her freshman year and begin attending the public high school, Colton Union. In the early sixties, just as the Beatles released their first albums in the States and the sexual revolution started to rock 'n' roll, an undersized girl with an inclination for the religious life began to seem freakish. Her classmates started teasing her about her diminutive size and boyish looks. The harassment escalated until a group of boys, watched by their laughing girlfriends, stuffed her into a locker, where Barbara nearly passed out before her panicked cries summoned help.

Of course, Barbara's mother also noticed that her daughter wasn't developing normally. Mary sent her daughter to Queen of Angels Hospital in Los Angeles, where at the age of sixteen she was told for the first time that she had Turner's syndrome. She was given relatively little information about what this meant, only that it was a chromosomal defect. She would always be small in stature and she would be unable to bear children.

She didn't mind being short, except when people made her feel bad about it, and her intention to pursue a religious vocation made her sterility of little account. Or did it? She began questioning what the diagnosis meant in terms of her worth as a woman. Was she less a woman for being sterile? Was she less of a person? Was she a freak? And were people justified in treating her that way?

Her mother acted as if the diagnosis did not matter—to spare her feelings, Barbara supposes. She wonders what her dad might have said, and whether he could have helped her understand that she could still be loved.

Into the void of authority in Barbara's life stepped the high school psychologist, Mrs. Eleanor Williams. She decided to take Barbara under her wing. She advised Barbara to wear contact lenses, lighten her hair, and dress more provocatively. Barbara found the contacts painful and less effective than her glasses, but she complied. She tried to understand what Mrs. Williams was saying about getting along with her classmates, especially boys. Mrs. Williams seemed to believe, like everyone else, that for Barbara not to pursue sexual relationships with boys was odd. It wasn't normal. She couldn't just relate to her male friends like brothers—that was definitely wrong. Reflecting back on this period, Barbara says, ruefully, "She tried to turn me into a sexpot."

Mrs. Williams also encouraged Barbara to join in group activities, to show some school spirit. She persuaded her to become the high school's mascot, Yogi Yellow Jacket. Stuffed inside the neon-bright insect, antennae bobbling from its head, Barbara danced around on homecoming floats and waved to the crowd.

Barbara's transformation from a Catholic school girl into a Yellow Jacket worked to a degree, or at least it impelled her to join up with the other locusts roaring into Egypt. She began to date, often seeing a friend named Dante. If she couldn't have children, she began thinking, at least she could marry.

Her consideration of marriage received a backhanded endorsement from the religious order she had long considered joining. Many of the local Immaculate Heart nuns, in the wake of Vatican II, had chosen laicization after quarreling over the traditional habit. The order's local house was closed. If the nuns themselves no longer believed in their way of life, how could she?

At the same time the distance between the "well-adjusted" young woman that her counselor envisioned and the person Barbara knew herself to be was so great that Barbara became desperate. (The emotional violence generated by this interior conflict would drive Barbara's wanderings for the next ten years.) As she was coming out of high school, the question seemed to be, how could she be normal and still escape the oppressively clubby atmosphere all around her?

Barbara ran off with a boy, eloping to Mexico. In the early summer of 1965, they took up residence for a short time in Arizona, before her mother informed the authorities that she was underage, and she came home, where the illegal marriage was quickly annulled. The marriage lasted long enough for her to recognize that her mother was right; she wasn't old enough to take on adult responsibilities. Her young husband and she parted as friends, and she thinks about him as a "beautiful young man" who was kind to her.

In the fall of 1965 Barbara matriculated at San Bernardino Valley Junior College, and became involved with a postman named Al. They married in 1966: a union that lasted ten years. Barbara put her heart and soul into the marriage, even though Al turned out to have a drinking problem, whose origins lay in his destructive family history.

In 1974, Barbara and Al were living in Oceanside, California— a run-down beachside community north of San Diego. Barbara had not given up on her Catholic faith and attended a charismatic prayer group, in addition to regular attendance at Mass and participation in a group of Third Order Franciscans. Barbara had long prayed for Al to seek treatment for his alcoholism, and her prayers were answered when he joined AA. But then he fell in love with a woman in the group and demanded a divorce. The decree was granted in December 1977.

Three and a half years later, in August of 1980, Barbara married for a third time, to a man I'll call Kenny. When they first met, he was living at the Salvation Army. She had discovered that she couldn't change someone else, but she thought Kenny was truly on the way to putting his life back together, and her impulse to care for those who needed her drew her to him.

He repaid her by lapsing back into his alcoholic problems as soon as he left his Salvation Army surroundings. This marriage quickly became far more violent than anything she had known before. After being married less than a year, Barbara claims Kenny put a loaded gun to her head and threatened to kill her. When he nodded off into a drunken stupor, she managed to slip away, summon the police, and run.

During Barbara's wanderings in the married state, she kept working and going to college, graduating in May 1983 from California State University at San Bernardino. She helped with the religious instruction classes (CCD) at her parish and pursued an active devotional life. Her failed marriages left her stricken, nevertheless, with shame, guilt, and embarrassment. She could hardly believe that she had lived such a life. She had aimed at something else entirely—hadn't she?

She found a good confessor in an African-American priest from New Orleans, Father Etienne, and opened her heart to him. He helped her see that ever since high school she had been playing a false role; she needed to rediscover the girl who had known she was meant for a celibate religious life. Barbara received this news with great gladness. She began hoping her true life hadn't been derailed forever.

In August of 1982, with Father Etienne's recommendation, Barbara entered Perpetual Rosary Monastery in Syracuse, New York. The contemplative life at Perpetual Rosary—six formal hours of prayer daily and a personal hour of adoration before the Blessed Sacrament—suited Barbara immediately. She had finally arrived at the life she had always meant to live.

Barbara stayed at the monastery for nearly six years, taking her preliminary vows after the first three years.

On the cusp of being a professed religious for life, the community informed Barbara that she would not be allowed to take her final vows.

The community had asked Barbara to undergo counseling with a psychologist, in order to understand how her failed marriages might affect her spiritual formation. The psychologist sent warning signals, it seems, to the community about the long-range effects of Turner's syndrome. The community had already noticed Barbara was hard of hearing and that she had difficulty completing unstructured tasks.

In any religious community, especially now that many orders are dominated by aging members, the health of younger members and their capacity to care for their elders becomes a prime consideration. The community seems to have believed that Barbara might soon become as much of a burden as a help.

Then, too, Barbara was already demonstrating an advanced devotion to prayer, recognizing in her interior life what Teresa of Avila calls the "seventh mansion," a transforming union. Some members of the community responded to her with jealousy and suspicion. Even her novice mistress, Sister Augustine, had questioned whether this could really be her first time living the religious life.

In the end, there's still a mystery about this chapter in Barbara's life. The only certainly here is that this decision caused Barbara tremendous suffering. Barbara prayed every night before the Blessed Sacrament, asking, "God, your will be done! God, your will be done! God, help me!"

Being sent away from Perpetual Rosary Monastery remains the greatest hardship in Barbara's life. When I spoke with her about her life there, she constantly slipped into the present tense. "We have a beautiful life that combines prayer, work, and recreation," she said. "When we pray the morning office . . ."

She was permitted to try a more active, less contemplative, religious life during an extended stay as an inquirer with the Hawthorne, New York, Dominican sisters. Again, it didn't work out.

Through communications to her family, the Dominican authorities arranged for Barbara to return to Los Angeles, to live with her brother Pat's daughter Karen and her family in Woodland Hills. Karen and her "aunty" were close, and this was a good place for Barbara to retire to and think.

Barbara says that she never blamed God or the Catholic Church. From the time of her nightly vigils before the Blessed Sacrament, crying out for God's will and God's help, she sought, through prayer, to transcend the dilemma posed by rejection. Would she rebel against what felt like injustice and seek redress, even vengeance? Or would she simply submit and agree in her persecution? Barbara found in her faith a third way of responding: she offered her suffering to God. In this way she fully acknowledged the reality of what was happening, but she was able to leave judgment in God's hands, in the hope that however hopeless her situation appeared, God would use it for God's own ends.

Barbara was now forty-three years old, with three failed marriages and two unsuccessful attempts to join religious communities behind her. She didn't have a nickel. She was living with her niece, and by virtue of her handicaps was disqualified for most jobs—all of this while being intelligent, more than bright enough to graduate from college.

Still, she had only one question: where did God want her to go next?

Absolutely convinced that she had a religious vocation, Barbara felt she only needed the right place to live it out. She quickly contacted a religious community in Orange County, made a retreat there, and came under the guidance of a senior member to discern whether she ought to join.

In the meantime she heard about an extraordinary event in Santa Maria, a midsized agricultural town—the world's broccoli and strawberry capital—on the coast between Los Angeles and San Francisco. A woman named Carol Nole had received several inner locutions—intermittent messages—from the Virgin Mary between March 24 and September 2, 1988. The Virgin had spoken of the need to repent and turn back to God. She wanted, it seemed, a shrine built—the Cross of Peace—on a particular Santa Maria hillside. The Virgin herself gave instructions as to how it should be built. There was to be no corpus (or hanging body) but instead holes filled with stained glass where the nails had been driven.

Press reports of these events initiated pilgrimages from every part of California to Santa Maria. Along with a busload of charismatics from Los Angeles, Barbara journeyed to Santa Maria to pray and rejoice with Carol Nole and her Catholic community. Barbara remembers the ride north to Santa Maria as a time of spiritual exhilaration; her bus mates and she sang praise songs—contemporary spiritual choruses—and prayed together.

Barbara and her fellow pilgrims went out to the designated Cross of Peace site. They couldn't actually walk up to the crown of the hill itself because the land was privately owned and the pilgrims had been forbidden from trespassing. So they stood on either side of Route 166, which runs along the base of the hill. Carol Nole, the Cross of Peace community, and the pilgrims began praying the rosary. The first decade was said in English, the second in Spanish, and so on through all the Glorious, Sorrowful, and Joyful Mysteries.

As Barbara was praying the rosary, she received an inner locution—the voice she had once heard report her father's death—to go over to the other side of the road and pray with the pilgrims there. She crossed and took a place amid the many clusters of people, their clasped hands draped with beads. She entered deeply into this prayer again, with her eyes downcast.

"Look up," she heard. She heard this distinctly, as if someone were standing right in front of her, speaking to her.

She looked up. She saw the Virgin Mary in a white dress with her blue mantle, her eyes gray, her lips soft and expressive. Barbara did not feel afraid, only joyful and full of peace. She wanted to stay in the Virgin's presence as long as possible, but even in the midst of this ecstasy, common concerns intruded. She was scheduled to go with the other pilgrims to Mass.

The Virgin told her to go. Barbara would see her again.

How soon? Barbara asked anxiously.

The Blessed Mother would take care of that.

When Barbara rejoined her friends, she told one of them, Elaine Wong, what had happened. Elaine urged her to tell Carol Nole.

Since many people approached Carol with "me too" stories, Carol reacted at first to Barbara's story with pessimism. Barbara's sincerity and transparent conviction soon won Carol over, though.

She accompanied the Nole family back to their house that night, where Carol's husband, Charlie, asked Barbara a barrage of detailed questions, including what the Virgin looked like and exactly where she had appeared. On a photograph of the Santa Maria hills, Barbara showed Charlie the apparition's location, which lined up exactly with the proposed Cross of Peace site. Charlie became convinced, too.

The spiritual care of the Cross of Peace project had been entrusted to a Monsignor Rohde. The Noles contacted him about what had happened, and he asked that the Noles and Barbara see him at nine o'clock that evening at San Roque Church in Santa Barbara. The long process of discernment as to the authenticity of Barbara's prayerful ecstasies had begun.

Barbara returned to Woodland Hills on Sunday afternoon and then came back to Santa Maria the following Wednesday, March 28, where she received another apparition. The Virgin promised Barbara that she would see her daily and instructed her to remain in Santa Maria.

As soon as the Noles became convinced of the authenticity of Barbara's experiences, they began integrating her into the Cross of Peace effort. They invited her to live with them.

By the time of Barbara's arrival, the Cross of Peace project had already encountered its greatest obstacle. The Newhall Land and Farming Company, the owners of the site, had no interest in selling the land or compromising its future uses by letting a pilgrimage site be erected. When the company's initial decision became known, Cross of Peace supporters, including the builders of a small, four-foot replica of the cross, backed away. They thought it imprudent to continue receiving donations for the cross's erection.

By nature an entrepreneur with group leadership and organizational skills, Charlie Nole became the driver of the Cross of Peace effort, which continues to this day. He saw in Barbara, at first, a means of energizing the Cross of Peace effort, to the end of sweeping away its opposition.

From mid-March through the first week of May in 1990, Barbara received daily apparitions among the pilgrims beside Highway

166 at the Cross of Peace site. The crowds swelled from gatherings of hundreds to thousands. Barbara's apparitions increased in length from thirty or forty minutes to over six hours. First Jesus and then Joseph joined Mary in these apparitions. She came to anticipate the character of the messages they would deliver by their demeanor and changes in apparel, as Mary would sometimes be adorned as the Queen of Heaven and at other times appear more simply.

Not being able to sustain concentration over that period of time, the other pilgrims prayed the rosary, sang praise songs, took breaks, and even cooked their dinners. Lay workers from the charismatic prayer group out of which Carol Nole's work had sprung ministered to the pilgrims, offering counseling and the laying-on of hands for healing. Many conversions and healings were reported. Anglos, Hispanics, and African-Americans joined together in a scene of great openness and reconciliation.

Barbara Matthias had brought something of Galilee to California.

While Barbara lived with the Noles, Charlie asked her to keep detailed records of everything she experienced in her apparitions—so much so that she often labored long into the night detailing that day's apparition and in the process mixing in her own feelings and projections with the accounts. The record she was creating would eventually compound the problems of discernment her experience demanded.

On May 8, after about six weeks of Barbara's residence with the Noles, Charlie launched a fund-raising campaign for the Cross of Peace project, essentially institutionalizing the effort as a ministry. The funds raised would support the roadside prayer vigils, lobbying with the Newhall company, and provide living expenses for Carol, Charlie, and Barbara.

In one of Barbara's next apparitions, the Virgin indicated her displeasure with the fund-raising effort. The money would come freely in time, she said.[3]

Charlie hotly disputed whether the Virgin could have said any such thing. He talked and remonstrated with Barbara ceaselessly, until in exasperation she said, "Maybe the Blessed Mother will just come and take me home, and all the turmoil will be over."

Because of the friction in the Nole household, Charlie asked Barbara to move out. They arranged for her to stay in the apartment of two young women who were part of the Cross of Peace project, before returning to Woodland Hills for a weekend stay with her niece's family. In Barbara's apparitions, she heard the Virgin predicting she would experience a time of persecution.

On May 19, her apartment mates drove Barbara out to the Cross of Peace hillside. Charlie met them there and wished Barbara well. After this strangely valedictory visit to the hillside, Barbara's companions began driving her south toward Los Angeles. The unusual visit to the hillside and Charlie's leave-taking cued Barbara to what was up. Charlie Nole meant for Barbara to leave town.

Barbara asked that her companions return her to Santa Maria. "Take me back to Santa Maria!" she begged. She threatened to jump out.

Her escorts flatly refused. Without Barbara's knowledge, they had packed all of her belongings into the trunk. She was suicidal, Charlie had told them, and needed to be with her family. Her elder brother, Pat, would be meeting her at her niece's home in Woodland Hills.

On Highway 101 at seventy miles per hour, there was nothing for Barbara to do but submit.

Naturally her brother Pat and her niece Karen, after learning that Barbara was seeing the Virgin Mary and being told that she was suicidal, drew a simple conclusion: Barbara had gone nuts. After all, hadn't she been expelled from two different religious communities, after three failed attempts at marriage? What other conclusion would anyone draw?

Barbara's confrontation with her family in Woodland Hills that day was heated. The atmosphere did not improve when she insisted on being alone between four-thirty and seven-thirty for her daily apparition.

Fearing that it was the only way he could provide his sister with the necessary care, Pat called the police, thinking this the fastest means to an involuntary psychiatric committal. He explained to the arriving officers that Barbara was seeing the Virgin Mary.

It's not our job to commit people, they said.

"She's seeing the Virgin Mary!" Pat insisted.

"So what?" they asked, chuckling to themselves. "That's not a crime, mister."

After several more hours of discussion, well past midnight, Barbara voluntarily checked into a psychiatric facility for evaluation. During the early hours of May 20, she was thoroughly examined and the doctors saw no reason to keep her. They sent her home with compassionate words.

By Monday, May 21, Barbara and her family were reconciled. Pat didn't believe she was seeing the Virgin Mary, but he also didn't believe she had gone crazy. He agreed to drive her back to Santa Maria, where he left her at an inexpensive motel.

The next night she found refuge at the Good Samaritan Shelter for the homeless, since she didn't have any money. Then she stayed with an elderly lady before becoming homeless once more. She ended up in a flophouse inhabited by hookers, drug users, and cockroaches, where, during her yearlong residence, one woman was suffocated with her own pillow. Nevertheless, the daily apparitions continued and Barbara was reassured that she would be provided for.

She was hired at McDonald's, which began easing her situation. When the ownership found that Barbara had trouble carrying out their instructions, however, they reduced her hours from twenty-five per week to two. They were freezing her out. Intervention by the Department of Employment on the basis of discrimination against the handicapped restored her half-time work schedule. Her health suffered during this time of persecution, though. She lost twenty pounds, dropping from one hundred to eighty.

On her knees in her transients' hotel, Barbara received comforting messages from the Holy Family—she would be taken care of. How, they did not specify. She was asked to exercise faith despite her present circumstances.

Barbara returned to Santa Maria at a time when the wisdom of Charlie Nole's fund-raising efforts was being questioned. Many in the community thought the efforts were unwarranted because of the property's not being available, and the regional bishop intervened, demanding the fund-raising efforts be stopped and all monies collected returned. The charismatic prayer group out of which the Cross of Peace project had been generated was informed on May 22 that the fund-raising effort was being canceled.

At the same time, the county authorities were becoming concerned about public safety issues related to the hillside prayer meetings. Route 166 is a common truck route and the minor accidents the prayer meetings had already occasioned seemed a prelude to the inevitable catastrophic collision between the pilgrims and a steam-rolling tractor-trailer.

In the midst of these conflicts, Charlie wanted nothing more to do with Barbara, and ordered her to stay away from the Cross of Peace hillside prayer vigils. While Barbara had been living with the Noles, Charlie had conveyed instructions from Monsignor Rohde, asking that Barbara request of the Blessed Mother that the apparition that day end at sundown. Monsignor Rohde was trying to gauge the length of the apparitions and their flexibility. Barbara believed she could not dictate terms to the Virgin and tried desperately to contact Monsignor Rohde. When her efforts failed, she refused to obey these instructions, fearing they might have come from Charlie himself or were simply unwise.

Charlie obtained a letter from Monsignor Rohde that questioned Barbara's stability (without directly naming her) because she had not obeyed his instructions as her spiritual director. For this reason he rejected the authenticity of the messages she was receiving. (Later, Monsignor Rohde would see the lack of wisdom in conveying instructions to his spiritual charge through another person and would recant the negative statements he had made about Barbara.) This letter was disclosed to the leadership prayer group on May 29.

When Barbara and a friend approached a Cross of Peace hillside gathering on June 2, Charlie read Barbara the riot act and threat-

ened to read Monsignor Rohde's letter to all the pilgrims in attendance. So Barbara just went away quietly.

At a subsequent meeting of the prayer group several weeks later,
someone asked what had become of Barbara. One of the leaders of
the Cross of Peace project said she was no longer associated with the
project and declared her a schizophrenic.

This statement angered Jerrie Castro. She was a longtime member of the leadership prayer group, and with her husband, Bob, a
mainstay of Santa Maria Catholic renewal circles. She had greeted
Barbara only once, but the manifest injustice of her being declared
a schizophrenic in a public gathering without any evidence being
presented wounded her for Barbara. She wanted to know the truth
of the matter and began to pray for her.

The Castros led a pilgrimage to Medjugorje that summer and
didn't have an opportunity to meet personally with Barbara until the
fall. They finally spoke with her on October 2, 1990, at a dinner
party with their mutual friends John and Barbara Gayton, the leading musicians in the Cross of Peace community.

Jerrie's occupational background, working with handicapped
children in special education for sixteen years, enabled her to see
Barbara clearly. She could look past Barbara's childlike, sometimes
headstrong behaviors to her true, gracious, bright personality. While
rumors continued to swirl through the town about Barbara's "hallucinations," "clairvoyance," and "schizophrenia," Jerrie became convinced of her sincerity.

This was a key turning point, but Barbara would still endure another nine months of subsistence living before people rallied to her
aid. Yet during this time of abandonment, as she received her apparitions in the cockroach-infested motel, a great work of healing in
Barbara's own life went on. Alone with God, she gave over all the
troubles of her past and present into God's care, relinquishing whatever resentments and bitterness remained. This time in Barbara's
life, although its specific spiritual transactions remain hidden in Barbara's private journals, prepared Barbara to be a channel of God's
mercies to others.

In July 1991 Barbara was graciously invited into the Gaytons' home, where she stayed for eight months. The psychological and spiritual healing that came through prayer combined with the compassionate care of others worked wonders. In February 1992, she was finally able to move into an apartment with another woman directly across the street from Saint Mary of the Assumption Church.

The summer Barbara went to live with the Gaytons, Jerrie Castro and a new supporter of Barbara's, Anna Marie Maagdenberg, her auditory specialist, arranged for the scientific investigation of Barbara's apparitions. Both Anna Marie and Jerrie were determined that Barbara would get the help she needed. If the doctors determined she was mentally ill, she would receive the appropriate treatment. If spiritual advisers found her apparitions were demonic, she would be exorcised. But if her apparitions proved to be inexplicable to science and in accord with the church's teachings, then the messages she was receiving should be evaluated and the fruits of her gift tested, in order that their purpose be understood. (One of the reassuring things about Barbara's case is that the people around her are totally down to earth.)

Through the testing process and by working with her spiritual advisers, Jerrie and Bob Castro eventually became Barbara's spiritual guardians. Jerrie and Bob make sure her life does not become a circus.

After Barbara's scientific testing and the spiritual guardianship of the Castros came into being, her life began to assume its present shape. Each morning she gets up, prays the morning office, a fifteen-decade rosary, and then goes to Mass. Afterward she eats breakfast and then walks to work. When her shift at McDonald's is over, Jerrie usually picks her up and takes her to the industrial park where Mission West Communications has its simple offices. No official organization has grown up around Barbara.

Small groups of people continue to come to the offices or other meeting venues to attend Barbara's apparitions. It's not hard to attend an apparition. There's nothing secret about it. One simply writes Barbara's spiritual director, Father Richard Culver, and asks.[4]

(Journalists and other writers should be forewarned, however. The local bishop strictly limits Barbara's media coverage; 60 Minutes, for example, was politely turned away.)

The people who come, like the women pictured at the beginning of this chapter, bring their hopes, fears, requests, longings—they bring themselves. A pilgrimage to attend one of Barbara's apparitions usually represents a desire to be totally in God's presence, and that brings with it an awful realization that nothing can be concealed or evaded.

Through Barbara's apparitions, God works many wonders. I became aware of Barbara through a woman who had long been alienated from both her father and her cradle Catholicism. This twin alienation seemed without remedy, as her father had died and the clutch of her anger against him kept her from experiencing God's love. But after she prayed with Barbara, she had a visionary dream of her father, and this mystical experience changed the emotional landscape of her life. She was able to forgive her father and soon reconnected with her faith. Her husband of many years, after having no interest in religion at all, began taking religious instruction himself.

In another case, a child was at risk in the womb. The baby had not gained sufficient weight and the doctors feared the child would be stillborn. The couple came to pray with Barbara. Over the next twenty-four hours, by the couple's doctor's reckoning, the baby gained an additional 25 percent in body weight. He was soon delivered as a bouncing baby boy.

These and other miracles are attested to in the many letters Barbara has received from people who have attended her apparitions. A great many of the letters, I noted, recount emotional healing within families, between spouses and between parents and their children, where love now reigns instead of hate. The Holy Family evidently can have a great effect on our own.

When I went to visit Barbara Matthias in the winter of 2000, I wondered what I would or wouldn't see and what impact this would have on my faith. Would the empirical wallpaper of this world peel off and the supernatural beyond be revealed? Did I want this to happen?

I prayed with Barbara during her daily apparition on three different occasions. I say "prayed with," which Barbara always found odd, since Barbara and Jerrie and others in the ministry speak of "attending" an apparition. Barbara herself, I believe, thinks of her own daily prayers as distinct from her visionary encounters with the Holy Family. But I was praying. As Barbara moved my hands to the Virgin's feet, as she extended my arms to embrace the Lord, as she put my hand up to receive a blessing from Saint Joseph, I was praying.

Beforehand I had many ideas about the prayer requests I would present during the apparitions, but I can tell you that the first thing that came to my mind when Barbara called me forward and began teaching me how to reach out to what she was seeing was simply this: "I want to be with you." My own desire for heaven, my fears of unworthiness, my doubts as to my faithfulness, my yearning to be with God bolted right through me with the force of an electric shock. If what I was doing there, in letting Barbara guide my hands in the air while I poured out my heart, was unreal, it was the fullest expression I had ever made of my desire for God to be real, and for that reason an honest human expression. So I resolved not to feel stupid. I was going to let the moment have its way, fully and completely, with no reservations.

This is what I have to report: I did not see Mary or Joseph or Jesus himself. I was always fully aware of my surroundings, and such bothersome realities as my extended arms tiring and hurting. I did receive, however, an unaccountable experience of peace, a deep, luxurious, delightful, yet utterly secure peace, in which I felt bathed, as if my true home lay in baptismal waters. It was extraordinary.

I questioned even this, of course. Maybe I had gotten myself so hyped up in anticipation of my visit with Barbara that this peace I was feeling was a natural reaction to having come through a personal ordeal. For this reason I was interested to see if the same peace would be present the second and third times I prayed with Barbara. While it diminished, this peace continued to rush in as we prayed.

As I reflected on the experience, I also realized one other thing: I knew where Mary and Joseph and Jesus were standing. Jerrie explained who was on the left hand and who was on the right before the first apparition, but I was too confused by my own anxieties to take this in. Maybe this information registered on a subconscious level, someone might say. Maybe so. But I still have to report that I continue to be surprised by my purely imaginative sense of the Holy Family's presence. There even seemed to be a twinkle in Joseph's eye as he heard of my family's needs and the anxieties these occasion. He knew what I was talking about. After Mary's surprise pregnancy, the journey to Bethlehem, the flight into Egypt, and caring for a son who began rebuking him at twelve, Joseph seemed to relate with sympathetic humor to all I was telling him.

So Barbara has been a tremendous encouragement to me, as she has been to many, many others.

Barbara Matthias, a repeated failure at both marriage and conventional religious life, now serves as a channel of grace to contemporary families—our primary communities—at exactly those points where she herself needed to be healed through prayer. Her daily apparitions have taken away the bitterness she experienced as a result of the sexual confusion of our times, the violence of men, and the weaknesses of her fellow believers. Her life shows us how, once we are called to a vocation, God is always ready to meet us in prayer, in order to empower us to fulfill that calling.

I know that many people who attend one of Barbara's apparitions are fascinated by her descriptions of the Holy Family—the robes, gowns, and mantles they wear, their facial expressions, the special feast days when Our Lady's head may be crowned with stars. I have to admit that I asked her almost nothing about this, although she was ready enough to give me detailed descriptions. What interested me about Barbara's experience and the clue I seem to have found to Jesus' own prayer as a result of our meeting lies in prayer as a *drama*.

Most of us think of prayer as specific acts of talking directly to God, either silently in our own thoughts or aloud with others in a worship setting. As I began to think about the story of Barbara's life, though, my attention was directed to a number of incidents in the life of Jesus that compose an inner drama that goes a long way in explaining the outward drama of his public ministry. Barbara's active life of prayer eventually unlocked and continues to accomplish her vocation—her purpose in this world. I began seeing how the same inner dynamic was at work in Jesus' life as well.

In the prayerful episode of Satan's temptation of Jesus in the desert, we see in miniature Jesus' entire mission, his championing of faithful humanity against evil. Through the temptation we see prayer as the primary battleground of this conflict, Jesus' fight to live in the truth while the father of lies seeks to make his corrupt appetites, desires, and manipulations Jesus' own.

We are tempted, I suppose, to see the devil's requests that Jesus turn stones into bread, worship him for the sake of worldly power, and throw himself off the parapet of the Temple to demonstrate his glory as a fablelike addition to the historical Jesus' life. We find belief in Satan embarrassing, part of a nonscientific way of looking at the world that is outmoded. The temptation is a necessary part of Jesus' life, however—in fact, key parts of Jesus' story wouldn't make sense without it. The temptation presents vital understandings of the spiritual drama within Jesus' prayers that is necessary to the outward, public action of the gospels. Jesus soon claims that he has *already* defeated Satan, especially when he exorcises a demoniac who is both blind and mute (Matthew 12:22–28).[5] Such claims make sense only if Jesus has already done battle with Satan.

Through Jesus' rebuffs to Satan we also learn the first principles of the Father and the Son's solidarity. From the beginning Jesus understands that his life depends utterly and exclusively on God. He will not turn stones into bread, because "man does not live by bread alone but by every word that proceeds out of the mouth of God." The supernatural precedes the natural.

Satan knows this, too, of course, since he's sought out Jesus—this new and suspiciously deadly opponent. The prince of this world then offers Jesus the whole of his kingdom, performing a miracle of his own by spreading out the nations of the world before him in an instant. There's a catch, though. Jesus must bow down and worship Satan, in order for everyone else to worship Jesus. " 'You shall worship the Lord, your God,' " Jesus remonstrates, quoting Deuteronomy " 'and him alone shall you serve' " (Luke 4:8).

Later, after his trial, when Jesus tells Pilate his kingdom is not of this world, he's reaffirming the truth he's been grounded in through his prayers. Although even his own disciples, right up to the time of his ascension, expect Jesus to usher in a temporal kingdom, Jesus knows his Father's instructions are directed to different ends.

Finally, in Luke's account, Satan takes Jesus to the parapet of the Temple and tempts him to prove his sonship by throwing himself down. Satan counters Jesus' former rebuffs by quoting scripture himself this time: " 'He will command his angels . . . to guard you' " (Luke 4:10). But Jesus replies, " 'You shall not put the Lord, your God, to the test.' " Jesus knows that his presence to his Father and the Father's care for the Son is not to be manipulated for his own glory or used to demonstrate his status in a prideful manner; he's to pour out his life for others and do so in a way that leaves people free to accept or reject him. The divine love never feels a need, as we so often do, to prove its worth. If Jesus had succumbed to this temptation, he would have proved himself merely the dupe of his own superstitions, for superstition consists in the attempt to exploit God for our own ends.

Jesus' encounter with Satan in the temptation reveals prayer as the primary battleground of Jesus' life. When Satan muscles in on Jesus' communion with the Father, Jesus does not cease to pray. Rather, he triangulates the dialogue, by responding to the tempter from the depths of his communion with the Father in words given by God to Moses—every word Jesus speaks comes from Deuteronomy. Significantly, these quotations occur in the context of Moses relaying Yahweh's instructions regarding the Promised Land. They set out what Israel must keep in mind—the conditions she must continue to meet as she comes into possession of Canaan. In quoting Deuteronomy, Jesus simultaneously cites first principles for the new Israel's kingdom—the reign of God he's establishing—and acknowledges their source in the Father. He knows that the Father is attending this dialogue, even if the tempter does not. Jesus' face-off with the adversary occurs in the midst of prayer.

Most important, the temptation prepares us to see that beyond the Romans with their political subjugation, and beyond the Jewish religious authorities' rejection of Jesus' mission, lies the primary opponent, Satan himself, whom Jesus claims to have seen "fall like lightning from the sky" (Luke 10:18). The outward battle to come is joined first through the inner battle of prayer. The understandings of his Father that Jesus reveals through this inner battle will also be played out in the public arena, where Jesus never fails to strike us as cognizant of the basic supernatural conflict that gives the outward action its shape. When Jesus first keeps silent before Pilate, for example, the Roman governor asks him, "Don't you realize that I have power either to free you or to crucify you?" Jesus is undaunted: "You would have no power over me if it were not given to you from above" (John 19:10–11). Jesus knows that Pilate is only one human actor in an essentially supernatural drama. He's been doing battle with his most formidable opponent from the beginning, and Pilate does not scare him.

In the temptation Jesus' life in prayer anticipates and in a sense already accomplishes Jesus' later victory on the cross—his defeat of Satan. What we might call this flash-forward principle of Jesus' prayer reaches its apogee in the transfiguration. The transfiguration is to the drama of Jesus' prayer what the ascension is to his public ministry.

Jesus leads Peter, James, and John to the top of a mountain, where "he was transfigured before them; his face shone like the sun and his clothes became white as light" (Matthew 17:2). Moses, who personifies the gift of the Law, and Elijah, the preeminent prophet, also appear. From the midst of a cloud as at Sinai, the Father proclaims, "This is my beloved Son, with whom I am well pleased; listen to him" (17:5). The Father's instruction to listen to the Son is particularly important because Jesus, both in Matthew and Mark, where the transfiguration accounts appear, has just begun teaching the disciples about his death and resurrection. Through Jesus' transfiguration, this epiphany of his resurrected glory, Peter, James, and John are given a preview—a flash forward—of events to come.

How is this possible? Jesus' presence to his Father already contains his accomplished work, and as such exists (as we can only think of it) in eternity, as opposed to the confines of sequential time. Although the Son completely emptied himself of his eternal glory in becoming man, as Saint Paul writes, his humanity also participated in eternity through prayer (Philippians 2:6–11). As the transfiguration shows, Jesus had access to the company of heaven, to the point of speaking with Moses and Elijah, through the opening into paradise that prayer is.

If our lives are "hidden with Christ in God," as Saint Paul writes, then prayer is the place where we enter into this secret dynamism of our providential destinies. Visionaries may enjoy, in an exceptional way, visible signs of their access to eternity as they "work out," as Saint Paul calls it, the drama of their salvation. But all such epiphanies of prayer's reality, from Jesus' own in the transfiguration through the saints', are meant to teach us all how close and available the power of God is.

Of course there is another important dimension of prayer, and that is the simple comfort we derive from God's presence.

In the garden of Gethsemane before his arrest and the onset of the passion, Jesus sweated drops of blood as he considered the rending of his flesh to come and desired that God would "take this cup" from him, if at all possible. That's probably the scene from the gospels most people think of when they consider Jesus' life in prayer. Most of the time when I'm on my knees it's because I'm facing a crisis I don't know any other way to face. (As the old joke goes, when all else fails, pray.) It comforts us that Jesus was clearly afraid of his own death and wanted to avoid the pain, suffering, and humiliation involved. We know that he prayed, "Not my will, but yours, Father," and we hope to find a similar courage. In Luke's account the Lord's agony is so great that the Father sends an angel to minister to him.

The angel's comfort was certainly a special mercy, and yet such mercies, such encouragements, abound in God's economy. Angels appear to Abraham and Sarah at Mamre to remind them of God's promise that they will have a son. There's a fourth presence with Shadrach, Meshach, and Abednego in Nebuchadnezzar's crematorium. As a sign of favor Yahweh himself passes by Moses and Elijah as they wrap themselves in their mantles. I've come to think of Barbara Matthias as one of those merciful comforts. Her daily visions are a gift to all believers. Her vocation encourages us in the practice of prayer, teaches of its reality, and brings about specific acts of mercy, the good fruit of a life lived in God.

The word of the Lord endures forever, and yet the Father is also mindful of our weakness, our mere flesh. In Jesus' ascension we see this mere flesh being raised into glory. In the midst of the Godhead exists a human memory of fear and the need for merciful comforts—Gethsemane is not only our point of identification but one of God's as well.

For this reason we are to be confident in prayer. Jesus tells us, "Therefore I tell you, whatever you ask for in prayer, believe that you have received it, and it will be yours" (Mark 11:24). In the same way, Saint Paul teaches us that the Lord "richly blesses all who call on him" and that the Holy Spirit intercedes for us when we do not know how to pray, "with groans that words cannot express" (Romans 10:12; 8:26). Saint Paul goes on to say that nothing, including the tempter who assailed Jesus himself, can separate us from the love of Christ, which we discover, first and last, in prayer.

In Thailand
The Liberator

From nearly the very beginning of Jesus' life, he was hailed as the great liberator. Zechariah, foreseeing the coming Messiah, sings out, "Blessed be the Lord, the God of Israel; he has come to his people and set them *free* (Luke 1:68; my emphasis). Jesus promises that "the truth will set you free," while proclaiming himself to be "the way, the truth, and the life" (John 8:32; 14:6).

Freedom and its personal dimension, self-fulfillment, are undoubtedly the preeminent spiritual concerns of our time, even for people who have no interest in God whatsoever. Western culture is rightly proud of its unprecedented degree of personal freedom, and the West's sense of mission consists in spreading the benefits of freedom around the globe.

Our world still includes a truly shocking amount of slavery, however. Experts estimate that 17 million children worldwide are held in conditions amounting to slavery.[1] One of the most common ways someone becomes a slave today is to be sold into prostitution as a young woman or girl. In fact, international trafficking in women victimizes an estimated 2 million every year.

I began reading accounts of the trafficking in women in the

mid-1990s as Thailand gained a reputation as the global capital of sex tourism. The problem of girls being sold into prostitution by their families was particularly acute there. In northern Thailand alone, as many as thirty-five thousand Hill Tribe women—the Thai equivalent of Native Americans or Australian Aborigines—are currently enslaved in prostitution.[2]

When I first thought of trying to find Jesus at work as liberator in relation to human trafficking, I was only guessing at what I might find or playing a hunch. Since I knew the problem to be widespread and horrific, I assumed that God must have called followers to address it.

It turned out there's a small cadre of Christians in the forefront of this battle.[3] One of the most prominent is Lauran Bethell, an American Baptist missionary whose work has attracted international attention, including visits by then first lady Hillary Rodham Clinton and Secretary of State Madeleine Albright.

In the late summer of 1999 Lauran invited me to visit her New Life Center in northern Thailand's major city, Chiang Mai. The New Life Center is a sanctuary for girls who either have been sold into prostitution or are at risk because of their family's circumstances.

In Thailand I came to know a world of violence and exploitation that is almost unimaginable. It's a world that must be exposed, however, so that the young women who suffer its violence can be freed. Lauran Bethell told me the following story about one of the young women she remembers best and how she came to work with her and others in similar circumstances. I've filled out the dramatic details of the story from what I saw personally in Thailand and from reading accounts of other young women being sold into prostitution.

❖

Myanmar (Burma), 1986

Beneath a triple-tiered canopy forest, through late afternoon heat and humidity so powerful it nettles the skin, a man in a flattened black turban and pajamalike shirt and pants walks along a mountain trail, followed by three children. Each child—the older girl and her two younger brothers whom she herds forward—has a shoulder bag stuffed with all that remains to them, an extra shirt, a pair of underwear, the dolls and stuffed elephants their mother sewed together. They are members of a tribal people called the Akha, an ancient people surviving on the margins of Thai culture. A month ago the children's mother died, and so they are making their way from an Akha village in Burma to another, Doi Huan, in Thailand's northern mountains, its Golden Triangle, where Myanmar, Thailand, and Laos intersect along the Mekong River. Their father has relatives there who will help him care for his children.

West of the town Sop Ruak, the exact meeting place of the three countries, flows a tributary of the Mekong, the Mae Sai River, that serves for twenty-five kilometers as Thailand's northernmost border. Only ten to fifteen kilometers south of the Mae Sai—a day's walk— lies the heart of Akha territory, with Doi Huan and other villages clustered in the mountains' folds. The family is going to cross the border at an unknown point along the Mae Sai, the easiest route from Myanmar into Thailand, although any crossing has its dangers.

In the girl's shoulder bag, buried so deep in one corner that it's partially caught in the weaving, lies the one coin—an Indochinese piaster—that the girl, Malee, rescued from her father's dismounting of her mother's traditional headdress. Her father took the others to buy opium. Malee has nothing else from her mother, except for the songs she taught her and memories of her comforting touch. When she hums under her breath, she can sometimes feel her mother's spirit watching over her—even recall her hummingbird pitch on their favorite lullaby.

> *Come be my protector, Ancestor,*
> *Hurry from the land of sleeping*
> *And take this day's cares away*
> *To keep this babe from weeping.*

Malee prays for her mother's protecting spirit to be strong now, for her father has told her of the dangers in crossing the river. There are bandits and she must keep her two brothers as quiet as possible.

"But we have nothing," she told her father. "What could they take from us?"

Her father sucked in his lips so that he looked like an old man without teeth. "They take girls," he said. "They take children too. The life they'll sell them into . . ."

They smell the river, the Mae Sai, long before they see it; feel its presence in the air, its touch, freshening. It smells like cold iron and cinnamon and contends with the boiling green of the jungle, pumping the air full of a breath-robbing humidity. They still have a full afternoon of walking ahead before their attempt. They will be crossing the river at twilight, the safest time.

When the river appears below them, a brown god snaking through the forest, with tall yang trees lining its banks, their father makes them hide back from the trail. He is going to find a place to cross, he says.

Her middle brother, Jaoo, wants to go with him, and his father slaps him so hard across the cheek that Malee has to stifle his screams against her chest with a suffocating force that increases his outrage.

With her father gone and Jaoo at last quieted, the screeching macaws sound louder and louder. Then she hears a monkey crashing among the branches in the denser forest behind them. In this dense green world the bandits could grab them before they were ever seen.

Her father finally returns and leads them down to the river. The place they cross is wide and the water runs no higher than her little brother's chest. With the river's silt bottom giving way beneath their feet, they struggle to cross all the same. Malee holds the youngest, Tan's, hand. In midstream he gives up walking, lets his feet float downstream, relying on Malee's strong tethering grip to tow him across.

Their father, reaching the far bank first, gestures for them to hurry. He scans the path ahead and turns back to them. He whips his hand at them—hurry, hurry. They struggle against the current and the soft river bottom until they begin to rise out of the water and the footing becomes firm once more. Malee grabs Tan's shoulders and sets him on his feet.

As they make their way onward, the brushing of their feet over the grass, the snap of twigs sounds too loud. Malee is moving into a territory whose inhabiting spirits she does not know; not only the bandits see her as prey, she's sure.

They keep walking, clearing the river-fed jungle, traversing mountain passes that take them into tallgrass meadows, back into rain forest, and out once along the ridges of hills from where they can see a few lights from dwellings in the valleys far below. The moon rises full and there are so many stars in the sky that Malee's body casts a well-defined shadow. Her family could easily be spotted. The trees and grasses are bejeweled with a crystalline light. Malee doesn't know whether to long for the heavier shrouding of forest or the freer air of the meadows.

Just when she thinks she's only walking straight into sleep, the ceremonial gates of Doi Huan village appear. The towering tripod of the village swing stands out against the empty air of the valley beyond. The village lies in the saddleback of a hill, its low, thatched-roof bamboo homes cradled amid higher and lower fields that are bare earth and stubble after the recent harvest. The cooking fires are still burning and the village dwellings almost glow like lanterns.

The first villager looks outside his hut, sees them, calls out, comes to their side. No matter when visitors arrive, everyone leaves his hut to greet them. The village soon clusters around. Malee feels the welcome and quietly thanks her mother for the safe passage. But where are her father's relatives?

Then, after a question or two from her father, she understands that her aunty has died and the rest of the family moved away, back into Myanmar, not far from where they started. They have come all this way for nothing.

A Yunnanese who lives among these Akha steps forward and offers them his home. Malee is suspicious. The Yunnan is not Akha but from a race who are itinerant traders, usually traveling from one tribal village to another, exchanging goods for opium—the Golden Triangle's gypsies. Wealthy Yunnanese sometimes establish stores within villages where the opium trade is particularly strong and become more settled, as this Yunnan must have. But why doesn't an Akha family offer them a place?

The Yunnan's home turns out to be large, with a loft space in the central hut and an adjoining hut for cooking and storage. When Malee and her family enter, she can hear the pigs that sleep in the pens below the floorboards rooting through the remains of the Yunnan's supper. The largest hog snuffles and squeals his warnings to the smaller ones as he takes the choicest bits.

Before she goes to sleep, Malee wonders if she will know where she is when she awakes. She looks around the women's side of the hut one last time and notices the family altar—at least these Yunnan act like Akha, knowing the proper sacrifices to make. This village seems more prosperous than the one they left. In the morning her father will probably find a real Akha family for them to stay with. Perhaps they will build a hut and stay.

Malee has been walking for days and yet she does not sleep immediately, but feels the march go on, as she listens to her father and the Yunnan talk of where they have come from and why. The Yunnan is interested in her father's story. She smells the heavy perfume from an opium pipe—no doubt her father's, the first bowl a welcoming present from the Yunnan, she guesses. Why should he be so generous?

In the morning Malee wakes and sees the Yunnan's sharp-faced wife bending over her with her feet planted on either side of her hips. She's looking at her like a rat whose head she means to crush. "Get up now," she says. "I want you to beat the paddy [to separate the rice grains from their husks] for our breakfast. You are working for us. You and your brothers."

Malee rises and makes a quick search for her father. She finds the Yunnan on the porch between the central hut and the cooking hut. He has a children's schoolbook—a book of simple line drawings that outline hats and cooking pots and animals, trees and other plants, each with writing underneath. The Yunnan tears out a page from this book and uses it to roll a long cigarette. He does not stop what he's doing even though she's standing before him, asking where her father is. "What has happened to my papa?"

The Yunnan lights the cigarette and draws on it several times, then relights it and blows on the lighted end. "Your father is gone," he says at last. "He cannot take care of you anymore. He says you are a good worker but three children are too much for him. So he gave you to us."

"Gave us?" Malee asks.

The Yunnan looks at her, daring her to challenge the arrangement. "You are going to work for us. You and your brothers."

"I told that girl to beat the paddy!" she hears the Yunnan's wife scream from inside the hut.

The Yunnan points to the cooking hut. "In there. Hurry up now. You'll have no trouble if you work hard. But see that your brothers don't get into mischief. Otherwise we'll send them away. We need Akha who know how to work, not just feed their bellies. If you want to keep your brothers with you, you'll do what we say."

Malee cannot live without her brothers, and she hurries to her task filled with panic. She should have known that the bandit they had most to fear would be opium.

Doi Huan Village, Late Summer 1987

The neighbor's rooster is her friend, she knows, although every time Malee hears his first piercing call, well before dawn, she wishes his carcass were in the cooking pot. The Yunnan's own cock won't start chasing his hens until first light. She needs the time to beat the paddy and set the black pot to cooking on the fire's trilegged stand. She has to cook the morning's rice, slice the durian melon, boil eggs, brew the tea, and see that her brothers are ready for the day's work before the Yunnan and his wife stir. Her brothers and she have more work than usual to do today. The remaining corn must be harvested quickly before it becomes dry and withers.

Her brother Jaoo wounded his foot yesterday; a broken-off stalk, as sharp as a bamboo *punji* stick, slashed the instep of his right foot. She cleaned the wound, applied bay leaves, and wrapped it so the bleeding would stop. He must be ready to work today or he will be beaten, as will she for not caring properly for the wound—or letting Jaoo injure himself in the first place, or whatever comes into the Yunnan's mind before the day's first pipes send him drifting.

After Malee serves the Yunnan and his wife breakfast, as well as her brothers, she feeds the pigs the leavings and then puts on her traditional headdress—a conical hat fronted by rows of aluminum coins and bands of silver appliqué, with strands of bright red and yellow gibbon hair hanging down at each side. The Yunnan often chides her for signaling her Akha pride, but she thinks it's helpful to remind him of where he's living.

When her brother rises, he's limping, but he isn't feverish, and Malee feels more hopeful about the day. On the way out to the Yunnan's cornfield they pass the village priest's house, where a water buffalo has been closely tethered, his feet hamstrung, in preparation for old man Geow's funeral. Tonight the priest will pierce the buffalo's heart while the boys quickly pour water down the beast's throat to keep his dying groans from disturbing Geow's spirit. Then the old man's canoe-shaped coffin will be carried through the village gates, out to the grave site.

As they walk down the dirt path to the cornfield, the valley below them is a patchwork of green and yellow and the mountains beyond rise up bigheaded, with the dark sheen of eggplant. The day is so gleaming bright that the valley's rice paddies flash back their silvery waters.

The Yunnan cultivates the most land in the village and there will be plenty to eat from this harvest, unless the rice field's soul departs in bad weather. The corn is nearly harvested now, but the rice has another two weeks to grow. Malee brings a sacrifice each day— a joss stick, some coffee beans—to the field's altar to persuade its soul to remain.

She worries the field's soul may be under attack by jealous spirits—the ones who injured Jaoo's foot yesterday. She asks her brothers to work close beside her so she can protect them from these demons.

After their midday meal, eaten in the field's temporary hut, Malee becomes distracted and loses track of her little brother Tan. She's relieved to find that he's crept underneath the neighboring coffee trees and fallen asleep. He'll still be there, she thinks, when it's time to walk back to the village, and then he'll be so full of energy that she won't be able to get him to sleep. After a year with the Yunnan, Tan still sings to himself and hunts out other children to play with and even yaps at the injustice of the Yunnan's beatings. His older brother, Jaoo, has become quiet, complains of being tired, and is more sad, Malee thinks, than he can express. She is worried about Jaoo. The evil spirits here probably sensed his weakness.

That night, while the villagers visit old man Geow's house, Malee and her friend Bua stand by the village swing, the place where, during the New Year festival, girls like Malee and Bua come of age. A girl's first turn on the swing means she's become a woman. She launches out into the sky over the swing's embankment and back again, showing off her new clothes, her readiness to be courted. Bua took her turn last New Year's but the Yunnan did not allow Malee to do so, even though her cycles started almost two years ago.

The whole village passes through old man Geow's hut, talking with the old grandmother, his grown children. This night will last for a long time; as the men smoke their opium pipes, people bring out their stores of alcohol and gambling games begin.

One of old man Geow's sons—the youngest, named Sheng— walks out to where Malee and Bua are standing. He's not wearing Akha clothing but jeans and a designer label T-shirt. He lives in the big city Chiang Rai now. When Malee first arrived in the village, she used to watch Sheng. His scowl too often spoiled his looks, hardened his expression. Despite his father's funeral, Sheng seems more at ease now; he stands up taller and settles his weight on his feet. She likes his full, wavy hair, how his T-shirt falls over his muscular chest and tapering waist.

He lights a cigarette and without saying a word, offers the pack to the girls. They giggle and cover their mouths. "You're old enough," he says.

"That's not for Akha girls," Malee says.

"Our women smoke." He looks pointedly at the swing. "I thought you took your turn last year."

"I did," Bua says.

"I should have," Malee says, "but the Yunnan wouldn't let me."

"You should have?" the young man asks, cocking his head and rolling his tongue around in his mouth.

Malee wraps her arms around one of the swing's poles, puts her cheek to its stripped smoothness, and peers at the boy.

"The Yunnan is a pig," he says, his voice suddenly sharp. "He lives here, but only to make money off the Akha. No Akha man would treat you and your brothers like he does. I've heard he paid your father for you."

Malee has never let herself think as much, although she's heard the rumor. "My father would never sell us," she says, suddenly angry. "He could not take care of us by himself."

"Then the Yunnan does not own you."

"No one *owns* me," she says. She cannot believe she is talking this much—about such private things—to Sheng. "My brothers must stay with the Yunnan for now, and so I do what the Yunnan says. It's for my brothers."

Sheng takes a drag of his cigarette. He flicks the ash away. "You could do better by them—your brothers."

Malee raises her chin, challenging him and listening at the same time.

"If you had money, a place to stay in Chiang Rai, you could bring them there. He couldn't stop you. Not if you had money. Real Thai baht. Not aluminum coins from a headdress."

She still has her mother's real coin—which might as well be aluminum for how far it would get her. "If you'll tell me how to get money like that, I'll bring the moon down for you," she says, thinking the whole conversation has turned absurd.

"You could work in the restaurant where I do. They always need girls."

"Like doing what?" Malee asks.

"It's a restaurant. Don't you know what a restaurant is?" He pantomimes picking up rice in his fingers and popping it into his mouth.

She does not like his being sarcastic. She knows about restaurants, and the fine temples in Bangkok, and even Western singers like Michael Jackson. The Yunnan has a radio and she tunes it to the Akha station when he's too stoned to notice.

"How much could I make?" she asks.

"Five hundred baht a week," he says.

Malee knows he is lying.

"Five hundred baht?" asks Bua.

"At least that much," he says. "Do you want to come too?"

"We could go together?" Bua asks.

"They always need girls. Chiang Rai is filled with Japanese and Westerners. They are building so many hotels and restaurants that even silly Akha girls can make money." He pauses, takes another drag on his cigarette. "If you know someone who can help you get started."

"How long would it take me to earn enough money to bring my brothers there?" Malee asks.

"A month. Two months. Once you have your own place, you can bring whoever you want there. You are paying for it." He flicks the cigarette butt and sends it sailing over the embankment. "Look, if you truly want to help your brothers, meet me here, right here at the village swing, when the first rooster crows."

He steps toward the girls and leans his head closer to their faces. He puts his hands on their shoulders, drawing the three into a tight circle. "Don't talk about this or I won't be able to help you. I mean it. Don't say anything. I always thought you were the nicest girls in the village. I don't want anyone to spoil this for you.

"You have to get away from that Yunnan, Malee. And if you want to come, too, Bua, you won't regret it. In a year you can come back to marry an Akha boy, only you'll have money to set up your house." He takes his hands from their shoulders, raises his head, and gives them an appraising look. "See you tomorrow," he says.

Malee and Bua talk long into the night about what they will do. If Malee had only her own happiness to consider, she would race Sheng to the highway. Her brothers' welfare is much more important than her own, though. Will the Yunnan give them away to someone else if she is not there?

When Malee returns to the Yunnan's hut, she watches over her brothers as they sleep. The clothes that lie neatly folded beside them are the same ones they were wearing the day they crossed the river with their father. The Yunnan has given them nothing, not even material for Malee to sew into new garments. Something else about the neatly stacked rags bothers her even more than the Yunnan's miserliness. Jaoo's clothes, as torn and threadbare as they've become, fit him. He has not grown, despite the meals she prepares so carefully for him. Have terrible spirits come into his soul? One kind is said to devour the organs. Is that why he is not growing? If she were to hold him night and day, she could not protect him from such evils. She has not let herself admit this before, but she feels as if he may be dying. Something in him is surely dying.

When the neighbor's fretful rooster crows, Malee gets up, kisses her brothers' cheeks, and heads resolutely toward the village swing. *Jaoo, Tan, please do not hate me. It is only for a little while. So I can help you.*

Highway 1, Northern Thailand, 1987
On the bus to Chiang Rai, Sheng sits between Malee and Bua and talks rapidly about the new life awaiting them. He will take Malee and Bua to his own apartment first and bring the restaurant owner there to meet them. If need be, they can stay at his place for a couple of days, until they find roommates among the other waitresses. They are going to enjoy themselves so much in Chiang Rai, watching television, going to movies, finding boyfriends who will take them to discos. They will need real clothes, not their village getups.

It's better if people think them Thai, and they are so pretty, they can easily pass for Thai. They must already understand some Thai, don't they? Of course he knows they have no money for new clothes, but the restaurant owner will lend them the money and then they can pay him back out of their wages.

"What if the restaurant owner doesn't like us?" Bua asks. "You said there were many people who would hire us. Don't we get to choose?"

"I can't go back to the Yunnan," Malee puts in.

"You are the prettiest girls in the village," Sheng says and puts his arms around them. "You will make the owner's restaurant more popular than ever."

Sheng leads them to a large, Western-style apartment building, which is guarded by a miniature spirit house—a tiny column-fronted palace, painted bright white with gilded doors and a crimson ceiling. It's a home for the *phis,* the evil spirits, that might haunt the residents otherwise.

Sheng's one-room apartment has a sink, stove, and bathroom. Its cinder-block walls are covered with posters: strutting pop stars stripped to the waist, their perspiration-matted hair flowing down over their shoulders, and naked women walking out of the surf or leaning over new automobiles. It smells of boiled cabbage, red peppers, cigarettes, sandalwood, soiled clothing, and the dank sweat of the walls.

Sheng has bought chicken and sticky rice and some soup with glass noodles. He asks Malee and Bua to set the food out on his Formica-topped kitchen table. He's going out to call the restaurant owner down at the corner bar.

When he returns, he says the restaurant owner is delighted they have come. He's coming over right away. Tonight they will have a party. The restaurant owner is very, very happy.

The three eat together, shoveling down the food, too hungry to talk.

After the meal, Sheng goes to the far end of the room where his altar sits. The altar is composed of a turban-wearing Buddha surrounded by joss sticks, votive candles, and smaller, finger-sized gods fashioned out of aluminum. Sheng opens a wooden box inlaid with ivory and takes out a cellophane bag filled with what looks like brown earth: rough heroin. He rolls a cigarette with the sticky substance. The girls' village is heavily involved in the opium trade; they are not surprised Sheng has the habit. It does surprise them when he offers to share the precious drug. Their polite puffs seem to disappoint him. He looks almost worried when Bua hands the heroin joint back for him to finish.

Sheng turns on his radio to a Western pop station, with men singing in falsetto voices. He rolls another heroin joint and begins dancing to the music, swinging his arms and hips, tentatively at first and then with burlesque exaggeration as the girls titter, more embarrassed than appreciative. He lifts his face to the sky and puts the joint to his lips, drawing hard, the joint flaring and shortening, as if Sheng's willing the smoke all the way down into his dancing feet. When the fire hits his fingers, he gives a yelp, shakes his hand, and explodes with curses. The girls laugh and he gives them a sharp look. Then he turns slowly around to them, waits until he has their eyes, and crushes out the joint between thumb and forefinger, taking vengeance. He eats the ashy roach.

Sheng reaches under the sink and pulls out a bottle of Mekong whiskey. He pours three glasses. Malee is more interested in the Mekong, having sipped the villager's homemade liquor on festive occasions. Mekong has a reputation for making the person dreamy. She feels like she's dreaming anyway, here in Chiang Rai, having a party in an apartment with naked men and women on the walls. She hopes the whiskey will help her act more confidently when the restaurant owner arrives. She takes a healthy sip and her throat and stomach catch fire. She chokes, takes another sip, and then breaks out in a sudden sweat as her breath won't come back to her.

Sheng is laughing. Bua is too. Malee feels that she's joined in, that she's catching on, however awkwardly.

When the restaurant owner appears, a tall man who wears pants that are cinched by a thin black silver-buckled belt and a shirt with a stitched monogram, he is all smiles. He has a big chin and a big Adam's apple and his feet are canoes.

After introductions, he stands apart with Sheng as they drink glass after glass of whiskey, speaking in Thai all the while. Their voices keep rising. Sheng shouts something and spanks the table with his open palm. The restaurant owner takes another drink, shouts something else, gestures with his fist, and slaps the table too. They keep this up, drinking, shouting, and banging the table—harder and harder.

Sheng finally turns to Malee and Bua as if remembering they are there. "Now we will have the interview," he says. "But my friend here wants to make it fun."

The owner speaks in their direction in Thai.

"He wants a drink," Sheng says. "He wants you to pour him a drink and bring it to him."

The restaurant owner crosses to the chair opposite where the girls are sitting on a rattan couch.

Sheng pours a drink and holds it up, sloshes it back and forth as a signal. "Malee, come take this and serve it to him. Show my friend what a good waitress you are going to be."

Why is the restaurant owner now Sheng's "friend"?

Still, Malee does as she's asked. She brings the man his drink. He doesn't take it from her hand right away but speaks again to Sheng.

"He wants you to serve it in a special way. Like you were his girl-friend. He wants you to sit on his knee and hold the glass to his lips."

The man splits his thighs apart and reaches for Malee's waist. He pulls her onto his knee. The men are drunk already, Malee realizes. They want to have their party. She will have to be careful.

Malee tries not to look into the restaurant owner's eyes as she puts the glass to his lips and tilts it toward him. She looks narrowly at his parched, wide lips, his big chin, his Adam's apple.

He raises his own hand underneath the glass and tips it all the way back, pulling her close with his forearm to the small of her back. The glass nearly drained, he suddenly brushes the tumbler from her grip, sending it flying into the wall. He grabs her head with both hands and tries to kiss her, jamming his tongue into her mouth. She bites down in reflex. He pulls away and strikes her hard across the face with the back of his hand.

She thinks that will be the end of it. She's been beaten before—many times. But the look he gives her now is steady and determined and absolutely ruthless. He grabs the collar of her blouse in his two big hands and tears it from her. Malee is so frightened she cannot utter a sound. Bua screams for her, only to be knocked over by Sheng's fist. The restaurant owner takes pleasure in stripping the last shred of her blouse away. He does it slowly, methodically. This is not over and won't be.

She cannot believe where she is and what's happening to her and there's no stopping it, so she becomes passive and endures his furious will. His violence has so little to do with her, she feels, although she bears its every horror. Silently, she screams to her mother for protection from this man and the spirits that possess him.

All that endless night the restaurant owner and Sheng take turns raping her and Bua. Long before the end, she wants to join her mother in the land of the dead.

Chiang Rai, Thailand, April 1988

After a year in the brothel, Malee has learned from the *mamasan* to make up her lips with a ruby red lipstick, a finer lining pencil, and a gloss that makes them look wet and luscious. Each day she dutifully applies rouge to her cheeks and eyeliner and shadow. After a lifetime of bowl cuts, her hair waves down over her shoulders. Her fawnlike legs skitter around the brothel in a tight silk dress and three-inch heels.

One year ago, when Malee awoke from the "restaurant owner's" brutal indoctrination into prostitution, she found herself chained to an iron bed. She was in great pain, bruised, bleeding, and cramping. The *mamasan* finally appeared, a tall woman in a long blue silk dress. She gave her a *pasin*, a dress slip, and her own frilly, scoop-necked gown. "I'm here to explain the rules to you," she said.

For the next three months, Malee was never allowed outside the brothel. She was chained to her bed every night. About once a week, she would be sold to a man as a virgin. The "restaurant owner," whose nickname turned out to be Click, visited her off and on for "lessons in lovemaking." He often beat her afterward for a poor performance. He never failed to end the beatings by shouting threats to kill her if she attempted to escape. She could see that his keenest pleasure came from beating her, and she had no reason to doubt him.

Gradually, she took her place, sitting in the brothel's front parlor in her frilly gown, waiting to be picked out. At first indifferently and then with the art she saw practiced all around her, she brought drinks to customers, petted them, hung on them, even sat herself down on their knees and poured drinks into their mouths—like that first time with Click. She likes the drink-serving part of the job best, because customers, when they become interested in her, often buy her drinks, too, and she prefers to stay drunk during working hours. When she has to, she downs the dregs of discarded cocktails to keep the numb feeling going.

Malee learns to show her breasts when that's requested by customers, who are mostly Thai, with the occasional off-the-beaten-track *farang* (foreigner) thrown in—usually Western export traders being entertained by their Thai partners. Soon she's no longer sold as a virgin but serves five to seven customers a day. As long as she maintains a good pace, Click stays away, and she's grateful for that. She thinks about only two things: how bad she feels for getting Bua into this and what has happened to her brothers.

One day, a *farang* who has wandered far from the usual tourist haunts comes in with a woman who must be his wife. He is tall, flushed, and florid. His fine rust-and-water-colored hair is chopped so that it falls in fingers over his high forehead. He has a trumpet of a nose and a way of looking around him, despite his impressive height, as if everyone were taller than he. The woman is thin, compact, Thai-sized, and she wears a blue seersucker dress, a tummy pack, and wooden sandals with a leather top strap. They are both beaming about something, perhaps just because they are so drunk, and the man talks long and loud, swaying back to laugh. A couple of girls come up and attach themselves to his arms.

Malee is making the mistake of watching all this. Only occasionally do couples come in wanting partners, and often there's trouble when they do. There's no illusion of courting to be maintained and it puts everyone off. The women are often accommodating their husbands' wishes and not as happy about it as they at first appear, especially afterward.

The woman looks into her tummy pack and takes out a Polaroid camera. She motions for the girls to get even closer to her husband, to rest their heads on his chest. The whole room flashes white as she takes pictures.

Then the woman looks around and sees Malee. She calls and motions for her to come over. Malee quickly grabs Bua. She doesn't know how far the couple's interest may extend and she doesn't want to be alone with them, even in the brothel's parlor. The woman motions for Malee and Bua to snuggle close with her husband. They put their arms around him and press their cheeks to his soft flanks.

He backs away suddenly. Malee tries to look around but feels his hand at the back of her head, squaring her face forward. Then the man places his hand on her shoulder. He's talking to the woman with the camera, his voice sounding alternately displeased, instructing, and conciliatory. He pats Malee's shoulder in a fatherly fashion. As drunk as he is, Malee surmises, he has noticed how young Bua and she are. He barks a last time at the woman. The lightning goes off once and again.

The man takes the photographs from his wife and waves them in the air to dry. He hands Malee one of the photographs. Its image is almost fully realized, the smear of brown at the edges clearing to reveal the brothel's putty-colored walls. Malee stares at her image. Her cheeks look too white from the makeup, her lips too red. The golden string she's woven through her hair glitters strikingly. Most strange of all, her eyes glow red. The way she looks reminds her of a spirit house—stark whites, stark reds, gilding. Her glowing eyes tell her it's true: evil spirits live in her now.

What power the camera possesses, showing even what has happened to her, the trouble inside. She fingers the corners of the hard-edged film and then tucks it away quickly next to her breast. Maybe someday she can find a spirit priest and show him the picture so that he will know what rituals to perform.

Bangkok, March 1986

Every morning on her way to language school, the missionary Lauran Bethell walks through one of the world's most infamous red-light districts, Patpong Road.

On Patpong Road the brothels are so open that many have big glass fronts. At night passersby can see dozens of girls sitting behind these windows, holding fans with numbers on them. Pick a number. Pick a girl. The flyers of the touts, which litter the early morning streets, bear obscene drawings of specialists—contortionists, dominatrixes, fetishists. The drunken men and women sleeping it off on Patpong seem as carelessly thrown away as the broken liquor bottles and used condoms.

Lauran can't help wondering why prostitution flourishes in the country. She knows it's illegal and that Thailand's dominant religion, Buddhism, teaches against it. Why have so many women given themselves to this life? Why do the authorities not only turn a blind eye but quietly encourage what's becoming known as sex tourism? Quickly, the prostitution issue becomes the one thing about Thailand that fascinates her.

Lauran is in Thailand in order to assume the chaplaincy of a prestigious girls' school south of Bangkok; she's supposed to learn the language before next year's spring semester begins. Unfortunately, she's not very interested in the job.

In fact, she doesn't really want to be in Thailand at all. She had a job teaching in mainland China at Nanjing in an elite agricultural university—a position she thought would turn into her life's work.

China was opening up again and missionaries like Lauran were finding that the Christian church, having gone underground during the Cultural Revolution, had actually grown while officially banished from public life. The churches were once again open and flourishing. The entire populace was eager to investigate spiritual questions, having been denied the opportunity for the long years of Mao Zedong's rule. But Lauran lost her job in China due to a pinched nerve that demanded she return to the United States for spinal fusion surgery.

She remains in love with everything Chinese, the literature, the painting, the architecture, the Chinese sense of fashion and taste in cuisine. She's not nearly as taken with their Thai equivalents.

The prostitution problem is different, though. While most people would regard walking along Patpong Road every morning as an unfortunate distraction, Lauran cannot stop thinking about the life so many women are leading there.

Learning about the Thailand prostitution problem becomes the way Lauran copes with her negative feelings about being in Thailand. On her weekends and the four days a month Lauran's allowed to skip language class without flunking, she undertakes her own research project. With her roommate Marcia, a missionary kid who grew up in Thailand and now works for the Peace Corps, Lauran begins contacting all the national women's agencies, gathering as much information as she can. She also volunteers to give English lessons to the Patpong prostitutes via Empower, a nongovernment agency that helps exploited women through education. She's interested in learning their stories—what brought them here, what their problems are, how they manage.

In teeming Bangkok, thousands walk by and choose either to ignore Patpong Road or exploit its women themselves, but Lauran Bethell feels called to help—for reasons she cannot fully explain.

Even today Lauran might not know how to explain why she became so involved with the prostitutes on Patpong Road. It has to do, certainly, with her own story, particularly her feelings of insecurity and entrapment.

.   .   .

Lauran grew up in the San Joaquin Valley, in central California. Her father was a Baptist minister and community activist, and her mother a behind-the-scenes dynamo who staged donkey-and-sheep-equipped Christmas pageants. Lauran describes her childhood as thoroughly happy, with her father's church in the small town of Lindsay a loving extended family.

As to high school, she hated it. In September 1965, the day before classes began, Lauran and her family moved from Lindsay to Atwater, California. Her new hometown, despite its outlying fields of almond trees and table grapes, derived much of its character from Castle Air Force Base. Atwater High was filled with teenagers who had lived in Germany, the Philippines, Iceland, and Kuwait, where they learned to make friends quickly, drop them as fast, and caught the air force's fighter-jock spirit.

Her aggressive peers shunned her socially, to the degree that Lauran wanted to become invisible. Already five feet four inches tall at the start of high school, she grew another six inches over the next three years—immediately out of every outfit she painstakingly sewed together. (She insisted on supporting herself as much as possible through part-time jobs and making her own clothes.) Rail thin, with Coke-bottle glasses and frizzy auburn hair, she felt herself to be a perfect gooney bird of a girl. She never had a date to the prom. She often wanted simply to disappear. This desire grew so strong at times that she experienced depressive episodes, with thoughts of suicide.

Why was Lauran's adolescence so painful? She should have been the "most likely to succeed" type, the girl who is elected to the student council and involved in every campus organization, from the drama club to the debating society. She was smart, ambitious, and naturally inclined to seek out challenges (which she will in the next years, despite continuing to suffer from depression). Her rage at being judged by her appearance turned inward with devastating and long-lasting effects.

Lauran's powerful desire for accomplishment led her to dream of another life. Paging through *National Geographic,* she longed to live and work in exotic locales. Her dreams and her high school night-mares would vie with each other over the next years.

After recouping some confidence at the University of Redlands, she put in six years of teaching in another San Joaquin Valley town, Merced. Her principal and peers became aware that Lauran possessed an uncanny ability to conduct the new-style open classroom, with its learning centers and children of different ages participating in several activities at once. Lauran turned out to be the pedagogic equivalent of a variety show's plate spinner, an educational magician. Her reputation enabled her to fulfill her girlhood dream of living in a place out of *National Geographic*. In 1978 she landed a job in Hong Kong.

The Hong Kong International School occupied a white high-rise that overlooked a channel of the black China Sea. Lauran had an apartment on an upper story and took the elevator down to her classroom. The school's pupils came from the children of the diplomatic corps, international financiers, corporate executives, and a few missionary families.

The prestigious Lutheran-affiliated school was a nearly ideal place to teach. Lauran soon discovered, though, that its social context encouraged her old self-doubts. As the year of teaching progressed, she felt the depressive spider drawing her nearer for its meal. The parents of her students had been educated at Harvard and Yale, Oxford and the Sorbonne. Their decisions determined the policies of nations and multinational corporations; their ideas caused international markets to rise and fall. They owned beach houses and mountain retreats and traveled internationally for holidays. They were exactly what Lauran had always suspected she could never be: members of the world's elite.

Her new boss, the school's headmaster, belonged to this class and intimidated her. One day he greeted her at lunch. "Lauran, how's the class doing?"

Flustered, she launched into a detailed description of the class's activities and continued breathlessly on with a justification of the open classroom setup—an unusual arrangement here. "If you study what Piaget says about childhood development—"

"A simple question, Lauran," the headmaster said, cutting her off with a dismissive wave. "A simple answer would have sufficed."

At times like these she felt as if she were back in high school, and her self-doubts started jackhammering at her confidence.

A simple answer would have sufficed. If only she had a simple answer to the horror and gloom such a rejoinder inspired.

In the summer of 1979, following her first year of teaching in Hong Kong, Lauran and her fellow teacher Judy decided to backpack through Burma and Thailand. Six weeks into the trip, though, while staying on a beach in the south of Thailand at a Christian guest house, Lauran became feverish. The missionary doctor attached to the ministry diagnosed dengue fever. Her back and neck grew stiff. Her joints ached so horribly that the thought of any movement filled her with dread. For days the fever kept her drifting in and out of a troubled sleep. She had a strange craving for mashed potatoes and grape juice. She had never been so sick before—not close.

As soon as she was able to walk again, she returned to Hong Kong, leaving her friend Judy behind to enjoy the rest of her holiday.

Back in her apartment at school, Lauran was still quite sick and would be for many days ahead. She did not as yet know that she had also picked up an intestinal parasite. The wasting parasite turned her depressive tendencies lethal—one of a parasite's most insidious effects. Lauran kept thinking she should feel better, but all she could do was sit in her apartment and look out over the hillside toward the China Sea. She couldn't hold anything in her stomach and had to force liquids to stave off dehydration.

Everyone else was gone from the school. She was more alone than ever. She had been dating a Mormon businessman, but their relationship had never progressed beyond sleeve tending to social functions. He was no help.

As she thought about the upcoming school year, Lauran didn't know whether she could cope any longer with its social demands.

She was so tired of pretending that she felt a confidence she had always utterly lacked. She began sinking into a severe, clinical depression.

One night, at the end of a day sitting alone, a day of reminding herself how utterly useless she was as a person, she could bear it no longer. Her adolescent thoughts of suicide returned once more, this time with serious intent. All the medications they gave her for the joint pain would end the useless struggle.

Her spiritual life had been on hold since her teaching days in Merced. She had as much as told God that she no longer understood the Christian faith. She had been a faithful Christian daughter and yet God had never deigned to address her crushing insecurities. What good was her faith? What practical effect did it have? What meaning did a word like "redemption" have for her—or the supposed freedom the believer has in Christ?

Yet she prayed one last prayer with all her heart. *I can't live this way,* she told God, *and I won't. You have to do something. Now!*

With that, she fell into an exhausted sleep.

In the morning, as the sun's low rays gilded her big front picture window, she awoke to find . . . that she was okay. She was . . . *okay.* In fact, she felt an unexpected lightness. She waited to feel foolish, for her doubts and fears to return. Instead, her mind remained quiet, peaceful.

For some reason she remembered racing as a child with her friends around the olive trees secured by the brick plant stands at her father's church in Lindsay—the freedom she had felt, which seemed to have returned.

I'm okay, she kept thinking over and over. It wasn't the most high-sounding oracle or revelation anyone had ever received, she thought, laughing to herself.

She knew immediately the enormous difference this would make. Literally overnight, she had been rescued from half a lifetime of insecurity and its accompanying depression. The enmeshing web of negative emotions no longer bound her. She was at last free. She could see herself in the company of the school's parents, with friends she especially admired at her church, Hong Kong International Baptist, and she imagined saying what she had to say, being who she was. What a relief! She couldn't get over what a transformation had occurred. It was a miracle—nothing less.

Lauran's unforgettable release from her own insecurities became the foundation of her adult life. She would always look back to that suicidal night and its resurrection morning as the time when her Christian faith became undeniably real.

In the late winter and spring of 1982, Lauran came to believe it was time to move on from the Hong Kong International School.

In her mid-thirties, Lauran had at last matured into her looks. She might have stepped out of an English portrait, the tall lady of the manor, all peaches-and-cream and thick, auburn hair, with a strong profile that promised strength and wise judgment. In the past couple of years she had enjoyed the most serious romantic relationship of her life, with an adventuresome, intelligent man who finally decided that he was incapable of sustaining a marriage—and remains, to this day, a lifelong bachelor. This was a blow she needed all of her reenergized faith to sustain.

Her relationship over, Lauran was ready not merely for the next challenge but to find her life's work—an alternative passion. She remembered how God vouchsafed her father's vocation when he leaped safely from his crashing World War II bomber. From that day on, he lived his life in grateful service. She wanted a similar wholeheartedness.

She began checking into possibilities, among them a new school being started by people in the diplomatic corps in mainland China and positions in Japan. She made a list of twenty life goals. The last item, surprisingly enough, turned out to be "attending seminary."

A month before she was scheduled to return to the States, a missionary at her Baptist church, the Reverend Noren, asked her, "What if you came back as one of us?"

A thousand objections immediately came to mind. Missionaries had to be linguists, dynamic organizers, people capable of great austerities, wonder workers whose leadership qualities translated universally. They had to be people like the Reverend Noren.

Then, on the threshold of leaving Hong Kong, Lauran spent a last Sunday at her church, assisting with the worship service. She asked the congregation to turn their hymnals to "When I Survey the Wondrous Cross."

As the chorus ended, with "Love so amazing, so divine, demands my life, my soul, my all," Lauran's voice broke and she was in tears, far too many to hide. She covered her embarrassment as best she could.

After the service, she asked the wife of the pastor to sit and pray with her. Lauran felt she was being called into ministry. She stopped worrying, as they prayed, about the objections the Reverend Noren's question inspired. With her call came the conviction that the gifts of the Holy Spirit would make up for whatever she lacked. If she was called, wouldn't she be equipped?

So, not quite five years after that Sunday morning, having been graduated from American Baptist Seminary of the West and ordained and commissioned by her denomination, Lauran found herself in Bangkok.

As Lauran teaches English on Patpong, she learns some startling things about her students and the Thai culture that has formed them. Almost to a woman, the prostitutes' driving ambition is to support their parents and brothers and sisters. They probably believe prostitution is wrong, but if their skills are limited and prostitution is the only way they can support their parents, then they are willing to be prostitutes. They resolve to keep the tenets of Buddhism that they can. Perhaps they will earn enough merit through supporting their parents that they will have a happier fate in their next life.

Also, Lauran learns the Thai prostitute's great secret, and its hidden meaning—the special allure that attracts sex tourism customers from all over the world. A Thai prostitute exudes an air of looking for love. She treats her client as if she were the man's girlfriend.

The retired brickyard worker from England, the widowed Australian insurance salesman, the socially inept lifetime American bachelor—all these and their Asian counterparts find young women who treat them like the man of their dreams. What they are too befuddled by lust to suspect is that the women are actually dreaming about how much money they can ship off to their families. One-night stands that turn into second visits, weeklong stays, and then an ongoing arrangement with an apartment keep increasing the family subsidy.

Lauran also learns that the sex tourism industry that flourishes in Bangkok represents only the high-dollar, hard-currency trunk of the elephant. It's estimated that 90 percent of Thai men use prostitutes, who are to be found in every village restaurant and barbershop, and even among the female caddies at golf courses. In Thailand, a polygamous legacy has given way to monogamy for the sake of rearing children, supplemented by prostitution. There's little expectation—at least on the man's part—of fidelity.

Another question begins puzzling her: why, in addition to the Thai women on Patpong, are there so many Indian, Burmese, Philippine, Korean, and Chinese women here? She begins to hear stories of women being sold into this life. One of her Empower students claims she was drugged and flown here from Pusan through Seoul. She has no reason to doubt her, and everything she's learning tells her such stories are not only true but common.

Because of her ambivalence about being in Thailand, Lauran makes minimal progress learning Thai. She remains discouraged. She'll put in her three years at the girls' school, she thinks, and then find something else. The prostitution issue interests her—and what it implies about the status of women in this country—but what can she do about that?

The prostitutes themselves are not particularly eager to have their situation addressed. In most cases, if a woman has chosen prostitution and has some negotiating power with her pimps, she won't leave. She'll even choose to come back to Patpong after realizing the dream of being a kept woman. The money is too good and the woman is often overwhelmed by addictions to sex, drugs, and the excitement of the bar scene itself.

One conversation changes everything for Lauran. A couple of months before her job is set to start at the girls' school, in December 1987, Lauran receives a call from Elaine Lewis.

Elaine and her husband, Paul, are legendary figures among Protestant missionaries in Asia, spending their lives working with the Hill Tribe peoples of the Golden Triangle, especially the Akha.

Elaine Lewis tells Lauran that she's formed a committe charged with establishing a ministry to help tribal women who have been sold into prostitution and those at risk of suffering this fate. As Lauran has been learning, women who have been sold into prostitution constitute the largest class of slaves in the contemporary world. It's a particular problem among the Hill Tribes.

Evidently news of Lauran's research into Thailand prostitution has impressed the missionary community and her name keeps coming up as a candidate for the new ministry's director. Would she like to run a safe house for victimized women? It will be located in Chiang Mai, Thailand's second city, in the heart of the northern region.

Before Lauran has finished talking with Elaine, she knows that she has found her life's work—or it has finally found her. There's suddenly a reason for the seminary years and the years teaching. There's a reason why her pinched nerve caused her to leave China. And there's now a great big reason to learn Thai as fast as possible.

In April 1987 the first safe house of the New Life Center opens in Chiang Mai, with eighteen young women in residence and Lauran as its first executive director.

Chiang Rai, 1988

The week after the tourists take her picture, Malee is chosen by a man who takes her arm and pulls her toward the back rooms without uttering a word. He's short and thin enough for his bones to show like spikes beneath his skin. His eyes are so whiskeyed up, ghosts seem to rise off them like mist from cold waters.

Once in her room, still without uttering a word, the man unbuckles his pants and lets them fall around his ankles. He removes his shirt. He rocks on his feet for a moment, not bothering to shield his genitals, only standing with his trousers still down around his ankles as if he needs their support to keep from falling.

He levels his bleary eyes at Malee and nods. She takes off her dress, her underwear, and lies down on the bed. He crawls on top of her and begins moving against her, muttering and grunting as if to encourage his erection. Still he has not spoken. When at last he is aroused, he pushes her legs apart and asks, "You want me, don't you? You want me, my lovely Tui?"

He's speaking Akha! Malee jumps up. "You are an Akha man!" she says. "You are Akha!"

"Tui," he says, beseeching, and reaches out to her.

"I'm not Tui," she says. "But I'm Akha, from the Doi Huan village. Do you know the village?"

The man looks up at her and she sees the confusion start to clear from his eyes. This sharpening reminds her of the photograph. She picks it up from her side table and points at Bua. "This is my friend," she says, excitedly. "She is Akha too."

Her nakedness suddenly shames her and she puts the photograph down and scrambles back into her dress. "You have to help us," she says, fitting and hitching the dress. "Bua and I don't want to be here. We were tricked. They won't let us leave. You have to take this photograph back to the village and get someone to help us.

"Look at the photo," she says. "You see how our eyes glow red? There are evil spirits in us. You don't want to sleep with a demon girl. You have to take the photograph back and have them help us go home so that the priest can entice the demons out."

"What family are you from?" the man asks.

"Zao Prung," she says.

"That family doesn't live in Doi Huan anymore," he says.

"My father gave my brothers and me to a Yunnan there. You know the Yunnan? My mother died and my father didn't know what to do with us."

"You still have brothers there?"

"Yes, and they need my help to get away from the Yunnan."

"I know that man."

"Then you know why I have to escape from here."

"But I paid . . ."

Malee stands tall on her feet and crosses her arms. Her jaw is clamped shut against what the man has just said. "What is your name?" she asks him.

He doesn't want to tell her.

"Aaaaaiiiiiii," she screams and smacks him hard on the ear.

"All right," he says, defenseless in his drunkenness. "Rae Po."

"Do you want two Akha girls to be slaves, Rae Po?" she asks. "To be owned by a Thai pimp?"

Rae Po hands the photograph along to the Doi Huan village headman, who talks with the missionaries Paul and Elaine Lewis, people the Akha often turn for help with the Thai authorities. Since this is a case of minors being held against their will, the police raid the brothel and bring Malee and Bua out. Bua's family has been longing for her return, and she's sent home. Malee is sent to Lauran Bethell's New Life Center.

At first, Malee is so confused she thinks she's been sent to another brothel—a mistake even the Chiang Mai police have made, showing up one morning in the first days of the center's existence to collect a payoff from the new brothel in town.

On arrival, Malee is brought into a room with desks and machines and an air conditioner in the window. Lauran and her assistant, Faith, come in. The Western woman is taller than any Akha man—she looks like a real-life version of a maternal spirit. When she hears the Westerner's assistant speak, she knows Faith must be Akha like her. No one but an Akha has ever spoken the language so naturally.

Lauran speaks to Faith in what Malee recognizes as Thai. Faith then asks her a question in Akha. They want to know where she has come from, what has happened to her.

She tells them about leaving her home village, about the Mae Sai crossing, even of her father giving her brothers and her to the Yunnan. She says, "I thought that nothing could be worse than working for the Yunnan. We were his slaves. We did everything for the Yunnan and his wife and he gave us nothing. So I ran away."

"That's when you came to Chiang Rai?" Faith asks. She turns to Lauran and speaks rapidly in Thai, catching her up on the story.

"That's when ..." Malee's voice catches. "It *was* worse," is all she can say. "It was so much worse, and I couldn't help my brothers at all."

Faith does not press her. She puts her arms around her and holds her.

It is so strange being touched now, Malee feels. She still longs to hold her brothers, but she is not sure she wants to be held herself. She remembers her mother lying with her at night and calming her into sleep, rubbing her back, stroking her hair. She will never feel her mother's touch again and her comforting seems the only power capable of freeing her from the spirits.

Lauran puts a kind hand on her shoulder and gives it a squeeze. Malee wants to reach out but can't.

Faith promises that they will all three talk again soon—only to make sure Malee is doing well. She doesn't have to say anything more about the past, unless she wants to.

The center's routine soon takes Malee into another, almost equally unexpected life. She's once again working in a kitchen, it's true—this one outside under a tin roof—helping to prepare meals for an even bigger household; but now she's not alone but with other girls as they prepare the paddy, chop cabbage, pare carrots. They are full of talk of school and lessons and giggling admissions about crushes on boys.

In her new home, Malee sleeps in an open teak-walled dormitory, where every girl has a pallet she folds up each morning and a few feet around it for personal possessions. It's crowded but like being back in a village, surrounded by a large family.

Malee is taught how to sew and make puffy-cheek dolls dressed up in traditional Akha clothing, complete with a vest under the chemise, leggings, and a headdress as elaborate as those of the most wealthy village women. She quickly becomes an expert seamstress and turns out doll after doll. Her housemother, Faith, praises her, and Malee likes to think she's helping to support this new place that's becoming a home.

When Faith tells her of the money she's earned through sewing dolls, she cannot believe it. Of course, they told her that the money from the dolls would come back to her, but some of the money from the men was supposed to come back to her.

What does she want to do with the money? Faith asks.

She wants to send it to her brothers, of course!

"We'll be happy to do that," Faith says.

She believes her—almost. When a letter comes from Paul Lewis reporting on her brothers and how the money has been used to buy them new clothes and treats, her mouth drops open. She sees a picture of Jaoo and Tan in their new clothes—they look so happy. Mr. Lewis says he will be keeping on eye on her brothers, making sure the Yunnan knows someone cares about their welfare.

Malee's worries have begun to lessen, except for one: no one here must ever take *her* picture. She doesn't want anyone to know that she's the demon girl. Jaoo's and Tan's eyes did not glow like hers.

After two months at the center, preparing meals, sewing, working with Faith on learning Thai, Malee walks out of the center one evening with the others to school. (The girls attend night school in order to help run the center themselves.) All the girls, in white, starched blouses and black skirts, trail in a line one after another, with Lauran Bethell in the lead, the mother before her uniformed ducklings. Malee is going to school! Faith tells her the center would like her to complete nine grades before thinking of a life on her own. Nine grades. She will be smarter than the headman.

.   .   .

Once Malee starts to learn Thai, she begins understanding the lessons taught at the center itself. Most mornings and evenings, Lauran sits in a chair and gathers all the girls around her. She places a book in her lap and reads from it. Lauran speaks of a loving God who compels the center's staff to show love to the girls. This God showed his love by sending his Son to die and then come back to life again. He makes the family altar and its sacrifices unnecessary, because the Son's death counted as the final sacrifice. The Son now has power over everything, the world that can be seen and the spirit world, too.

The talks always end with candy for everyone, Nestlé's chocolate and M&M's and hard candy—a little sweetening in the life of girls who live more austerely than monks.

One evening Lauran Bethell talks to the girls about a man named Legion. This man has so many demons inside him he lives among the caves and tears his own flesh. God's Son, Jesus, meets this man and the demons are so fearful they throw the man to the ground and cry out for pity. Jesus sends the demons into a herd of pigs that dash off a cliff and drown themselves, returning the man to his family and home village.

Later that night, after Malee comes back from school, she asks Faith about Jesus and the evil spirits. Does he still have power over them?

"Yes," Faith says.

"Do you know the Jesus ritual for casting out evil spirits?" Malee asks.

"Yes," Faith says. "I can even perform it. But you have to help. If you'll talk to Jesus with me, we'll ask him to throw the demons out."

"It's all right if I talk to him?"

"Yes."

"In Thai, or Akha?"

"It doesn't matter. The loving God and his Son, Jesus, know all languages."

"Okay," Malee says. "You start talking to him. You tell me what I have to say."

"It doesn't matter what you say. You ask for what you want, and if you mean it, he'll do it."

"I'll mean it," Malee says eagerly. "Why *wouldn't* I mean it?"

Doi Huan Village, Northern Thailand, 1996

Lauran is driving up to Doi Huan village to visit Malee. She's married now to a gifted linguist from a Chinese family. Prior to the traditional Chinese ceremony the young man's parents planned, Lauran performed a Christian ceremony for the couple, for Malee's husband is a strong Christian as well. Malee has a new baby, who is close to his first birthday. Lauren takes a carload of presents with her.

There was always something extraordinarily *light* about Malee—she fairly skimmed over the earth, Lauran remembers. And she was always singing. She had the gift of many tribal girls for singing and harmonizing to an extraordinary degree. Lauran began calling her Hummingbird.

From the center Malee went on to work for a Western family, completing her high school education and seeing that her brothers were delivered from the Yunnan and were cared for, during their own educations, in a youth hostel.

When Lauran arrives in Doi Huan, she walks straight to Malee and her husband's hut. She's so eager to see her. She finds the young husband on the hut's porch, giving the couple's fat baby a bath in a metal tub. Malee is at the village church, he tells her, leading a pre-school class. She should go see her there. The baby and he will wait for their return.

The church that has been built in this Akha village is much like any other Akha hut, bamboo walls and floors and a thatch roof. It is marked only by a cross over the front entry.

As Lauran nears, she hears children singing. She's caught off guard because the children are singing not in Akha or even Thai. It's English.

Lauran's through the door when she hears, in high-pitched earnestness:

Yes, Jesus loves me,
Yes, Jesus loves me.

Yes, Jesus loves me,
The Bible tells me so.

Malee stands at the front, conducting, wearing a yellow dress with a big yellow bow in her hair. She's teaching her students English, as another preschool teacher might teach French with "Frère Jacques." Lauran has brought her camera and quickly pulls it out to take a snapshot of Malee with her students. Malee sees what she is doing, opens her eyes wide, and smiles.

The secular imagination generally views not only sexual slavery but all oppression as the result of outside forces that work against the individual, usually through the exertions of a privileged class or group. Even when the restraints exist within us, like Lauran Bethell's insecurities, we presume that they properly belong to others—or more accurately, bad environments that have been falsely internalized. Secular analysis immediately looks at "the system"—the economic and cultural forces that encourage sexual slavery, or the family system that promotes insecurity—to explain individual problems. Responsibility lies not in the person but in surrounding conditions that shape the person's actions.

Jesus questioned the truth of any purely external analysis. "What goes into a man's mouth does not make him 'unclean,' " Jesus says, "but what comes out of his mouth, that is what makes him 'unclean' " (Matthew 15:11). And, "The good man brings good things out of the good stored up in him, and the evil man brings evil things out of the evil stored up in him" (Matthew 12:35).

Jesus' liberation begins not through politics but through the person. It begins when God's love comes to reign in the heart. As I suggested in the Introduction, in the Christian view the "good things" in a good person are there by virtue of Christ's indwelling presence. "I in them and you [Father] in me," as John records.

In his earthly life Jesus showed God's love to people in ways that were, for the time, not merely politically incorrect but scandalous. The scandal of Jesus' sharing meals with publicans and sinners consisted in its contradiction of the religious leaders' external analysis of what it would take for Israel to throw off their Roman oppressors. These leaders—as ours do today—had their own understanding of freedom's demands.

Israel's leaders believed that their Messiah would come, their deliverance occur, only if they kept the covenant. As a "holy nation," they might be worthy of Yahweh's redemption. This could hardly be the case, though, if public immorality were in any way encouraged. So Jewish religious leaders marshaled society to shame the immoral into changing their ways. To those who abided by the religious law, Jesus was undermining their national-liberation efforts by countenancing sin.

These tensions are present in the famous scene of a prostitute washing Jesus' feet. Invited to a Pharisee's house for a meal, Jesus allows a woman who has led a sinful life to bathe his feet with her tears, kiss them, dry them with her hair, and anoint them with alabaster perfume. The Pharisee has his negative suspicions of Jesus confirmed, thinking Jesus must not know the woman's trade, and therefore he can be no prophet. The Pharisee cannot imagine anyone who cares about Israel's plight coming so close to the appearance of evil.

Jesus rebuts the leader's prejudices by saying, "Her many sins have been forgiven—for she loved much. But he who has been forgiven little loves little" (Luke 7:47). For the Pharisee, freedom is all about the corporate status of Israel—its collective or external righteousness. For Jesus, freedom is first about the interior disposition of a single heart. Then it's about community, because the forgiveness Jesus shows to the prostitute is meant to reunite her with the community—to restore her to it, rather than run her out of it.

Through reaching out to his society's untouchables, Jesus announces that our freedom lies first of all in God's love for us—God's *care*. God's love makes everything else possible.

> See how the lilies of the field grow. They do not labor or spin. Yet I tell you that not even Solomon in all his splendor was dressed like one of these. If that is how God clothes the grass of the field, which is here today and tomorrow is thrown into the fire, will he not much more clothe you, O you of little faith? (Matthew 6:28–30)

Such statements not only call Jesus' hearers to a profound trust in God's care but also reveal Jesus' understanding of people's common wants and needs. He doesn't neglect these things for the sake of a higher purpose. He tells us we can rely on God for them; we can let go of our common anxieties and begin living out the reality of God's love.

In his best-known teachings, the Beatitudes, Jesus responds to our natural desire for freedom and the happiness it brings. Each of the famous short sayings—"Blessed are the poor in spirit ... blessed are those who mourn ... blessed are the meek"—begins with a description of a state of being, "blessedness," that may be much more than happiness but never less. The word used in the Greek New Testament, *makarios*, describes in pagan Greek literature the state of happiness and well-being the gods enjoy. Jesus is saying that the freedom he offers—the life he brings—actually fulfills the divine element in each person, the image of God in which we are made.

How can this be? we wonder, because Jesus associates his understanding of well-being with many categories we'd rather not: like mourning, meekness, and poverty. We think our freedom and its joys exist in bright contrast to these shadows.

Outside of religious speculation, though, what is happiness? I remember a character in an Iris Murdoch novel (who was herself a professional philosopher) defining human happiness as the "temporary remediation of difficulties." It's only the result of a fleeting improvement in our circumstances.

Much of what we know as happiness can be readily accounted for in this way. A promotion at work, an Adonis inviting us on a date, our son knocking down the winning three-pointer in his basketball game—all these bring their sudden exhilaration; but the promotion, the new relationship, and the next contest soon bring their own challenges and accompanying anxieties. Our satisfactions are purely momentary creatures and can be maximized only to a limited degree, as the life of any billionaire shows.

By contrast, Jesus' blessedness is so powerful it can exist in the midst of negative circumstances. Through the Beatitudes Jesus claims that those who follow in his way will find even difficulties transformed into joys. Every suffering will find its just compensation, and every virtue its present and future reward. All that rises from our mortality will converge in Christ's immortality. There will be a peace that passes all understanding in whatever circumstances we may find ourselves, including wholly negative ones. Blessedness is freedom in the midst of any circumstance.

A life that had this measure of happiness and well-being truly would seem godlike. It would also release whatever dynamic powers we already possess. We sense this, don't we? If only we could escape our persistent flaws or character deficits, our habitual fears, we could step out into an amazing freedom. Jesus says this is possible through belief in him. "I am come that they might have life, and that they might have it more abundantly" (John 10:10). That is, indeed, what Lauran Bethell began experiencing after her breakthrough experience of God's love.

Not only are our native capacities unleashed through Christ; Jesus also claims that God himself, through Christ's indwelling presence and the Spirit's ministrations, will supply whatever we are lacking in the accomplishment of God's purposes. In the post–Last Supper discourse in Saint John's gospel, Jesus says:

> I tell you the truth, anyone who has faith in me will do what
> I have been doing. He will do even greater things than these,
> because I am going to the Father. And I will do whatever you

ask in my name, so that the Son may bring glory to the Father. You may ask me for anything in my name, and I will do it. (John 14:12–14)

Faith gives us the freedom to enter into Christ's ongoing work, to do "greater things than these," Jesus' own mighty works or miracles. As individuals experience freedom in God, they become a mighty collective force, the kingdom of God in action, Christ's Body at work in setting the rest of the world free.

In Rome

The Prophet

The gospels report that people thought Jesus must be a prophet—
that was his obvious role, in their eyes. "Some say that thou art John
the Baptist: some, Elias; and others, Jeremias, or one of the
prophets" (Matthew 16:14). The first stated theme of Jesus' public
ministry is, after all, a prophetic call to repentance: "From that time
on Jesus began to preach, 'Repent, for the kingdom of heaven is
near' " (Matthew 4:17). Jesus' call to repentance, while issued generally, most often was directed specifically to the religious leaders of
his day, the reform-minded Pharisees and the Temple authorities.

Today we have politicized the role of prophet. Gandhi and Martin Luther King Jr. and Nelson Mandela are the most frequently
mentioned prophets of our time. Like the archetypal prophet,
Moses, these leaders brought their people into a new land of freedom.

How, then, would I discuss Jesus' prophetic role in our world today? I suspected I would have to find a religious leader calling his
peers to repentance, and doing so in a way far surpassing the usual
ecclesiastical squabbles. The person would also have to be a leader
whose call to repentance came out of a profound understanding of
freedom.

In 1994, through the document *Tertio Millennio Adveniente* (As the Third Millennium Draws Near), Pope John Paul II began to prepare the Roman Catholic Church for the Jubilee 2000 celebrations. Jubilee 2000 would be a time of repentance as well as forgiveness, the pope said. The church needed to recall those times in history when her sons and daughters

> departed from the spirit of Christ and his Gospel and, instead of offering to the world the witness of a life inspired by the values of faith, indulged in ways of thinking and acting which were truly forms of counter-witness and scandal.... A painful chapter of history to which the sons and daughters of the church must return with a spirit of repentance is that of the acquiescence given, especially in certain centuries, to intolerance and even the use of violence in the service of truth.[1]

The pope's statement immediately alerted close observers to the possibility the church might actually address itself to the Crusades, the Inquisition, the forced conversion of indigenous peoples, and the church's role in the anti-Semitism that fueled the Holocaust—to the whole litany of historical sins its opponents often cited. During his many travels, John Paul II had already shown a willingness to speak of these historical errors, most notably on a pilgrimage to Auschwitz. What was he planning this time? How would he call the whole church to a collective act of repentance? What significance would this have for the future direction of the church?

When the calendar of celebrations for Jubilee 2000 was announced, the first Sunday in Lent, March 12, was proclaimed a Day of Pardon. On that day, the world was informed, the whole church would be called to a collective act of repentance for the historical sins of the church's sons and daughters.

The Day of Pardon announcement occasioned commentary from all sides, which steadily intensified as the event neared.

External communities, particularly the Jewish community,

watched to see whether the church would not only confess but make a *good* confession. Would the church confess to its legacy of anti-Semitism?[2] Would it go so far as to name names?

Those within the church wondered whether the church *should* repent of its historical sins and even whether it could. Do not sins belong by their very nature to individuals? Only God looks on the heart. Do we have a right to judge people in the past by today's standards?[3]

The most interesting questions tended not to be asked. Why was this being done—particularly, why now? And what implications would the Day of Pardon have for the church's future? These, at any rate, are the questions that drove me to investigate the story.

After traveling to Rome, interviewing the papal household theologian Father Georges Cottier and the director of the Archive of The Congregation for the Doctrine of the Faith, Monsignor Cifres, as well as reviewing all the published material on the Day of Pardon, I found that the *why* and *why now* questions had one answer: John Paul II. Although discussions about the Day of Pardon involved outside scholars, theologians, and several congregations and councils within the Curia, John Paul II led the church toward the Day of Pardon from first to last.

This led me to wonder, when did John Paul begin to think of this, and how? Only John Paul himself knows the answers to those questions, but in this chapter I've tried to capture the gist of what he might say.

So this is a story about one man, a prophet of our time, Karol Wojtyla—whom the world knows now as Pope John Paul II—and one day, the Day of Pardon, March 12, 2000. It's also the story of a thousand years of history and the innumerable evils committed in the name of Christ that John Paul finally brought to the altar of Saint Peter's. To tell the story I'll skip a stone across this great sea of time, because its meaning depends, in a sense, on skipping identifications of one prophetic figure with another—a walking-on-water power that finally lifted another Peter out of history's drowning sea.

✢

Like many Poles, Karol Wojtyla came to think of Poland as a suffering servant among the nations—a Slavic Israel. Poland's sacrificial history began as far back as the fourteenth century, when some of the people bordering its territories, the last of the pagan tribes left in Europe, the Samogitians, were among the first to experience genocide—not only mass slaughter but a *principled* slaughter.

The fourteenth century's experience of genocide came out of the Crusades and the problems entailed in the church-state alliances that followed after Constantine legalized Christianity in the late Roman Empire (325 A.D.).[4] The Constantinian bargain eventually resulted in a profound confusion about what belonged to the kingdom of God and what to the secular state—and who decided these questions. By the second millennium the keys of Christ's kingdom and the sword of earthly rule jangled against each other on the habits of monks and the armor of princes alike. Popes administered their own states and princes appointed important churchmen; heresy became a capital offense in civil law and simony—the selling of church offices—a concern of Holy Roman Emperors.

Within the Crusades germinated the perfect expression of the Constantinian confusion of the secular and the spiritual: the chivalric orders. The Hospitallers of Saint John, the Knights Templar, and the Teutonic Order all began when crusaders established makeshift hospitals to care for their fallen comrades. The knights of these chivalric orders were given the status of religious; they belonged to the church as monks did, and took the same vows of poverty, chastity, and obedience, with this crucial addition—fighting the infidel. Their principal activity was not prayer but war.

As the Crusades in the Holy Land were winding down in the thirteenth century, one of the chivalric orders, the Teutonic, began a long retreat to Germany, where it searched for another Crusade.

At that time the Christian church was still evangelizing Europe. Missionaries were sent to the peoples of the easern Baltic coastlands, to Prussia, and border areas between Lithuania and Poland. Many of the missionaries were martyred.

In 1217, Pope Honorius III preached a Crusade against the pagan tribes of these regions, the Pruthenians, Curonians, Semigallians, Samogitians, Lithuanians, and other tribes within the Letto-Slavic race. In 1225, a Polish duke, Conrad of Masovia, claimed his territory had been invaded by these peoples and requested the assistance of the Teutonic Knights. The Holy Roman Emperor, Frederick II, endorsed this request by "incorporating" Prussia into the empire by a bull of 1226. Since Prussia was now formally part of the Holy Roman Empire, at least on paper, armies could be sent in to defend it—even from its own peoples. Frederick's land grabbing was further based on his own pragmatic theology. In Frederick II's understanding, the empire and the church were one, and so the gospel could be spread by the sword. He saw no difference between subjugation to the empire and conversion to the Christian faith.[5]

Within twenty-five years, the Teutonic Knights had conquered all of Prussia. Acknowledging this, Frederick II, in two golden bulls of 1245, granted the governance of Prussia to the Teutonic Order. The emperor's reasoning in these bulls endorsed the Teutonic Order as "a State and a Church . . . whose only *raison d'être* was permanent war against infidels . . . for the conquest of their lands as far as its victorious army could reach," says historian Stanley Belch.[6]

About the same time, the Teutonic Order was authorized by Pope Alexander IV (1254–61) to take possession of all lands it could conquer within the Islamic territories of the Holy Land. "By this grant," says Belch, "the Pope tacitly confirmed the principle of conversion by force and the principle that infidel nations have no rights vis-à-vis Christians."[7]

The Teutonic Knights' practice would soon show what the equation of conquest with conversion against a people considered without rights, or subhuman, could mean.

The Samogitians, who lived in border areas between Poland and Lithuania, resisted the rule of the Teutonic Knights over the next two hundred years. The war the Teutonic Knights fought against the Samogitians was marked by the Germans' overwhelming military superiority. "Perhaps not until the Spaniards encountered the Aztecs was such a dramatic disparity of technology to recur in a major conflict," says military historian Norman Houseley.[8] The Teutonic Knights had mailed cavalry, giant catapults and trebuchets, and crossbows as its disposal; the Samogitians, bows and arrows, swords, and running away. Tens of thousands of Samogitians and other Baltic tribesmen lost their lives as the Teutonic Knights established fortresses from Prussia into Lithuania.

The systematic destruction of the Samogitian and other Baltic tribes proceeded through raids, or *Reisen*, the Teutonic Knights launched against isolated civilian populations. Usually these *Reisen* occurred on either the feast of the Assumption or the feast of the Purification of the Virgin Mary as a religious tribute.

For example, in 1314, the Teutonic Order attacked throughout the province of Medininkai, employing all of its military might against small lowland farming villages beside the Nevezis River in central Lithuania.

In one of these villages, August 15 dawns with mostly clear skies, except for gauzy patches of fog that cling in the treetops of the forest behind the village. A dozen small farms are strung out along the Nevezis between a marsh headland and a great forested bend in the river. Each farm has two groups of dark wooden buildings: the long, wide *troba*, or dwelling house, with its central chimney, besides which stands a granary—and across a clean yard, barns for threshing and livestock, small outbuildings, and pens.

The villagers' wheat fields beside the river stand tall and golden in the still blue-shaded morning light. White smoke from the farms' central chimneys spirals upward against the backing evergreens as pigs grunt and rustle in their cages and goats crop the ground around their ties.

Out of the forest at the right, a horse and its bareback rider appear. Flashes of the horse with its rider's head pressed forward against the beast's surging neck show their speed as they trace the path on the other side of the wheat fields from one farmhouse to another.

After each stop, the farmers and their wives and children rush out of their *troba* and begin running toward the marshland at the head of the village. The shouts of fathers and mothers to their children and their neighbors spark from one farm to another. Some of the men, even if they have children clinging to their necks, carry scythes or pitchforks. The women, their heads covered by brightly colored scarves in henna and yellow and gentian blue, keep spreading their arms wide to shelter their children along, retracing their steps to grab up little ones, as they make their maddened way toward the marsh.

Out of the forest from all sides come the Teutonic Knights' footmen, armed with crossbows, pikes, the heavy, slashing swords called falchions, and their favorite, the flail—three spiked-lead balls tied to the end of a stave for bludgeoning and battering.

The knights appear behind on their caparisoned horses, wearing blue mantles charged with black crosses and skirted white tunics over full plate armor. Their helmets, with wide circular brims, look like upended spittoons, and their swords are so heavy they require two-handed hilts.

At a signal, the knights break fast from behind the footmen's ranks toward the marsh themselves. The Samogitian farmers' chief means of defense lies in their underground fords, the tunnels they've dug through the marshlands, that lead to their own fortresses.

In the race to the tunnels, the knights' horses cut off escape to all but a few, and the knights begin driving back the villagers toward their foot soldiers. To terrorize the women and children, whom they want to keep as slaves, the knights decapitate the first pitchfork-wielding men and carry their heads at arm's length as they curse the villagers back into the encircling footmen.

The remaining men who attempt to stay with their families, covering their children with their bodies, are quickly dragged away to be bashed to death with the hideous flails. Those who run to the forest are shot by crossbows or intercepted by the reserves that now come forward.

None of the men who have been unable to reach the marsh are

allowed to escape. Their bloodied stares express shock, horror, outrage as they fall one by one amidst clusters of attackers.

After the women and children are herded together, the footmen begin tying them up. The women and the older children have their hands bound. Younger children who cannot walk or might not be able to keep pace with a forced march are tied to their mothers, often back and front, where they scream and scream and scream.[9]

The Teutonic Knights cart the pigs and other livestock that can be taken away and then begin putting the torch to the Samogitians' houses and fields. The few who have escaped will have nothing to return to.

Since this scene is repeated throughout the district of Medininkai, with over seven hundred slaves taken in this one incident from 1314, the remaining few from the district's villages can only give up their homes and flee to their tribal neighbors elsewhere.

In this way, the Teutonic Knights subjugated one area of the countryside after another, building fortresses afterward in order to consolidate their rule. In its efforts to "convert" the Samogitians, the order made over one hundred *Reisen* against the population. They did not introduce the women and children they made slaves to Christianity, for converts could no longer be slaves. Their mandate to convert the Baltic tribes turned out in practice to be strictly a policy of extermination and enslavement, because living converts were useless to them.

The Teutonic Order's conquest of the eastern Baltic coastlands eventually boomeranged against Poland itself. In 1386 the grand duke of Lithuania, Jagiellon, married the heiress to the kingdom of Poland and embraced Christianity.[10] From this time forward the Poles and the Lithuanians were Christian allies, and yet the Teutonic Knights did not cease their *Reisen,* going so far as to burn whole villages of Lithuanians in their newly constructed Christian churches. The Teutonic Knights insisted that the conversion of infidels could not be trusted, and as the Spanish Inquisition later declared against the Jewish-convert Maranos in the sixteenth century, false converts must face death. Here we see genocide not only in its practical character (the physical extermination of a people) but also in its theoretical character: the basic identity of an entire people becomes the reason for its death.

This led the Poles to defeat the Teutonic Knights in a direct confrontation at Tannenberg in 1410, and yet the order's genocidal campaigns against Samogitia continued until a second defeat in 1422 and even afterward.

The Teutonic Order's principled slaughter did have one redemptive outcome. It led to the work of a Pole who is to international law what Copernicus is to astronomy. He was the rector of the University of Krakow from 1409 to 1432, and his name was Pawel Wlodkowic. (He is usually referred to in English as Paulus Vladimiri, as I will do here.) The story of the Teutonic Order's slaughter of the Baltic tribes became important to Karol Wojtyla because of Paulus Vladimiri. In fact, although their lives are separated by five hundred years, Paulus Vladimiri, in terms of his thinking about religious liberty, stands behind Karol Wojtyla as the prophet Elijah—in Jesus' thinking—shadowed John the Baptist.

In order to understand the full importance of Paulus Vladimiri's work, however, Karol Wojtyla would have to experience persecution himself.

In 1944, on August 6, the feast of the Transfiguration, in the city of Krakow—three hundred miles south from that long-ago Samogitian village—on what will come to be known as Black Sunday, the twenty-four-year-old Karol Wojtyla crouches behind locked doors in his basement apartment on Tyniecka Street. He can hear shots being fired almost as frequently as during the 1939 invasion. Jeeps, motorcycles with sidecars, and Black Marias roll through the streets as squads of Gestapo arrest every able-bodied man they can find. The Nazis hope to forestall any repeat in Krakow of last week's Warsaw uprising, a last resistance by the Polish people to Hitler's occupation.

Warsaw is now being razed by overhead bombing as the last hope of an independent Poland dies.

From the time of the German occupation, September 1, 1939, Karol Wojtyla has been engaging in underground activities that could have resulted in his being arrested and imprisoned in Auschwitz—or simply shot in the street. For the Germans don't merely mean to occupy and exploit Poland; they intend through their Kulturkampf, or culture struggle, to wipe any vestige of Polish culture from the face of the earth. Engaging in cultural Polish activities and unsanctioned religious devotions has become a capital crime. Karol—or Lolek as he is more often called during this period—has consistently flouted these edicts. He's a member of Unia (Union), an organization of ideological and cultural resistance to the occupation that promotes clandestine cultural activities, aids Jews, and seeks to keep Catholic social ideals alive. Lolek has also continued his studies in the underground Jagiellonian University, formed soon after most of the faculty was arrested and deported by the Nazis. He's pursued his interests in acting and the great works of Polish drama through the Rhapsodic Theater. The troupe members have put their cultural principles to the test (and risked their lives) in twenty-two formal performances and over a hundred clandestine rehearsals.[11] What's more, Lolek is a key leader in Jan Tyranowski's Living Rosary groups, where young people meet together to learn to live with God in the midst of the occupation. Any one of these activities, as benign as they may strike us today, could already have led to Lolek's death.

Lolek's greatest offense, however, lies in the life commitment he's only recently made. He's one of Archbishop Sapieha's underground seminarians. Since the occupying Nazis shut down the seminary, Archbishop Sapieha began accepting candidates for the priesthood on the basis of clandestine studies and examinations. Lolek goes to his job every night at the Solvay chemical factory in Borek Falecki, where he works in the plant's water purification unit, stealing time, with his coworkers' assistance, for his seminary studies. The job has so far protected him from deporation into slave labor within Germany, as his *Ausweis,* or identity card, states that he's employed in an industry essential to the German war effort. None of the Germans or their Polish informers have found out he's been studying and taking exams in secret.

This morning when he came home from working all night through a double shift, he was informed that the archbishop was calling in all of his underground seminarians to his own residence. Lolek was to go into permanent hiding.

But the Gestapo are at the door of Tyniecka 10 before Lolek can make any effort to cross town to the archbishop's residence. He can only hide in the dark basement apartment and wait, praying for deliverance as his heart pounds. As he waits, he cannot help remembering the carnage on the road to Tarnow during an abortive escape attempt at the beginning of the occupation. Whole families were cut down on the road by the strafing aircraft of the Luftwaffe. Old classmates like Jozef Wasik have been publicly executed for underground activities. The women of Jerzy Kluger's family—a Jew, his closest friend in high school—have been shipped off to the extermination camps. The Salesian priests in his own Debniki parish have been arrested and deported as well. Just last April, the boy he served so many morning Masses with, Jerzy Zachuta, was taken by the Gestapo in the middle of the night. Zachuta's name has been listed on a Gestapo poster with Poles to be shot.

Lolek has little doubt of the outcome if the Gestapo find him. For five years now he's lived, as have all his countrymen, with the possibility of death from day to day. He knows how easily it can happen.

He can hear the soldiers' boots scraping the floors above and then hammering the stairs up to the second floor. "Our Father . . . ," he prays. The soldiers' voices are muffled but he catches the sense. They are asking if anyone else lives here. A young man is often seen going in and out.

No one else lives with them, his loyal neighbors reply, truthfully, evasively.

"No one out to Mass this morning?" the Gestapo question.

"No one is out," they say.

Lolek's apartment, the one he shared for so long with his recently deceased father, is often referred to by friends as the catacombs. The first saints in the time of the Diocletian persecutions, in the real catacombs—could they have been as frightened as he is now? "Blessed art thou . . . ," he prays. He's cold and sweating at the same time.

Lolek waits a hellish eternity, but the Gestapo finally leave without discovering him. He has been saved once more. But why? Why did they leave? The entrance to the apartment is obvious enough from the street. Was this providential? Has he been saved *for* something? Or only until the next time?

His friend Irena Szkocka, whom he calls *Babcia*, or Granny—most of the Rhapsodic Theater performances take place in her flat—then helps him wend his way across town to the archbishop's residence, walking a block ahead as a scout.[12] They are aided as well by a priest, who watches his back and side approaches.

The three walk past the many posters listing the names of hostages who are waiting to be shot in reprisal for resistance activities, and go over the Debniki bridge, which is guarded. Somehow the soldiers pay him no attention. From the bridge they have to walk up toward Wawel Cathedral into Old Town and finally to the archbishop's residence. Immediately adjacent to the residence sits a police station with an armory. But here again, they are not stopped.

As soon as Lolek enters the archbishop's residence, he's given a cassock, disappearing into a prophetic disguise.

Soon the Nazis make inquiries about what has become of their chemical plant worker, but underground channels arrange for his name to be stricken from the payroll. The Germans "were unable to find my trail," as John Paul writes later.[13]

In September of 1965, the fourth session of Vatican Council II begins in Saint Peter's Basilica. The tremendous nave has been turned into an *aula*, or hall, with ten tiered rows of felt green chairs to each side, for the more than two thousand council fathers, as well as *periti* (theological experts), religious, staff, and ecumenical observers.

Karol Wojtyla, recently enthroned as archbishop of Kracow, sits amid his fellow bishops, doing two things at once. While listening to the speeches, or "interventions," by other council fathers, Archbishop Wojtyla is writing one of his own, which he'll deliver in less than a week's time, on the twenty-second. (Wojtyla is famous within his diocese for being able to write correspondence and memoranda while conducting meetings. He flabbergasts newcomers by summarizing these discussions at their end, giving due weight to different points of view, before articulating his own thoughts.)

The most contentious issue at Vatican II, religious liberty, will soon be debated one last time, with the chances of the vitally needed "Declaration on Religious Liberty" being promulgated growing longer. The *schema*, or draft, of the declaration currently before the episcopate faces stiff opposition from members of the Curia and others. Last year, Cardinal Tisserant, dean of the council presidents, went so far as to pull the document off the agenda. Because of extensive revisions suggested by the Secretariat for Promoting Christian Unity, Cardinal Tisserant said, further discussion would have to wait until session four.

In response, more than a thousand council fathers signed a document asking Pope Paul "urgently, more urgently, most urgently" to overrule Cardinal Tisserant.

Pope Paul declined.

The council fathers now have one last chance to find a way through the impasse.

The proposed "Declaration on Religious Liberty" would reposition the church vis-à-vis the Constantinian legacy. Its opponents worry that the declaration may involve, in the words of historian and papal biographer George Weigel, "such a dramatic development of doctrine as to suggest that the Church had been gravely mistaken in the past."[14]

In nations where Catholics constitute a substantial majority, the church has long sought a privileged position within society—what in American constitutional terms we would call "establishment." Cardinal Ottaviani of the Holy Office and others believe the church's privileged position in Catholic-majority states desirable, in order to maintain a moral witness in culture. In 1965, the church operates this way in many countries, particularly in Latin America. (In Ecuador, for example, the church not only is supported by the state but has the right to outlaw any cult—meaning competing faith—it deems harmful.) Opponents of the declaration go on to argue that "error has no rights." They fear abetting the moral relativism sweeping through Western culture.

Many among the Western European bishops, influenced by the *nouvelle théologie* of such theologians as Yves Congar and Jean Daniélou, see the necessity of a "new evangelization" that renounces the old altar-throne alliances. The privileged position once afforded the church in these countries has resulted in the church losing its dynamic witness.

The United States contingent, influenced by Jesuit theologian John Courtney Murray, wants the universal church to embrace the free exercise of religion over against establishment.[15] The Americans point out that the United States is among the most religious nations in the world precisely because the Roman Church and other Christian communions do not suffer from the anticlericalism that results from compulsory taxation. Christian communions in the United States are free to be the moral witness in culture that is needed *because* they are institutions purely of witness, not compulsion.

Archbishop Wojtyla and others from the Soviet bloc find the Western European and American arguments sympathetic but lacking theological depth. To Wojtyla's mind, in fact, the present draft of the proposed declaration is based too much on "positive law"—legal guarantees. Wojtyla lives in a society where religious freedom supposedly enjoys a full range of legal and even constitutional guarantees. This does not keep the Polish government from building new towns, like the infamous Nowa Huta, without providing space for any churches. Nor does it prevent his government from interdicting free discussion even within the Catholic community itself—the archbishop, when he wants to communicate with his parishes, must have his messages delivered by hand. It does not prevent his government from arresting clergy for organizing devotional groups in churchless neighborhoods.

As the sometimes sonorous and often quite stumbling Latin of the council fathers' interventions echoes through Saint Peter's, Archbishop Wojtyla ponders again how to find the needed basis for a declaration on religious freedom that speaks from the heart of the faith—an approach that the whole church can agree upon. At his enthronement ceremonies back in March of 1964, he was reminded again by Professor Franciszek Bielak's welcoming speech of the work of Paulus Vladimiri, the rector of the Academy of Krakow in the fifteenth century.[16] At the Council of Constance, Paulus Vladimiri argued before the church fathers of his day that the Teutonic Order's forced conversion—their slaughter—of the Baltic tribes must end. Their *Reisen* against the Samogitians and others were criminal, no matter how many papal bulls and edicts of the emperor stood behind them.

Wojtyla has brought the works of Paulus Vladimiri with him today and is refreshing his memory as to how the gospel allowed Vladimiri to grasp truths that eluded so many in his time.

It is not allowed to compel infidels by arms or oppression to embrace the Christian faith, for to take this way is to wrong our neighbor, and bad things most not be done in order that good things should result. . . . No one is to be compelled to the Faith, because Faith must not be from necessity, since forced services do not please God. . . . And in particular the Jews should be tolerated because we prove our truth and faith by their books.

Wojtyla thinks again, as he often does, of his high school friend Jerzy Kluger's family—the matriarch, Grandmother Huppert; his mother, Rozalia; and his sister Tesia, killed by Hitler's Holocaust. After fifteen years he's reconnected with Jerzy himself, oddly enough, by virtue of the council; his friend now works in Rome as an engineer. In his mind's eye, Wojtyla sees the Jews of Kracow being driven into the hastily constructed ghetto where so many died from disease and malnutrition even before the deportations. Vladimiri had contended with a similar horror.

> And what is said of the Jews applies thoroughly of every infidel, and therefore the same law applies and those who use power rather than charity pursue their own ends and not Jesus Christ's, and the rule of divine law is therefore broken. And whenever one prefers to dominate rather than to bestow care, honor inflates pride and what was provided for concord tends to damage.[17]

The Council of Constance embraced Vladimiri's reasoning, Wojtyla knows, and officially declared that an infidel is a human being. A pathetic victory, it might seem, but if the Nazis had accorded the Jews the same status, the Holocaust would never have happened. Of course, the same council went on to burn the Wycliffe sympathizer Jan Hus at the stake; there's no shirking the church's responsibility through flattering comparisons.

The notion of responsibility gives Wojtyla an idea, a way to frame his final argument to his fellow churchmen. Religious liberty must be considered within the context of its God-given purpose. God gave humankind free will in order that we might choose to love God—"since forced services do not please God," as Paulus Vladimiri wrote so long ago. The rule of divine law is the rule of charity, the rule of love, not power. Only those who are truly free can respond to God as God longs for them to. How can the church, in any way, compromise this God-given freedom? Only the free human person can be responsible, as God intended.

When Archbishop Wojtyla steps to one of the microphones in the *aula* on September 22 to present an intervention on the "Declaration on Religious Liberty," he delivers a pivotal speech, and much of its language will be picked up and used in the final document itself. He begins by delivering what seems criticism against his theological allies—the Western European bishops and the Americans. Any statement on religious liberty must not simply embrace Western liberalism, he argues. The world is waiting for the church to speak to this issue not on the basis of human convention and law but from theological revelation.

"The Declaration," he states, "is made in part to the civil authorities but primarily and directly to the human person himself."[18] Because religion is a matter of relationship between God and humankind, the declaration should stress that the rights of conscience entail this fundamental relationship—their meaning in fact derives from it. "It is not enough to say in this matter 'I am free,' but rather 'I am accountable.' This is the doctrine grounded in the living tradition of the Church of the confessors and martyrs. Responsibility is the summit and necessary complement of liberty."[19]

Archbishop Wojtyla's appeal to the foundations of humankind's relationship with God, as known through revelation, helped the council to arrive at the final text of the "Declaration on Religious Liberty," which was formally promulgated on the penultimate day of the council, December 7, 1965.

> The Vatican Council declares that the human person has a right to religious freedom . . . the right to religious freedom is based on the very dignity of the human person as known through the revealed word of God and by reason itself. . . .
>
> One of the key truths in Catholic teaching . . . is that man's response to God by faith ought to be free, and that therefore nobody is to be forced to embrace the faith against his will. The act of faith is by its very nature a free act.[20]

The "Declaration on Religious Liberty" also distinguishes between the church's teaching about religious liberty and the historical practice of many churchmen. The declaration acknowledges that "through the vicissitudes of human history there has at times appeared a form of behavior that was hardly in keeping with the spirit of the Gospel and was even opposed to it," but insists, "it has always remained the teaching of the Church that no one is to be coerced into believing."[21]

Archbishop Wojtyla left Vatican II, this "second Pentecost," as he described it, knowing that humankind's God-given freedom and accountability demanded that the church do more in terms of addressing that antigospel "form of behavior." It would take another "vicissitude of history," the almost unimaginable event of a Pole being elected pope, before he would see how this unfinished business of Vatican II might be accomplished.

On March 12, the Day of Pardon for Jubilee 2000, Saint Peter's is filled to capacity, its great colonnades sheltering thousands of ticket-holding congregants from the central nave out to the arms of the transept. Behind Saint Peter's crypt, under Bernini's great bronze spiraling baldachino, stands the altar. The altar itself is banked by choirs, row after row of boys and men in white surplices over black cassocks.

The liturgy begins as two dozen candle bearers enter in pairs, followed by an army of violet-vested bishops with tall, white miters. They stroll forward, nodding to friends they see among the crowd, at ease with the pomp and splendor. At the beginning of this celebration the atmosphere is more like a huge graduation ceremony than a solemn Mass, with the crowd's curious whispers competing with the introit music.

John Paul II emerges at the right-hand side toward the back, where Michelangelo's *Pietà* rests behind shatterproof glass. (His initial seat at Vatican II was located at about the same place.) The pope wears violet vestments as well—the Lenten color of penitence. The staff he holds is silver, as are his miter and the lace embroidery on his stole. The pattern woven into his miter shows innumerable small crosses within windowlike squares.

Now seventy-nine years old, the once extraordinarily youthful

John Paul has aged—albeit he still keeps up a schedule that would exhaust most young men. This morning as the service begins his head rests crookedly on his shoulders. His staff shakes in his hand. His eyes are downcast and he breathes so heavily that it's hard not to count each one.

John Paul makes the sign of the cross. He says that on this Day of Pardon the church, like Mary, embraces her crucified Savior and asks the Father for pardon.

Then he mounts a three-step rolling platform and is wheeled by attendants in white cutaways up the long, long aisle.

"Attend to my voice and listen to my prayer, O Lord!" the choir sings.

Then the litany of the angels and saints begins. "Holy Michael . . . Holy Raphael . . . pray for us . . . Holy Lucy . . . Holy Cecilia, pray for us . . ."

A fifteenth-century cross from the Church of San Marcello al Corso goes before, the corpus carved from wood, its face twisted by the wrenching death. John Paul keeps making the sign of the cross as the procession moves forward; the people applaud in the midst of the chanting and the singing, and the seated cardinals doff their red caps.

The Mass moves quickly to the readings. John Paul's homily will take up these words from the epistle: "God made him who had no sin to be sin for us, so that in him we might become the righteousness of God" (2 Corinthians 5:21).

John Paul sits as he delivers his homily, his miter off, wearing a white skullcap. He picks his way through white note cards with shaking fingers. As he speaks, he draws strength from the words themselves, his voice becoming more expressive, his presence full of life. He's meditating on the thoughts of Saint Paul, the former inquisitor who saw men to their deaths for what they believed.

"Although Christ, the Holy One, was absolutely sinless," John Paul says, "he agreed to take our sins upon himself; he agreed to bear our sins to fulfill the mission he had received from the Father, who—as the Evangelist John writes—'so loved the world that he gave his

only Son, that whoever believes in him . . . may have eternal life' "
(John 3:16).

As John Paul speaks, the atmosphere in Saint Peter's changes.
The speaker's own conviction begins to become the crowd's as quiet
reflection replaces curiosity and the spectators become worshipers.

" 'Because of the bond which unites us to one another in the
Mystical Body, all of us . . . bear the burden of the errors and faults
of those who have gone before us,' " John Paul says, quoting from *Incarnationis Mysterium*, the papal bull that called the church to celebrate Jubilee 2000.[22] "We cannot fail to recognize," he says, "*the
infidelities of the Gospel committed by some of our brethren*, especially during the second millennium. Let us ask pardon for the divi-
sions which have occurred among Christians, for the violence some
have used in the service of the truth, and for the distrustful and hostile attitudes sometimes taken toward the followers of other religions. Let us confess, even more, *our responsibilities as Christians for
the evils of today. . . .*

"Yes, man is the only creature on earth who can have a relationship of communion with his Creator, but he is also the *only one who
can separate himself from him.*"

After John Paul's homily, seven representatives of the church,
five cardinals and two bishops, join him in prayerful repentance for
the historical sins of the church's sons and daughters. They step forward to offer prayers for sins committed in the service of the truth,
such as the Crusades and the Inquisition, the use of torture, the
burning of heretics, and the forcible conversion of indigenous peoples; for sins against Christian unity; for sins against the Jews; for sins
against love, peace, and respect for cultures and religions; for sins
against the dignity of women and the unity of the human race; and
for sins related to the fundamental rights of the person, the rights of
conscience being chief among them. After each cardinal and bishop
offers a prayerful petition, John Paul replies with his own.

Cardinal Ratzinger, who heads the Congregation for the Doctrine of the Faith, the successor to the old Roman Inquisition, prays
for sins committed in the service of truth. "Let us pray," Cardinal

Ratzinger says, "that each one of us, looking to the Lord Jesus, meek and humble of heart, will recognize that even men of the church, in the name of faith and morals, have sometimes used methods not in keeping with the Gospel in the solemn duty of defending the truth."

To this, John Paul replies, "In certain periods of history, Christians have at times given in to intolerance and have not been faithful to the great commandment of love, sullying in this way the face of the Church."

The great cloud of witnesses we are taught watches over us—Paulus Vladimiri and the slaughtered Samogitians among them—must be cheering.

At the end of the prayers, John Paul approaches the fifteenth-century wooden crucifix—a crucifix lovingly crafted, as it happens, in the time of Paulus Vladimiri and the Council of Constance. He pauses to kiss the crucifix and then looks up at its victim.

As the bright television lights catch John Paul's upturned face, the aged pope looks transformed, absolutely vital. He looks up at Jesus and his eyes are filled with gratitude and satisfaction.

As I've explored the life of Karol Wojtyla and his actions as pope, I've come to see the Day of Pardon as a profound expression of John Paul's inner drama—his spiritual formation. John Paul knows what it is to crouch in fear while mortal enemies knock at the door and to pray for God's deliverance. That was just a brief episode, yes, but it's also an emblem for his deep and long-lasting experience of totalitarianism and its many uses of coercion. His life impressed upon him that the fundamental freedom that exists between God and humankind must never be compromised by any human agency.

In John Paul we once again see a Christian and a Christianity of the catacombs, and like the early church fathers, especially Tertullian and Saint Cyprian of Carthage, he knows that the church, like its Lord, may employ only the means of witness, never power. "Those who use power rather than charity pursue their own ends and not Jesus Christ's," as Paulus Vladimiri wrote so long ago.

When he became Peter's successor, John Paul did not forget the church's commitment and his own at Vatican II to ground the church's witness first and foremost in the Christian understanding of the human person—who we are, how God has made us, and what God wants for us.

As Archbishop Wojtyla emphasized to the council fathers of Vatican II in 1964, the freedom of conscience that God extends to the human person demands accountability. How can the church lecture the world on this point unless it is willing to be accountable? As Monsignor Cifres told me in Rome, "When John Paul goes to other countries, he speaks very directly about the most important moral issues. But to speak the truth about others, one must first be willing to speak the truth about oneself."[23]

On the Day of Pardon, March 12, 2000, the Catholic Church finally repented of the Constantinian legacy, its centuries-long attachment to religious establishment. It turned to go in an utterly different direction—the true way of the cross. Only the greatest of contemporary prophets could have led such a historically bound and politically sensitive institution to such an act of self-examination. Behind the prophet John Paul II, the church marched out of the past into something closer to "the glorious freedom of the children of God" (Romans 8:21).

We may still be uncertain about calling John Paul II and even Jesus prophets. After all, what is the true nature of prophecy and the prophet's role? Aren't prophets wild characters like Elijah, who was whisked off to heaven in a whirlwind?

The true prophet is first of all a spiritual doctor—a diagnostician. Like John Paul, the prophet sees the world in the light of God's reality, and for that reason can see beyond the world's illusions. He or she speaks from the depths of a personal encounter with God to the contemporary situation, diagnosing how Israel—and more broadly humankind—has alienated itself from God. Most often this opposes the prophet to the status quo and those in authority who benefit from it. Nathan tells the story of a rich man who slaughters a poor man's one ewe lamb in order to entertain a traveler. King David, shouting imprecations against the injustice, then learns that *he* is the rich man—the one who has murdered Uriah for the sake of bedding Bathsheba.

The prophet who speaks hard truths always calls those who are living a lie to repentance—to amending their behavior for the purpose of once more enjoying God's fellowship. Jonah calls Nineveh to repent and much to his surprise and even displeasure, Nineveh does.

The prophet also warns of the consequences if the people choose not to obey the Lord's command. Sometimes these warnings are not only proclaimed but enacted: Jeremiah wanders through Jerusalem under a wooden yoke, showing the people how the king of Babylon will lead them away into slavery (Jeremiah 28).

Prophecy includes future prediction, too—the aspect we often think of. Sometimes a prophet's analysis of the contemporary situation is so insightful that the prophet can reason out how events are likely to unfold. (John Paul II predicted the end of communism in Eastern Europe long before the Velvet Revolution of 1989 because he knew communism radically misunderstood the nature of humanity.) At other times, the prophet is simply so caught up in communion with God that the prophet's words resonate far beyond his own imaginings. In the psalms David speaks of the sacrifice of the Lord's anointed in terms that Christians have always taken as strikingly like the crucifixion (Psalm 22:16–18: "A band of evil men has encircled me, they have pierced my hands and my feet. I can count all my bones; people stare and gloat over me. They divide my garments among them and cast lots for my clothing"). Isaiah speaks of a suffering servant who is "wounded for our transgressions," "bruised for our iniquities," by whose "stripes we are healed" (Isaiah 53).

We rarely think closely about Jesus as a prophet because we fail to discern these aspects of prophecy within his public ministry. After all, what was his diagnosis of the contemporary situation? (Did he even speak to the contemporary situation, or were his words always meant for the ages?) Can we say in specific terms how and why Jesus thought Israel had alienated herself from God? Did he warn of the consequences of this alienation? Did he predict the outcome of the nation's wrongful behavior?

The last chapters of Matthew, those immediately preceding the evangelist's depictions of the passion, show Jesus most clearly as a prophet. His diagnosis of the contemporary situation, his warnings of the consequences of this behavior, his call to repentance from it, and even his predictions of future events are found in Matthew 23 through the beginning of Mathew 26. There's an added dimension as well, the place where Jesus' prophetic vocation opens into his messianic mission. Jesus not only predicts the catastrophic events that will result from Israel's failure to respond to his call to repentance, he prepares the means by which his followers as the new Israel will survive the coming destruction.

Jesus begins by blistering his chief opponents, the religious authorities—or as we would say, the churchmen.

> Alas for you, scribes and Pharisees, you hypocrites! You shut up the kingdom of Heaven in people's faces neither going in yourselves nor allowing others to go in who want to. . . . Alas for you, scribes and Pharisees, you hypocrites! You pay your tithe of mint and dill and cumin and have neglected the weightier matters of the Law—justice, mercy, good faith! . . . You blind guides, straining out gnats and swallowing camels! . . . Alas for you, scribes and Pharisees, you hypocrites! You clean the outside of cup and dish and leave the inside full of extortion and intemperance. Blind Pharisee! . . . You are like whitewashed tombs that look handsome on the outside, but inside are full of the bones of the dead and every kind of corruption. . . . You are full of hypocrisy

and lawlessness. . . . You are the children of those who murdered the prophets! Very well then, finish off the work that
your ancestors began.

You serpents, brood of vipers, how can you escape being
condemned to hell? (from Matthew 23:13–33)

Paradoxically, Jesus accuses the legalistic Pharisees of "lawlessness." He says they have neglected the most important part of the
Law—justice, mercy, good faith—for the sake of extortion and excess. Like those who killed the prophets, they are people not of the
Law but of violence. Their violence manifests itself both in the
manner in which they control others—by imposing essentially gra-
tuitous religious observances—and in their intentions toward those,
like Jesus himself, they cannot control. They carry death in their
hearts and visit this death both spiritually on those who follow them
and physically on those who refuse to do so.

This prophetic diagnosis and indictment has to be seen in the
context of the Pharisees' self-conscious intention—what they told
themselves they were about. In terms of their worldview, Jesus could
not have been more wrong or more offensive.

Like Jesus and his disciples, the Pharisees composed a lay movement with the purpose of renewing Israel. By demanding of themselves and others the strictest keeping of the Law—and protective
hedges around the Law such as sacrificing spices like dill and
cumin—they would help bring about a collective sanctity that God
must one day honor by liberating Israel from Rome's subjugation.
That was their purpose. They were a liberation movement. They
were not shutting up heaven; they were bringing heaven on earth
through the true and final return of Israel from exile, which they
conceived as an independent Jewish state where fidelity to God's law
reigned.

The background story to Jesus' dispute with the Pharisees and
the other religious authorities of his day involved two questions:
How should the nation of Israel respond to Roman subjugation? And
what did it mean *to be* Israel in this situation? The background story

to Jesus' own—much like John Paul's background story—concerned living in an occupied nation. How should the people respond to this manifest evil? The Pharisees had their answer. Jesus evidently had another.

Each major "party" we meet in the gospels has its answer, in fact. Even after being conquered by Rome, Israel enjoyed a measure of independence, of self-governance, which was made possible by the Jewish authorities who interposed themselves between Rome and the people. Although Rome's own prefect, or governor, Pilate, wielded the ultimate power of the sword, its Jewish head of state, King Herod, administered much of the old northern kingdom, including Jesus' Galilee. Herod and his ilk were outright collaborationists, of course, as were the small bureaucrats, the hated tax collectors, that we meet with in the gospels. Herod's power depended in large part on his ability to keep the lid on trouble—to prevent revolutionary parties such as the Zealots and the terrorist Sicarii (Assassins) from leading violent revolts.

The head priest, Caiaphas, and his Sanhedrin—who were drawn from the class known as Sadducees—administered public morality and religious observance. The Sadducees and priests played a double game: they favored social stability (Caiaphas, remember, says about Jesus, "It is expedient for us that one man should die for the people, and not that the whole nation should perish" [John 11:50], while insisting absolutely on their own religious prerogatives (the Sanhedrin won't actually come into Pilate's court when they bring Jesus to him, in order to avoid ritual impurity).

As a lay movement, the Pharisees had no legal power. They were more like the advocacy groups we know—from Greenpeace to the Anti-Defamation League to the old Moral Majority—which engage in symbolic actions that effectively influence culture. The Pharisees were so engagé in the cause of freedom and justice that they accepted and were ready to justify the use of violence. It's likely, in fact, that many among those who eventually led the revolt against Rome in 67 A.D. were Pharisees.

That's why Jesus blasted them as men of violence: those who, in their own day, were willing "to use violence in the service of the truth." They had mistaken their politics for righteousness, and were all too ready to justify any means toward their temporal ends.

But how were the people to be free? Jesus endorsed neither militant nationalism nor collaborationist double-dealing. He espoused living the truth whatever the cost. His way forsook violence and depended entirely on living witness—the freedom even enslaved peoples have to live and perhaps die for the truth. Jesus' radical proposal is found in the Sermon on the Mount and particularly, once again, the Beatitudes.

> Blessed are the peacemakers: they shall be recognized as children of God.
>
> Blessed are those who are persecuted in the cause of uprightness: the kingdom of Heaven is theirs. Blessed are you when people abuse you and persecute you and speak all kinds of calumny against you falsely on my account. Rejoice and be glad, for your reward will be great in heaven; this is how they persecuted the prophets before you. . . .
>
> You have heard how it was said: Eye for eye and tooth for tooth. But I say this to you: offer no resistance to the wicked. . . .
>
> You have heard how it was said, You will love your neighbor and hate your enemy. But I say this to you, love your enemies and pray for those who persecute you. . . .
>
> You must therefore be perfect, just as your heavenly Father is perfect (Matthew 5:9–12, 38–39, 43–44, 48).

Love the Romans? Pray for them? Offer no resistance? We can read the Beatitudes and listen to the Sermon on the Mount with equanimity only because we fail to imagine the tyrannical enemy that immediately leapt to everyone's mind in Jesus' audience. How could what he was saying be true? Jesus might well have been accused of religious quietism. But Jesus embraced the love of our enemies as the most radical and dynamic solution to others' violence. He was trying to start a self-sacrificial movement of pure witness, believing that Israel's blessing to the nations depended upon her holiness, not her independence. (Likewise John Paul, following Jesus, believed Poland's ultimate freedom depended on a church of witness.)

Jesus stakes the truth of what he is saying, the credibility of his proposed solution, on his powers of prediction. The Temple—for all of Jesus' opponents the ultimate symbol of Jewish nationalism—will soon be destroyed. The violent faith of his opponents will find a violent end. "In truth I tell you, not a single stone here will be left on another: everything will be pulled down" (Matthew 24:2).

Whether Jesus knew this by divine inspiration or simply through astute analysis cannot be known, of course. But as a prophet, he was accurate. The Jewish revolt of 67 A.D. under John of Gischala and Simon son of Giora led to the destruction of the temple in 70 A.D., as Titus led the Roman legions back into the city. By Tacitus's account, more than six hundred thousand perished by the sword, disease, or famine. Josephus puts the number at more than a million. Those remaining in the city became the gladiators' prey or were sold into slavery. With this catastrophe Temple Judaism came to an end.

Jesus' prophecy of the Temple's destruction informs the most forceful action we ever see him take. When Jesus cleanses the Temple, overturning the money changers' tables and letting loose the livestock, he says that his Father's house is meant to be a house of prayer, but the authorities have made it a den of thieves. Once again, we usually think of this as part of Jesus' indictment of a legalistic and therefore corrupt Judaism. But his action carries a far greater significance—one that makes his trial and crucifixion far more understandable, the rage of his opponents easily anticipated. Symbolically, Jesus is saying that the present religious leaders have sacrificed their authority. Since they have "shut up heaven," the Temple might as well be closed down. He was not only prophesying the "abomination" to come (Matthew 24:15)—the destruction of the Temple—he was laying the blame for it at the feet of the religious authorities. Like Jeremiah carrying the yoke of slavery through the streets of

Jerusalem, Jesus enacted his prophetic message—he put the Temple out of business temporarily, as a means of predicting its ultimate fate. No wonder his opponents sought his execution.

Often when predicting the fall of Jerusalem, Jesus also articulates how his personal fate will bring about the reconstitution of the people of God—what we know today as the church, the "new Israel." Jesus predicts not only that the Temple will be destroyed but that he "will build it up again on the third day" (John 2:19). From now on, the Temple "not built by human hands," the resurrected Jesus, will alone command the new Israel's worship. Here his prophetic vocation becomes messianic, for in the midst of the failure of his call to forsake violence, Jesus prophesies his triumphant resurrection and the crown of victory given "to all who have longed for his appearing" (2 Timothy 4:8).

His mockers laughed at this prediction as Jesus hung on the cross: "So! You who are going to destroy the temple and build it in three days, come down from the cross and save yourself!" (Mark 15:29–30).

His followers find in this prophecy their continuing hope in the living Christ.

In Iran

Christ the Martyr

Most of us think of Christian martyrdom in terms of antiquity, the lions ravaging Christians at the behest of the Roman emperor Diocletian or Saint Sebastian's chest full of arrows. Unfortunately, when I began to consider Jesus' death and those who follow him today in martyrdom, I had a world of stories to choose from. In more than sixty countries, Christians are harassed, abused, arrested, tortured, or executed for no other reason than their faith. The expert Paul Marshall estimates that 200 million Christians throughout the world live in fear of political repression and discrimination.[1]

In a telephone conversation I asked Paul Marshall which story among the store he knows best exemplifies Christian martyrdom today. He suggested I investigate the courageous deaths of three evangelical pastors in Iran in the mid-1990s. It's a story that involves the current conflict between Islamic fundamentalists and Christians—a conflict with global repercussions that becomes more acute day by day.

In November 1993, not far from ancient Babylon, where Daniel was thrown into the lions' den and Shadrach, Meshach, and Abednego were pitched into Nebuchadnezzar's fiery furnace, the Reverend Mehdi Dibaj huddled in a Mazandaran Province prison cell, praying about how he could defend himself against capital charges. A compactly built sixty-year-old man, his short salt-and-pepper hair bristled above his deep-set, dark eyes and his bunchy cheeks. His cell contained a cot, a hole-in-the-floor toilet, a line of small snapshots of his four children at eye level opposite his bed, and under the high window that afforded light if no view, a cross fashioned from twisted palm fronds.

Dibaj was accused of being a Christian—more particularly an *apostate,* one who has given up Islam to accept Christianity. For him, Daniel and the three stiff-kneed brothers were not the stuff of Sunday school lessons, flannel graphs, and cotton-haired stick figures. They were as close as his impending death. Two years before, Dibaj wrote to his seventeen-year-old son, Yousef, "If we want to walk close with God, we must go into the fire."

Since Dibaj was imprisoned the first time, in 1983, for sixty-eight days, and then beginning with his rearrest in 1984, the Assemblies of God minister had spent almost ten years behind bars for his faith.

The few visitors he had been allowed, usually at six-month intervals, always came ready to offer encouragement. Mehdi Dibaj proved of greater encouragement to them, however, for they sensed how close Dibaj had grown to Shadrach and company's "fourth man"—the accompanying presence of the Lord.

The authorities tried their best to break him. Their first approach was to cajole him back into conformity, telling him they knew him to be a good Muslim at heart. He need only sign a paper to that effect and he could go home.

Dibaj had reason to suspect that the interrogating religious authorities really did want him to sign their paper and be on his way. He was a member of a family with relatives in the religious hierarchy, an embarrassment they could no longer afford following the Ayatollah Khomeini's Islamic Revolution of 1979. They might have instigated his arrest as a way of demanding his return to the fold of Islam. But since the day in 1953 when he had begun his Christian journey by reading a simple gospel tract, a world of love unconditioned by status considerations had opened up and he wasn't tempted to bargain away such freedom.

His wife, Azizeh, found the authorities' control irresistible. Threatened with stoning if she did not recant her faith, she unmade her vows, renounced the life they had led with their four children, and allowed herself to be given to a Muslim husband. An orphan raised by Christian missionaries, Azizeh must have experienced Mehdi and her children's loss—they remained faithful to their father and his faith—as another catastrophic desertion. Mehdi grieved for Azizeh, cast away into another's home once more.

The authorities' methods of coercion then became more violent. Dibaj remembered awaking to a swollen face and battered ribs from the previous day's interrogation, even as a horsehair rope went around his neck. He strained to open his blackened eyes to the first light of day in the prison courtyard before a hood shuttered his sight again. He heard verses from the Qur'an being read aloud.

Someone was leaning close, asking, would he sign a statement recanting his faith?

The speaker pressed a pen into his hand. No one removed the hood, though. They wanted him to sign a paper he could not see.

His thigh and shoulder muscles quivered in the freezing morning cold as he half knelt on bare ground with the noose starting to haul him upward. He had so little control over his body he couldn't get his feet under him; his knees and feet were icy and clumsy. He struggled to pray, wanting his last moments to be filled with God, not terror.

They let him strangle for a moment or two, to feel the rage of his body struggling to survive, and then, without a word, took him back to his cell. His body kept shaking and he wanted to howl out his fear and anger.

The beatings and mock executions were at least of limited duration. When he began his two years of solitary confinement, however, in a three-yard-square unlit cell, he thought he understood the eternity of the damned.

It had taken him a month or more before he understood how available the Lord was to him in solitary. At first he kept formal times of prayer and then began learning to let the Lord keep him company from moment to moment. The darkness of the nights in his stone-hewn dungeon gradually became luminous—like the evenings when God walked out with our first parents. For him solitary removed Raphael's blazing sword from the entrance to that first Mesopotamian garden and allowed entry back into God's company. He tried to describe this later and all he could say was that God had performed many miracles for him.

Much worse, and a humiliating testing it had been, was to be back with the normal prison population, where his fellow prisoners called him "unclean Christian" and beat him for praying. Their contempt cut him off from God far more effectively than solitude. When they went to sleep, Dibaj kept his night watches, and yet his sense of God's presence dwindled. Ashamed to be such a poor witness, he asked to go back into solitary confinement.

The prison authorities thought him mad, and sent him to a psychiatrist. Then they turned these events to their own advantage by asking him to sign a document attesting to his mental instability. He could be released if they could ascribe his faith to mental illness. To be a Christian convert in Iran was to be insane! He was the only one who saw the humor.

Twice before, in 1982 and 1986, the courts had convicted him of apostasy and sentenced him to death. Each time he had chosen to appeal the sentence to the High Court, as was his right. In these appeals he pointed out that nothing in the Qur'an explicitly requires the death of an apostate. This view is based only on some reports of Sunna and other traditions. There must be a *shubha,* or element of doubt, as to the appropriateness of any conviction rendered against an act that was not a crime at the time it was committed. He had been a Christian since 1953. No part of the *shari'a*—the Islamic legal code being invoked against him—had been in effect until after the Islamic Revolution of 1979. The criminal code was amended to make apostasy a capital offense only this year.

As the Reverend Mehdi Dibaj sat in his cell and prayed over his course of action, though, his thoughts began to center more and more in the stark truth. The authorities wanted to take his life because he was a Christian. Did he mean to deny this or compromise his stand by legal maneuvering? At that moment, by virtue of all he had suffered, Mehdi Dibaj decided to let the fundamental issue of his faith be the court's issue.

Like the saints of the second and third centuries, Justin and Tertullian, Dibaj chose to defend himself by writing an apologia—a reasoned explanation—of the Christian faith itself.

"With all humility," the prisoner began writing, *"I express my gratitude to the Judge of all heaven and earth for this precious opportunity, and with brokenness I wait upon the Lord to deliver me from this court trial according to his promises. I also beg the honored members of the court present to listen with patience to my defense and with respect for the name of the Lord."*

In 1993 the several power centers of the Iranian Islamic Revolution—the clergy, the judiciary, and the Ministry of Information through SAVAMA (the secret police)—directed both a legislative campaign and a campaign of intimidation against the evangelical Christian community. Many among the most powerful players in the Islamic Revolution had decided, it was becoming clear, that Iran's pure Islamic state was being compromised by the growing witness of evangelical Christians.

In May the government required that all shopkeepers post signs stating religious affiliation, a significant step toward isolating religious minorities, the beginning of a commercial apartheid.

The Ministry of Culture and Islamic Guidance approached all the Christian churches in June and pressured them to pledge that they would not evangelize Muslims. To the best of their ability they would not allow them in their worship services and they would not conduct worship in Farsi, the common language of the Muslim people. This demand had little effect on Christian communions like the Roman Catholics and the Orthodox, who ministered almost exclusively to ethnic communities and conducted their services in the languages of those people. But the measure struck directly at the heart of the evangelical community, as was intended.

The *shari'a*, the most conservative of Islamic legal codes, which provided in its *huddud*, or criminal code section, for the stoning of adulterous women and the mutilation of thieves—as well as the death of apostates—was becoming more and more the law of the land. The deep traditions of Muslim tolerance, especially for Christians and Jews as "People of the Book" *(Ahl al-Kitab)*, were being swept aside as the people's fidelity to the revolution waned and extremist elements became ravenous for scapegoats. A harbinger of things to come occurred in 1990 when the Reverend Hossein Soodmand was hanged in Mashhad on charges of proselytizing, apostasy, and operating an illegal Christian bookstore and church.

Since 1990, when the Iranian Bible Society had been closed, both Christians and Jews—who had counted on the society for copies of the Torah—had to go without new copies of scripture and other religious publications. In that same year, the Garden of Evangelism, a retreat center in north Tehran, had been closed as well.

The new legal measures of 1993 prompted local officials to take frightening actions against evangelical churches suspected of proselytizing. In the holy city of Isfahan, police scaled the walls of a private garden where the Assembly of God church was gathered and demanded to see everyone's identity card. The fifteen Muslim converts attending that church were later interrogated. Their lives would be in danger, they were told, if they continued attending.

In Kermanshah converts were rounded up, hanged upside down, and beaten with thick wires. The same happened in Mashhad and Gorgan.

In Ahvaz, Sari, Kerman, and Orumiyeh the evangelical churches were simply closed down.

.   .   .

Because of Dibaj's impending trial and the evangelical community's widespread persecution, the Reverend Haik Hovsepian-Mehr asked for an appointment with the director for minorities' affairs at the Ministry of Culture and Islamic Guidance. As chairman of the Protestant Council (a body representing all of Iran's Protestant denominations) and superintendent of the Assemblies of God, Reverend Hovsepian-Mehr often represented the interests of the evangelical community before government officials. These officials were the ones who began calling him Bishop Haik, which even his fellow Protestant clergy adopted afterward.

Bishop Haik was a little dynamo, with a short frame built like a clenched fist. His potato-shaped face gave him a comfortable, avuncular look, and he might have been mistaken for a cobbler but for his clerical collar and sharkskin suit. He came alive in conversation. His arching eyebrows, long, sharply tipped nose, and mobile lips leant an extraordinary range of expression to his naturally dramatic speech.

His appointment with the director took place on a cold early-December afternoon in the ministry building on Sepah Street. While Bishop Haik waited in the office's anteroom, the director's secretary poured him a tall, lipped glass of tea held by a filigreed silver handle. Bishop Haik's thumb worked over the handle's geometric detail, diamonds inscribed by circles in a typical Moorish pattern. His first sips burned his tongue and he wanted to put the glass down but could not find a nearby table.

He remembered his four interrogations by SAVAMA, the Iranian secret police. Although today's appointment came about by his own request, he felt almost as nervous.

Bishop Haik had long wanted to see the evangelical church's persecution as a fanaticism that would pass. An ethnic Armenian, Bishop Haik felt as much an Iranian as anyone. His people had been in Iran for four centuries, since Shah Abbas during the Safavid dynasty brought Armenian artisans to build and decorate his capital,

Isfahan. *Isfahan nisf-I-jahan:* Isfahan was "half the world," or as
much as half the creation to anyone who had seen its wonders after
Armenian tile workers, bricklayers, goldsmiths, carpet weavers, and
dyers had finished.

Bishop Haik did not know exactly what he hoped to accomplish
at today's meeting. Registering a formal protest of the church's persecution simply seemed the right thing to do. "Think not what you
will say when you come before the judge," the Lord advised. Did this
mean he had been sinning ever since calling the director for an appointment?

The last time the two had met, Bishop Haik had refused the director's request that the Assemblies of God abide by the government's June antiproselytizing measures. The Assemblies conducted
many of their services in Farsi. They nurtured Muslim converts.
Bishop Haik hoped he could steer the conversation clear of the Assemblies' noncompliance.

A half hour past the appointed time, Bishop Haik was ushered
into the director of minorities' affairs' office. The tall, slight young
man was fully bearded. He wore a white muslin turban *(a'am-
mameh)*, a flowing camel's hair robe *(a'aba)*, and a white, pleated,
collarless shirt with a black onyx stick pin. He stood at the side of his
desk for the briefest moment to extend his greetings.

He retreated behind his desk, then, saying, "Just another moment while I finish this note." He pulled his chair over to the corner
table on which his computer sat. He kept Bishop Haik waiting another five minutes as he scratched his beard and hunted and pecked
out another sentence. Then, after leaning back in his chair and in-
specting the still-unfinished note, he finally turned around and
scooted his chair back behind his desk, where he lined up two stacks
of paper and opened his black appointment calendar. "What business have we today?" he asked Bishop Haik.

"As I told your appointment secretary," Bishop Haik said, "we
have many things to discuss."

"We'll need to cover only the most important, I'm afraid. When
you made the appointment, my schedule looked more open. The

days have a way of filling up." He cocked his head and put a hand to his throat below his beard, pulling at his whiskers.

"The welfare of the people, the poor, is always the most important issue, as I'm sure you'll agree," Bishop Haik said, beginning with a common strand of their theologies. "In Mashhad, Gorgan, Kermanshah, Isfahan—all over the country my people are being interrogated, often beaten."

The director drew back in his chair. He stared at Bishop Haik. First composure, then contempt, then indictment came into his clear young brown eyes. "That's a broad charge. One I know nothing about. But I do want to know this. Are these truly your people? Are they Armenians?"

"In some cases. In all cases they are people who have been attending our churches."

"If they are Muslims, they need to return to Islam. For their own good. You know the consequences of apostasy. They become dead to their families."

Bishop Haik had to bite back a smart reply about death-dealing. "I'm sure you've read UN special investigator Pohl's report," Bishop Haik said. "The one from this past July. The world knows of the growing persecution of the evangelical church here. The International Covenant on Civil and Political Rights, which has been ratified by Iran, states that no one should have his freedom to adopt a religion impaired. The world wants to know why Iran is not abiding by this agreement. Shouldn't our community be able to ask the same question?"

"What I believe some within the government want to know, Mr. Hovsepian-Mehr," the director said, "is why your sect refuses to abide by last June's agreement not to proselytize. It's well known that your group is seeking to ensnare Muslims. Even the most direct actions of the authorities must be considered merciful under these circumstances. Jesus himself cautioned us to fear those who can kill the spirit, the soul. Are Muslims wrong for guarding the souls of their people?"

The director's allusion caught Bishop Haik off guard. How

much did he know of Christianity? "Our faith, Director," Haik said, "compels us to share it with others, just as yours does. We coerce no one. All Iranians are hospitable to guests. When guests come to us, we speak in their language, we offer them the best we have."

The director glanced away. "Soft words, but they will not help me serve your interests. You know how things stand."

"Perhaps if Investigator Pohl were invited back into the country," Bishop Haik said, rushing and trying not to, his breath catching, "his influence could help you reinstitute greater protections for our people."

"Investigator Pohl? You spoke of hospitality. Mr. Pohl has abused ours, we feel. We do not need such outside influences. To be frank, these international accords, shaped as they are by Western hegemonism, mean little to us. We have surer guides ourselves." He glanced—with irony, or satisfaction?—at the dominating portrait of Ayatollah Khomeini hanging on the wall.

Bishop Haik remembered Dibaj. "Perhaps we have not been as careful as we might have been—in our ministry. Our sharing of the faith. But there is one matter that we have found agreement upon in the past. At least in terms of what suits both communities' long-term interests."

"Reverend Dibaj?"

"Yes, Reverend Dibaj. His case is before the court again. With the law amended he may be in great danger."

"A danger of his own—"

"But forty-five years ago. Forty-five years. When Iran was so different."

The director folded his hands and looked at them as if he might offer up a parting gift after all. "I think everyone wishes this matter resolved," he said. "I will look into the new developments."

Bishop Haik's mouth was now so dry it felt seared. "I have taken up enough of your time, then. The evangelical Christian church is not Iran's enemy. Our Lord's kingdom continues not to be of this world."

"Take that admonition of His Holiness Christ's as seriously as possible, then. At present Iran is not the place for another Crusade, not even an evangelical one. It will be a long time before Mr. Billy Graham comes here."

"They say, 'You were a Muslim and you have become a Christian,' " Mehdi Dibaj's apology continues. *"No, for many years I had no religion. After searching and studying I accepted God's call and I believed in the Lord Jesus Christ in order to receive eternal life. People choose their religion but a Christian is chosen by Christ. He says, 'You have not chosen me but I have chosen you.' From when? Before the foundation of the world."*

Soon afterward, Haik learned the effect of his visit. The director of minorities' affairs wrote an article for a local Tehran newspaper stating: "At the moment, there is not a single person in our prisons who has been jailed for his personal or religious beliefs."

The often-repeated justification for such a statement rested in the political cast given to evangelical and other non–Shiite Muslim groups by Iranian authorities. An article in *Keyhan* newspaper stated, "One of the major intrigues of the West to continue their domination of the Islamic communities has been the creation of trivial sects."[2] Remarking on the persecution of evangelical churches, Iranian deputy foreign minister M. Javad Zarif told the *New York Times:* "We consider them to be a political organization. If someone wants to start a political organization they must go through the process to obtain permission, as is the case for Muslims."[3] Repeatedly Iranian officials told their people that Christianity fostered Western imperialist designs and brought with it the Western evils of materialism, sexual exploitation, the use of drugs and alcohol, and liberal attitudes toward women.

Bishop Haik suspected worse might be coming. He regretted bringing up the United Nations report and Investigator Reynaldo Galindo Pohl, remembering the director's glare. The government was hypersensitive to outside opinion, always courting—in the paradoxical Persian way—both approval and condemnation.

The director soon confirmed Haik's suspicion by demanding that all of Iran's Christian churches write letters to the United Nations attesting to the full religious freedom they enjoyed.

"I have been charged with 'apostasy'! The invisible God who knows our hearts has given assurance to us Christians that we are not among the apostates who will perish but among the believers so that we may save our lives. In Islamic law an apostate is one who does not believe in God, the prophets, or the resurrection of the dead. We Christians believe in all three!"

Four days before Christmas, December 21, 1993, the following document arrived via fax in Haik's office from one of his government back channels:

> Verdict No: 1766/72
> Branch No. 7 of Punitive Court 1 of Sari 7

> According to the contents of the file no. 1690/69 K 7 of this court, Mr. Mehdi Dibaj, son of Hassan, age 59, from Isfahan, resident of Babol, is accused of apostasy and cursing the Prophet of Allah [Muhammad] and all the saints and insulting Ayatollah Khomeini. . . .
>
> Hereby in reference to the contents of the file on the cursing of the Prophet . . . he is declared innocent. But on the charge of apostasy . . . he is sentenced to execution.

Haik could hardly believe this. Immediately, he worried that Dibaj's own reaction would prove almost as troubling as the court's decision. Dibaj had long talked of martyrdom. He never had any understanding of what his own heroic gestures might cost the larger church. (Bishop Haik was remembering those times when the authorities gave Dibaj medical furloughs, sending him off with broad hints that he take flight. Dibaj always appeared promptly back at the prison at the appointed time.)

Haik wanted Dibaj to appeal and do so quickly. All the other Protestant ministers were much like Haik himself—middle-aged men with families to support. The Protestant Council expected Haik to keep the situation from devolving into open conflict, although they knew such a time might come. But now? Over the intransigent if admirable Dibaj? Haik's diplomatic instincts told him to keep managing things, not to throw down any gauntlets.

Haik dispatched a communication to Dibaj, urging him to appeal.

Dibaj's return letter, although full of spiritual encouragement, embraced the sentence—at least on its surface. "When they gave me the verdict," Dibaj wrote, "my heart was filled with joy because I saw that my name would be listed with those martyred for their faith in Jesus Christ."

Medhi Dibaj appended to this letter his immediate response to the court, in which he made five stunning requests.

To Public Punitive Court of Sari: Ref. to the verdict 1766–72
    With greetings, I, Christian prisoner Medhi Dibaj, son of Hassan, with respect to the Name of God and the faith in Jesus Christ our Lord and Savior, accept the court verdict with joy and peace. Please:
    1. Expedite the process of carrying out the sentence.
    2. Submit my body to Babol Medical College for their medical use.
    3. Allow the cross to remain around my neck.
    4. Before carrying out the sentence allow Holy Communion to be given to me by Bishop Haik Hovsepian-Mehr and Reverend Vartan Avanesyan.
    5. I donate my belongings to the church and give my children into the hands of God, who is able to keep

them safe so that they grow in the grace and knowledge of our Lord Jesus Christ. Amen.

Paradoxically, Dibaj's letter to Haik also included speculations
that contradicted his unabashed desire for martyrdom. About the
verdict, Dibaj wrote to Haik, "The judge is not permitted to perform
his own verdict. He has to refer it to the High Court for the fourth
time, which will for certain be quashed. It will stay in the High
Court for two years to await its turn and then another year in Sari!"

To ascertain Dibaj's settled thoughts on the sentence, Bishop
Haik urged Dibaj's son Yousef to visit with his father in prison. In
case Dibaj had been prevented from preparing an appeal, his fellow
clergy wrote one up and sent it along with the young man.

The response that came back through Yousef was unequivocal.
"Please tell Brother Haik and all who pray for me," Dibaj wrote,
"that I believe this is my hour of trial like Abraham. I will not bow
before the worldly people and beg them for my release or forgiveness! I am quite ready for execution. This is a privilege that no one
has the right to take away from me!"

Yousef further reported that he had spoken with the judge, who
said, "Since he has written his will and delivered it to us and has
asked us to hasten the time of his execution, no one can stop it. Even
the UN cannot help his case."

Had all the authorities discussed his UN threat? Bishop Haik
could only wonder.

Since the sentence had been handed down on December 21 and
Dibaj had effectively waived his right to appeal, his execution could
be carried out in another week or two.

*"The good and kind God reproves and punishes all those whom he
loves. He tests them in preparation for heaven. The God of Daniel, who
protected his friends in the fiery furnace, has protected me for nine
years in prison and all the bad happenings have turned out for our
good and gain, so much so that I am filled to overflowing with joy and
thankfulness."*

.   .   .

On January 9, Bishop Haik received a fax at his home office. It came through Cyprus from his main contact in the United States, Ebrahim (Abe) Ghaffari. One of the men that Haik had mentored, Ghaffari ran a support organization, Iranian Christians International, Inc., that directed aid to the Iranian evangelical church, both supplies for evangelism and resources for Christians who needed to flee the country. Ghaffari had learned that Dibaj's execution might be imminent. Pastor Soodmand had been hanged before the larger world knew of his plight. Should Ghaffari publicize Dibaj's case? Or was Haik already employing his own quiet diplomacy?

At that moment Haik's wife, Takoosh, came into the office to call her husband to dinner. He would be there in a moment, he said, and took another look at the fax.

"What is it?" she asked.

He handed it along.

He watched her reaction as she read. Lately, she was wearing her dark hair down to her shoulders. The style always reminded him of the early days of their marriage. That period had not been carefree either, as a car accident took the life of their first child and almost crippled both of them. The three children of the missionary friends riding with them also died. Their marriage had been forged in a holocaust. They never stopped delighting in each other's company, though, and as many hard years as there had been, which of course took their toll, Haik thought their love for each other had grown ever finer.

She lowered the fax paper and asked, "What will you do?"

He shrugged, pressed his lips together, crossed his eyes, and made an idiot's face.

She tilted her head and shared the laugh. Then she said, "Tell me now. The way things have been going ... I've had my own thoughts. We should talk about it."

"The situation—I mean the whole situation, not just this—it's getting worse day by day." Haik chose his words carefully, even in his own home office, as he was sure it was bugged. "All the outside organizations counsel patience—the denomination and those at the World Council. But I'm wondering if we have been too patient."

She nodded slowly. "I think Ebrahim's right," she said, shaking the fax paper.

"You do?"

"Yes."

"But he's not the one to do it, you know."

They looked at each other as husbands and wives do—those communicating looks that record life's sudden patterning, the lines of their shared history inscribed in the other's face.

Had the time truly come for heroic gestures? Was he prepared to make one? He must do what he could for Dibaj and the church without regard for the personal consequences. Otherwise his life had been a sham. "Perhaps you should consider visiting Aunt Tasbi." This was their code for emigrating. As the persecution had grown worse the past several years, Haik and Takoosh had agreed that the children and she should emigrate whenever she thought best.

"Will you come too? When you can?"

He shook his head.

"What are you going to do?"

"Just open the window." This meant dramatizing the situation to the world, by every means available.

She crossed her arms and held herself tight. She began shaking and stomped her foot. "Open it, then," she said, squeezing the words out. "Open it." She handed the fax back and turned toward the door.

He caught her, taking her into a close embrace. He already felt deprived of her. What he did now he must do with all the will he could muster. He would open the window—wide. No more stumbling threats, but vigorous and direct action in the hope he could win this fight, not only for his Lord but for Takoosh and the family as well.

"Christ has asked me to deny myself and be his fully surrendered follower, and not fear people even if they kill my body."

.   .   .

Two hours later, on that same day, January 10, Abe Ghaffari went into his filecrammed office and found a fax had arrived: Bishop Haik's response to his query. As he read through it, the back of his neck began prickling. Bishop Haik had written an open letter to his global contacts, from Norway to London to South Korea. He sent it to the major human rights groups like Amnesty International and Human Rights Watch and even Investigator Pohl at the United Nations.

In his open letter Bishop Haik detailed the specifics of "Brother Dibaj's" case, then provided background on the persecution being suffered by the entire Iranian evangelical church, in Mashhad, Isfahan, Kermanshah, and elsewhere. He laid the blame squarely on the Iranian authorities.

Bishop Haik went on to say, "The policy of 'Let us keep silent and see what will happen next!' is a satanic policy. If we die or go to jail for our faith we want the whole Christian world to know. . . . You may wonder why I am writing so openly. We have nothing else to lose. . . . I am quite ready for anything. I believe that in the same old Persia, God is going to repeat the story of Daniel in the twentieth century."

The fax was not Bishop Haik's only action either. In late November or early December he had given an interview with Middle East Concern and sent a letter to United Nations special investigator Reynaldo Galindo Pohl. Both dealt with the worsening of persecution. Middle East Concern published Haik's interview on December 13. In the interview Haik issued an open invitation to the United Nations special investigator to visit Iran in order to verify his charges.

These developments shook Abe Ghaffari because his own life had been so much formed under Bishop Haik's influence.

As a college student in Oregon, Abe Ghaffari read the Christian scriptures and felt drawn to the faith. He knew of no Iranian Muslim converts, though, except through books. The Christians in his hometown, Neyshabur, were the ones who owned the liquor stores and ran the movie theaters! It took him three years to decide firmly that he believed in Christianity and was willing to pay the price—all the while hoping the price wouldn't be too high. He had no desire to share his faith.

Abe and his bride, Marie, returned to Iran in the summer of 1971. While touring the countryside, they set out for Mashhad, but couldn't find transport other than a minibus that went only as far as Gorgan. It was the time of spiritual pilgrimage called *hajj*. The minibus dropped them off in Gorgan in the middle of the night. They knocked on the door of one inn and then another. Everyone shouted they were full: go find another place to sleep.

Abe and Marie had heard about Gorgan's Pastor Haik from an Armenian missionary. At one o'clock in the morning, Marie finally persuaded Abe to approach his door.

They found the light on in the church building next to the pastor's house. Pastor Haik had been in the church praying. Abe stumbled through their story about trying to find a place to stay. Haik questioned him suspiciously—even at that stage he had to guard church property against Tablighat-e Islami radicals.

Marie pulled Abe back behind her and told Pastor Haik that they were Christians. A missionary in Tehran suggested they should visit, and unexpectedly, here they were.

"Why didn't you say so at the beginning?" Haik asked.

They slept on the Persian carpet behind the church's pulpit that night, since Pastor Haik had other guests as well. Abe told Marie they would get up early in the morning and be on their way, suspicious of an Armenian who evangelized Muslims.

Instead, Abe and Marie spent three days with Pastor Haik and his wife, Takoosh. Abe would never forget driving out with Haik to the flat-roofed, mud-brick villages of peasants in the surrounding area. The pastor stopped here and there along the roads to talk with people, chatting about the harvest, their family's prospects. The charismatic way he struck up these conversations and how quickly they led to deep exchanges of religious views was astonishing. Abe had never known an Armenian with such a heart for Iranians. His cultural prejudices began to fade. Might he one day be able to share his faith with his fellow Iranians as well?

Before they departed, Haik told Abe and Marie he would be praying that they return to Iran to minister.

Three and a half years later Abe and Marie found themselves back in Iran helping to establish a house church for Muslim-convert Christians. But in 1979, at the beginning of the Islamic Revolution, they were forced to leave Iran, Marie because of her health—medical care became almost nonexistent—and Abe because he was an intellectual and a convert.

Ten years later, back in the United States, Abe would leave a successful academic career as a business professor specializing in organization theory and labor relations to found Iranian Christians International, Inc. His mentor, Bishop Haik, had become his colleague and partner in ministry.

Abe didn't know the situation on the ground in Iran as well as Bishop Haik, but his position as an outside observer made him more aware of relevant global developments.

The 1993 Christmas season just ended had seen worldwide Islamic authorities rallying opposition against the Vatican's recognition of Israel. On December 30 the two parties signed a "Fundamental Agreement" that would lead to full diplomatic relations.

The agreement provoked statements from Islamic leaders that revealed their understanding of global politics and what they took to be the West's satanic use of Christianity. The imam of Tehran, meeting with Christian leaders as part of their Christmas celebrations, warned that Vatican City's recognition of Israel could only be seen as part of the West's global assault against Islam. He implied that this Christmas might be the last celebrated in Tehran.

The spiritual leader of the nation, Ayatollah Seyyed Ali Khamenei, delivered a Christmas message (broadcast on Iranian TV on January 3) in which he excoriated the Western powers for using Christianity as a means of access and destruction in the Muslim world. "The dominant powers and governments, under the pretext of Christianity but in truth materialist and ignorant of the teachings and traditions of His Holiness Christ, have made life difficult for the innocent nations and peoples, and commit all sorts of injustice against them."[4]

On January 7 the head of the Iranian nation himself, President Hashemi Rafsanjani, detailed the historical context of the Islamic world's reaction in a sermon. Islam had been born after seven centuries of Christianity's failure to bring man to God, Rafsanjani said. The rise of Islam quickly proved there is no longer any validity for other religions—the world should have been converted to Islam long ago. Yet much of the world continued to turn away from Islam. He called on Iran and the entire Muslim world to adopt "the Prophet . . . and *Jihad* [holy war] as a model."[5] He predicted that just as Muhammad and his followers had been able to conquer the Christian world around them, today's Muslim world, despite its current Christian opposition, would inevitably triumph over its enemies.

The imam's, Khamenei's, and Rafsanjani's statements were being echoed in many other quarters. The London-based Islamist *Al-Ouds al-Arabi* wrote: "The Vatican's recognition of Israel on Israeli terms is an insult to all Arabs and Muslims without exception because the consequences of that recognition will be a catastrophe for all, without exception."

"I would rather have the whole world against me but know that the Almighty God is with me, be called an apostate but know that I have the approval of the God of glory, because man looks at the outward appearance but God looks at the heart, and for him who is God for all eternity nothing is impossible. All power in heaven and on earth is in his hands."

Bishop Haik's January 1994 open-letter fax stimulated several worldwide campaigns on behalf of the church in Iran.

Executive director Andrew Whitley of Middle East Watch, a division of the international civil rights advocacy group Human

Rights Watch, wrote on January 11 to Ayatollah Seyyed Ali Khamenei to protest Mehdi Dibaj's sentence. "After nine years' imprisonment, often under poor conditions, and subject to mistreatment in
jail, the Reverend Dibaj has already suffered more than enough for
the sole 'offense' of exercising his right to freedom of religion. His
ordeal must not be prolonged. We urge you to use your authority as
faqih to quash his unjust sentence and release him immediately."

A communiqué of January 12 stated, "Amnesty International
fears that Dibaj is at imminent risk of execution. . . . He may have
merely exercised his right to freedom of religion and speech. . . .
These rights are guaranteed under the International Covenant on
Civil and Political Rights to which Iran is a state party."

On January 13, Reuters reported, "The United States has called
on Iran not to execute an Iranian citizen facing a death sentence for
the crime of converting from Islam to Christianity. . . . State Department spokeswoman Christine Shelly said the man, Mehdi Dibaj, had
served 10 years detention without trial."

Agence France-Presse ran a story on the Vatican's diplomatic efforts on the prisoner's behalf. "The Tele-Pas television, close to the
Vatican, announced on Friday that Vatican diplomacy will be mobi-
lized to save the life of Mehdi Dibaj, the Iranian priest who was
Muslim by birth but has been sentenced to death in Sari for converting to Christianity."[6]

*"The love of Jesus has filled all my being and I feel the warmth of his
love. . . . God, who is my glory and honor and protector, has put his seal
of approval upon me through his unsparing blessings and miracles."*

On January 16 Abe Ghaffari picked up the phone and heard the
ocean-in-a-seashell sound of a long-distance call coming through.
Then two clicks and, "Ebrahim! Ebrahim!"

"Yes. Yes? Who . . . ?"

There was Persian music playing in the background and many
voices. "He is free! Mehdi is free! They released him."

"Haik?"

"Yes, this is Haik. Ebrahim, it's true. Had you heard already? They've released Dibaj. He's here with us. And some of the brothers and sisters. We are here celebrating. Praying and celebrating!"

"How?"

"They just let him out. He had to sign some papers saying he would stay nearby. His charges haven't been dismissed—that's important for people to know. We have to keep up the campaign. But it's working. They've released him."

"Is he well? How does he look?"

"You should see. Maybe we should all spend some time in prison. It's the next best thing to a resurrection!"

"You think they'll let him stay out? Is the danger passed?"

"Well, this is still Iran, my friend. They made him write a letter of thanks to the judicial authorities for their leniency. He also had to promise to return to court at any time for questioning. But I don't see what they can do now that he's free again and the world's watching."

Abe's own joy was tempered by thoughts he was reluctant to express. "You should continue to be careful," he said. "Maybe more careful now than ever." This transcontinental phone celebration was far from careful.

"I don't know," Haik said. "Perhaps we were careful too long. The Lord gave us courage and is blessing the steps we have taken."

"It's still a shadowed valley," Abe said, wondering what the bug listener would make of the biblical allusion.

"Shall I fear evil then?" Haik asked.

Abe could not help thinking, *I fear it for you.*

The next day, Monday, January 17, the spokesman of the Judiciary of the Islamic Republic of Iran, Hujjat-ul-Islam Ali Hoseini, announced that "the press reports indicating that Rev. Dibaj was sentenced to death for converting to Christianity are groundless and that contrary to foreign reports, Mr. Mehdi Dibaj had been out on bail and his case was still under investigation."[7]

"Now because God does whatever he desires, who can separate us from the love of God? Or who can destroy the relationship between the cre-

ator and the creature or defeat a heart that is faithful to his Lord? He will be safe and secure under the shadow of the Almighty!"

On Wednesday, January 19, Bishop Haik left home for the Mehrabad Airport in west Tehran to pick up two Armenian women arriving from Isfahan who were to leave for a conference in England the next day. His office soon received a call from the arriving party wondering where Bishop Haik might be.

Hours went by without Bishop Haik turning up. His family and coworkers scoured the airport. They could not find his car.

By the end of a long, agonizing day, they could no longer deny his probable abduction and notified the police.

The police reported they had no information on his whereabouts.

How could this be, his family wondered, since he had been under the government's twenty-four-hour surveillance?

At any moment they expected a phone call from one group or another claiming responsibility.

A week went by, and they heard nothing.

In the United States, Abe Ghaffari sent out a press release, "Iranian Pastor Missing, Feared Tortured or Dead." Abe was already starting to grieve, knowing how the story must play out.

Ten agonizing days after Bishop Haik disappeared, his family received a phone call from the Tehran Office of Investigation. Haik's body had been found days earlier. His assailants had left it by a police station located on Old Shemran Road in Tehran. The Office of Investigation had a photograph of the corpse and wanted a family member to make an identification.

When Bishop Haik's son Joseph looked at the photograph, he saw many of the twenty-seven stab wounds that caused his father's death. The photograph also showed stitches on the abdomen that the coroner's office attributed to an autopsy.

Joseph asked how and when the body would be released to the family.

The police did not actually have the body in their possession. Bishop Haik was already buried in an Islamic cemetery, Beheshta

Zahra, just outside Tehran. They claimed not to have the authority to exhume the body, even though a Christian corpse desecrates Islamic holy ground.

The family would have to appeal for the exhumation to be carried out, and eventually the district court of Shah-re Rey (on President Rafsanjani's personal recommendation, sources reported[8]) ordered this to be done.

The next week Iran's Permanent Mission to the United Nations stated that "a suspect has been arrested and is under investigation" for Bishop Haik's murder and that police were searching for accomplices. The report specified that the prosecutor in Tehran had ordered a full investigation "to arrest and bring the perpetrators to justice." The report speculated that Haik was at the "wrong place at the wrong time" and was probably killed by "unknown assailants with unknown motives."

The authorities refused comment, however, on why they initially failed to identify the body of a well-known public figure, why no photograph of Bishop Haik's body was published in the newspapers, as is standard practice with unidentified victims, why they failed to continue calling the phone numbers of church associates found in Haik's pockets.

Most in the human rights community concluded that Bishop Haik was murdered by a group of contract killers on order from the Iranian secret police, SAVAMA. He was quickly buried, they guessed, as a cover-up and to hide traces of torture.[9] The supposed autopsy might have been an additional means of covering up torture. Who could doubt the cause of death of a man stabbed twenty-seven times?

On Tuesday, February 1, the family was allowed to view the body and prepare it for burial. Police and agents of the Information Ministry insisted on delivering the body to the church two days later. The family was advised that the police would stay on duty to assure that the body was interred immediately.

"Our refuge is the mercy seat of God, who is exalted from the beginning. I know in whom I have believed, and he is able to guard what I

have entrusted to him to the end until I reach the kingdom of God, the
place where the righteous shine like the sun."

On the day of Bishop Haik's funeral, the police prevented a formal
cortege by requiring three-minute intervals between all cars arriving at the cemetery. They carried their automatic weapons at the
ready among the graveside mourners and confiscated video and still
cameras, preventing any photographic record of the event.

The authorities influenced press coverage of Bishop Haik Hovsepian-Mehr's funeral to such an extent that the *New York Times*
falsely reported that the family was allowed to conduct an independent autopsy and misleadingly stated that three hundred Armenians attended the funeral.[10]

Three hundred church members did pack the small church service. Then two thousand mourners and more stood for three hours
in bitterly cold weather at graveside to honor Bishop Haik, including
the ambassador of Norway and innumerable Muslims. When a Roman Catholic priest threw his handful of dirt on the coffin, he declared, tears in his eyes, "This man is a saint and a martyr."

The Reverend Mehdi Dibaj commented, "I should have died,
not Brother Haik."[11] The funeral brought the evangelical Iranian
church together as never before and spurred interest among many
Iranians: if such men were willing to die for their faith, perhaps
there was something to it.

Bishop Haik's assassination also provoked worldwide protest.
Demonstrations broke out in front of the Iranian embassies in Paris,
Seoul, and London. In Seoul the Yoido Central Church of the Assemblies of God, the largest church in the world, with seven hundred thousand members, tied up the Iranian embassy's switchboard
with phone calls and faxes for days. These fellow Christians brought
so much attention to the issue that Iran recalled its ambassador for
consultations. Thousands of Scandinavians also participated in a let-
ter-writing campaign. Middle East Watch and other human rights
organizations called for a thorough investigation of Bishop Haik's
death.

. . .

"They object to my evangelizing. But 'If you find a blind person near a well and keep silent then you have sinned' [a Persian poem]. It is our duty, as long as the door of God's mercy is open, to convince evildoers to turn from their sinful ways and find refuge in him in order to be saved from the wrath of a righteous God and from the coming dreadful punishment."

Despite Bishop Haik's fate, Mehdi Dibaj undertook his pastoral journey to Iran's evangelical congregations. About his presence, one Iranian Christian remarked, "From the day he came out we all noticed how his face was shining. The light and love of Christ just shone from his face. God had truly made him a saint."[12] The sight of so many who had become Christians moved him to tears. He now understood how he had survived his years in prison; the new converts were the face of his strength.

The authorities did not forget about Dibaj or cease their surveillance and intimidation of the evangelical church, however. In April a *fatwa* (religious edict) was issued against Mehdi Dibaj in a Tehran newspaper, calling for his execution.[13] Like the *fatwa* against novelist Salman Rushdie, this declaration meant that anyone who took Mehdi Dibaj's life would be acting at the religious leaders' request.

The authorities' eagerness to remove Dibaj from the scene, one way or another, was also expressed through the return of his passport. Released criminals in Iran are generally not allowed to travel outside the country for at least three years. But Dibaj was simultaneously threatened with death and given the means of escape from the country.

Once again Dibaj chose to stay, but many Christian leaders, particularly Muslim converts, made preparations to emigrate.

Surveillance of the churches increased. A Muslim imam as well as armed intelligence agents attended every worship service at Bishop Haik's old church in Tehran.

Then in June and the first days of July church leaders began receiving terrifying "heads up" phone calls informing them that the government could no longer protect them. They should be on their guard or get themselves out of the country, if possible. The threat was confirmed by a mole high up in the government: a hit list existed, according to this source, with the names of top evangelical leaders.[14]

The Christian community speculated on whether they should attribute these new persecutions to the government itself or to an extremist faction within the government that more moderate leaders could not control. President Rafsanjani was positioning Iran to be more open to the West, a policy at odds with the persecution of evangelicals. People very high up, including those in the Ministry of Information, must be behind the terror.[15]

The ongoing persecution made use of past events. One convert coming out of Iran said that his interrogator confessed the authorities made a mistake by officially executing Pastor Soodmand in 1990. In the future, he said, such converts would simply disappear, as Bishop Haik had.[16] The same could be arranged for anyone unwilling to cooperate.

"I am a Christian, a sinner who believes Jesus has died for my sins on the cross and by his resurrection and victory over death has made me righteous in the presence of the holy God. The true God speaks about this fact in his holy word, the gospel. Jesus means Savior 'because he will save his people from their sins.' Jesus paid the penalty of our sins by his own blood and gave us a new life so that we can live for the glory of God by the help of the Holy Spirit and be like a dam against corruption, be a channel of blessing and healing, and be protected by the love of God."

During the week of June 20–24, the Reverend Mehdi Dibaj held a Christian conference with a small group of believers in the Sharon Garden in Karaj, a suburb of Tehran.

Although he entitled one of his talks "Prison Experience," he never spoke of his own personal trials directly. He stressed 1 Thessalonians 5:18, "In everything give thanks." Whether the taste of our experience was more like chocolate candy or medicine, he said, the Lord meant everything for our good. We are the apple of his eye.

He quoted Deuteronomy 32:11: "As an eagle incites its nestlings forth by hovering over its brood, so he spread his wings to receive them and bore them on his pinions." When a mother eagle teaches her eaglet to fly, Dibaj said, she bears her young up into the air and then casts the eaglet into free fall before snatching him out of the air once more. As the young bird falls, flapping his wings awkwardly, he must be terrified. The mother knows what she is doing, though.

When we try out our wings of faith, Dibaj continued, we may find ourselves plunging downward, helpless and frightened. Even in these moments, we are secure in the Lord's care. The Lord is only initiating us into our true lives as creatures made a little lower than the angels.[17]

So if we listen, God speaks, Dibaj said. If we pray, God performs miracles. If we are humble, God is glorified.

On Friday afternoon, at the conference's end, Pastor Dibaj left to celebrate his daughter Fereshteh's seventeenth birthday. The whole extended family was taking the occasion to stage a reunion—the first such gathering since their father's imprisonment ten years before.

When Dibaj failed to arrive at the party, the stark fear of another murder gripped everyone immediately. Had Dibaj been released from prison only to suffer martyrdom like Bishop Haik? His family soon had no choice but to report him missing to the authorities, who once again could be of no immediate help.

The next day, Saturday, the scholar, translator, and pastor Tateos Mikaelian was preparing to preach to the Central Assembly of God Church in Tehran, Bishop Haik's old congregation.

Mikaelian was the evangelical community's most distinguished scholar, with a whimsical nature springing from a deep spirituality. He spent his days translating Christian books and his evenings ministering to Saint John Armenian Evangelical Church. With a round head, worn bald with thinking, tar black eyebrows, and dancing, sharp eyes, his countenance held a contemplative depth like a saint in a Byzantine mosaic—the outward sign, perhaps, of the severe spiritual disciplines he kept, such as fasting for forty days and drinking only water.

Mikaelian's church conducted its services in Armenian. Because of the Presbyterians' ethnic base, Mikaelian and his people had not been drawn as immediately into the latest conflicts.

Tomorrow Tateos Mikaelian would be speaking in Farsi, with an imam and SAVAMA agents in attendance. The people would be thinking about Dibaj, as was he right then in his study. His sermon might be received as the most confrontational action he had undertaken in a long time.

The scholar had been subject to the wrath of the authorities in the past, though. Early in the Islamic Revolution, when the government insisted Mikaelian's Armenian schools must teach Christianity out of a government-approved text—which specified that Christ was not crucified or the Son of God—Mikaelian gave an interview to a French magazine protesting the government's interference. The Iranian newspapers picked up the story and Mikaelian became notorious. The clerical authorities interrogated him over and over again until he began joking about his "new friends." His life had been in danger from that point on. After the onslaught of interrogations passed, Mikaelian became far more cautious. The experience left him with long-term fears that he battled, which he had admitted to intimates such as Haik.

Even though Mikaelian had replaced Bishop Haik as chairman of the Protestant Council, he did not believe his own life to be in danger. Mikaelian might well be speaking to the next person taken, though. What would he want to know if he found himself in that situation? How should he be preparing himself?

When the Reverend Mikaelian delivered his sermon the next day, he spoke directly to the issue of martyrdom, with prophetic courage.

In these times of persecution, with Bishop Haik gone and Dibaj missing, who were the church's opponents? Mikaelian asked.[18]

Their opponents were religious leaders who believed that holiness consisted in obeying God's commands. Holiness belonged not only to individuals but also to nations, who, through collective worship and right behavior, could make Iran the habitation of God and his justice. A holy people could induce God to fulfill his promises through strict observance.

Toward that end Muslim leaders found themselves driven to eliminate the influence of those who distracted the people from this enterprise. The zeal with which they pursued these ends declared their righteousness. Muslims took faith seriously enough to fight for it.

If Christians were not of a like mind, why not? Mikaelian asked. Who were they as a religious people?

Christians believed that God's love for his people could not depend on their own holiness. They were sinners incapable of deserving God's love. But, as the apostle Paul declared, while we were still sinners, Christ died for us. God's love came to us in Christ without our having done anything to deserve such a love.

Islam taught how humankind approaches God. The faith of Christianity teaches how God approaches humankind.

Without Christ, Christians believe, we are nothing. But who are we in him?

In Christ we are all things.

Mikaelian read from 1 Peter 2:9. "You are a chosen race, a royal priesthood, a holy nation, a people of his own, so that you may announce the praises of him who called you out of darkness into his wonderful light."

Who are we? Mikaelian asked again. We are the Body of Christ within the world, the living presence of Christ, and just as our Lord did, we take our faith seriously enough to pour out our lives for God's glory.

Jesus asked his disciples, "Are you able to be baptized with my baptism? To drink from my cup?" He told his followers to rejoice when they were misused and slandered and persecuted. For if men reviled them, the Father would remember them. "In the world you will have trouble," Jesus said, "but rejoice and be exceedingly glad, for I have overcome the world."

So his fellow Iranian Christians, Mikaelian said, were not to be perplexed or afraid of martyrdom but prepared to face it. Not as others, who have no hope, but in the certain faith that Christ's triumph over the world manifested itself in the resurrection. To face their own deaths was to identify wholly with Christ, for, as the apostle writes, to live is Christ and to die, gain.

"Therefore I am not only satisfied to be in prison for the honor of his holy name but am ready to give my life for the sake of Jesus my Lord and enter his kingdom sooner, the place where the elect of God enter everlasting life."

As it happened, Tateos Mikaelian was preaching to—or for—the next life taken. Three days after delivering his last sermon in Tehran, on June 29, Reverend Mikaelian received a mysterious phone call at his home about 4:30 P.M. He drove off and, like Bishop Haik and Mehdi Dibaj, disappeared.

Of the two, Dibaj and Mikaelian, the scholar was found first. The police called Mikaelian's son Galo at 5 P.M. on July 2, asking him to identify his father's body at the coroner's office. The pastor had been shot three times in the back of the head.

Then, on July 5, police informed Mehdi Dibaj's family that they had run across his body in a Tehran park as they searched for Mikaelian's killers. Officials claimed he had been stabbed to death, but others noted rope burns around his neck, as if he had also been hanged.

Human rights activists said both deaths looked like "extra-judicial executions."[19] Once again the police refused to release the bodies to anyone and insisted on custody until their interment.

Mikaelian's family was warned against speaking of his death to anyone. Mehdi Dibaj's four children hardly needed to be warned; six short months after their father's release from prison, they had lost him forever.

The world did take notice, with protests from many quarters. The United States Department of State called on Iran to "abide by its obligations" under the UN Human Rights Declaration. "Harassment and brutal attacks on some religious minorities are all too commonplace in Iran," said acting spokesperson Christine Shelly. Members of Parliament in the United Kingdom discussed urging their government to use their seat on the United Nations Security Council to call for action against Iran. Amnesty International, Human Rights Watch, Christian Solidarity International, and Jubilee Campaign notified Iran they would hold the government responsible for any further action taken against the evangelical church.

Memorial services were held from London to California. The Presbyterian Church U.S.A. designated August 28 as a day of prayer in support of the Iranian church.

Iranian officials quickly denied any new crackdown on religious minorities. Hossein Nosrat, spokesman at the Permanent Mission of the Islamic Republic of Iran to the United Nations, described the deaths as "isolated cases," and "in no way, under no circumstances" were they part of a new effort against Iran's Christians. Nosrat said the Iranian government suspected an opposition group that was "trying to create an atmosphere of fear for the minorities" as part of a "new campaign against the Iranian government." He pledged his government would carry out an extensive investigation.[20]

Within days Iranian authorities clarified what they meant by an "opposition group." They charged three women members of their chief political rival, the Mujahedeen Khalq Organization (MKO), with the murders of Dibaj and Mikaelian. Authorities brought the families and other Christian leaders to meet the purported MKO ringleader, Farhanaz Anami. In their presence she "confessed" that the pastors were killed in order to stir up sectarian violence between Muslims and Christians.

A statement from the Mujahedeen office in Paris, however, called the official version of events "foolish fairy tales" and blamed the Iranian Intelligence Ministry.[21]

The Christian community in Iran did not know what to believe: whether the assassinations were committed by the government, by an extremist faction within the government, or by the Mujahedeen. These cumulative events caused widespread depression and fear. Not only was the Christian community being scapegoated by political groups intent on power, but now they were being used as a pawn in international politics—a pawn horribly useful to all sides.

"He is our Savior and he is the Son of God. To know him means to know eternal life. I, a useless sinner, have believed in his beloved person and all his words and miracles recorded in the gospel, and I have committed my life into his hands. Life for me is an opportunity to serve him, and death is a better opportunity to be with Christ."

In many evangelical churches of Iran today members do not use their real names. They are known to one another only by fictitious first names—Ali, Hossein, El Nathan[22]—so as to limit any interrogator's success. Congregations must remain small, quickly creating new cell communities when growth occurs. They meet mostly in randomly rotating private homes, as their public churches remain for the most part shuttered. Any potential convert must be investigated extensively, as SAVAMA agents are always trying to infiltrate church circles. The Iranian evangelical community, especially the part that ministers to Muslims, has become largely clandestine. The persecutions of 1993 and 1994 have been successful, in this sense.

Nor have these persecutions ceased. On September 28, 1996, Iran gave the church another martyr, Muhammad Bagher Yusefi. He was found hanged in a forest near his home city of Sari. The pastor of the Assembly of God church in Mazandaran, he also ministered to Bishop Haik's old congregation in Gorgan. He had helped raise two of Mehdi Dibaj's sons during their father's imprisonment.

The truth about the 1994 killings of the three pastors has begun to come out, however. In 1999, prodded by the work of investigative journalists like Akbar Ganji and Emadedin Baghi, Iran's president

Muhammad Khatami forced the Intelligence Ministry to own up to the 1998 murders of four dissidents—two writers and a reform-minded politician and his wife.[23] Fifteen agents were found guilty of planning and carrying out the murders, and the intelligence minister, Dorri Najafabadi, resigned. In the course of these disclosures, intelligence agents confessed to carrying out many other murders as well, all in extrajudicial-execution style. Bishop Haik Hovsepian Mehr, Mehdi Dibaj, and Tateos Mikaelian were alluded to in press reports as among the probable targets.[24] Unfortunately, those who were suspected of ordering the killings, such as former intelligence minister Ali Fallahian and the high-ranking judge Mohseni Ejei, were never seriously investigated. The most senior ministry official to be arrested, Saeed Emami, a possible source of countless other disclosures, was said to have committed suicide while in jail.[25] It has become pretty clear, though, that the arrest of Farhanaz Anami and her two MKO coconspirators was a sham concocted by the true perpetrators of these executions.

The sacrifice of the three pastors and many others within the evangelical community has not been in vain, despite the church's underground status. The blood of the martyrs remains the seed of the church. In 1977 there were only twenty-seven hundred evangelicals in Iran out of a population of 45 million. Of these only three hundred were former Muslims. Today, there are close to fifty-five thousand believers, of whom twenty-seven thousand are from Muslim backgrounds. About half live in Iran and the remainder are dispersed among more than thirty countries. The large Christian Iranian émigré community contains a dynamic strength that replenishes and extends the work of those in Iran itself.

In the parable of the seed, Jesus predicted the good seed would produce five, ten, one-hundredfold. The sacrifice of Iran's contemporary martyrs has helped accomplish, despite ferocious opposition, the literal fulfillment of this divine calculus.

Abe Ghaffari, as he works for the welfare of Iranian Christians all over the world from his base in Colorado, remembers a time prior to the Islamic Revolution when Iranians were almost completely closed to Christianity. Paradoxically, according to Ghaffari, the Islamic Revolution has actually opened many Iranians' minds to Christ. He now sits in his office and receives transcontinental phone calls from Iranians asking, "What does it mean to be a Christian?"

As I was writing about those three brave men, Haik, Dibaj, and Mikaelian, I began to wonder, how did Jesus himself come to believe that he would die a martyr's death? And what meaning did he believe his death would have?

Jesus had reason to think about martyrdom virtually from the inception of his public ministry. After he reads out a portion of Isaiah's messianic prophecy in his home synagogue, or sends Legion's demons into the Gadarene swine, or declares before the religious authorities that Abraham exulted to see Jesus' day—on all these occasions and others his life was imperiled. The trip to raise Lazarus from the dead takes Jesus through such hostile territory that Thomas declares, "Let us also go, that we may die with him" (John 11:16). Many times Jesus must have thought, as any person would, what meaning his ministry would have if his life ended violently. He needed no particular prescience to anticipate his martyrdom. Jesus forecasts such a fate so early in his ministry, in fact, that he may have anticipated the outcome of his campaign as a distinct possibility from the beginning.

Jesus came, as the evangelist Mark tell us, announcing God's liberation. "Repent, for the kingdom of God is at hand." Most believed, including Jesus' followers, that such an announcement heralded the end of Israel's present exile—its subjugation by Rome. Political freedom would enable Israel to fulfill her calling as light to the nations. Israel might become the world power of her day, blessed by the Lord's hand, led by the anointed one, Messiah.

Jesus did claim to be the Messiah. He tells Caiaphas this straight out, and adds, "And you will see the Son of Man sitting at the right hand of the Mighty One and coming on the clouds of heaven" (Mark 14:62).

But he conceives of the Messiah as a servant—he takes Isaiah's personification of Israel in the prophet's songs of the suffering servant and makes this personification his literal role. As his public ministry fails, Jesus chooses to be the man of sorrows acquainted with grief, one wounded for our transgressions, by whose stripes we are healed. Further, he will be the cornerstone the builders reject, on which everything eventually rests, the Temple not made by human hands that is willingly destroyed in order to be raised up again on the third day.

In this conception lay his final mission—his understanding of calling—and the basis on which he wagered that his death would prove a martyrdom, a death that convicts its perpetrators.

Jesus anticipates his death and its meaning by inaugurating a new rite—a thanksgiving, or Eucharist. The new rite captures both the promise of God's fellowship and what Jesus prophetically understands as its cost. He will, as the Lamb of God announced by John, willingly receive the death that his opponents harbor in their hearts, and put that death to death by showing the world its true character.

The theology of the cross—of martyrdom as a redemptive act— is a genuine construct of Jesus' own religious genius. Jesus saw what was coming and understood its purpose in a way that has held his followers' imaginations ever since.

Still, how did Jesus come to understand that his death would be his vindication in more than historical memory? How did he anticipate that when he laid down his life for his friends, his heavenly Father would raise him to glory? A dying and resurrected Son of God had no part in Jewish tradition. Jesus forecasts this event repeatedly without the disciples believing it or even being able to take it in. Their faith had no such concept.

The most that can be said, perhaps, is that the resurrection of the dead was always a sign attached to the end of Israel's exile—to the coming of the kingdom of God. The famous passage from Ezekiel about the valley of dry bones represents just such a prophecy.

> I prophesied as he [the Lord] commanded me, and breath entered them [the dry bones]; they came to life and stood up on their feet—a vast army.
>
> Then he said to me: "Son of man, these bones are the whole house of Israel. They say, 'Our bones are dried up and our hope is gone; we are cut off.' Therefore prophesy and say to them: 'This is what the Sovereign Lord says: O my people, I am going to open your graves and bring you up from them; I will bring you back to the land of Israel. Then you, my people, will know that I am the Lord, when I open your graves and bring you up from them.' " (Ezekiel 37:10–13)

If the gospel accounts are to be believed, Jesus performed the raising of the dead, most notably in the case of Lazarus, as a sign that God's kingdom had come through his ministry. There is a logic, I suppose, in one who personifies Israel enjoying her prophesied restoration—as the firstfruits of those who sleep, as Saint Paul writes. But it's an unprecedented logic. Jesus' faith in the heavenly Father's vindication through his own resurrection breaks the bounds of any usual analysis.

Our portrait of Jesus has relied, principally, on historical ways of thinking. What can possibly be said historically about Jesus' resurrection? Only that Jesus' expectation was so popularly known that his last hecklers used it to scorn him. "You who are going to destroy the temple and build it in three days, save yourself! Come down from the cross, if you are the Son of God!" (Matthew 27:40).

If Jesus expected to be raised from the dead, his expectation existed in hope, not certainty. His martyrdom was not playacting, which it might be considered if he had not suffered his death as any martyr must, at complete risk of being only another deluded fanatic. On the cross Jesus cried out, "My God, my God, why have you forsaken me?" He experienced the full measure of human trial—the desperation of searching for God when God seemingly refuses to respond. His spiritual desertion testifies to the authenticity of his martyrdom.

Yet that desertion takes place within the context of faith; Jesus' echoing call is issued in words from Psalm 22, which concludes with a cry of celebration.

> *For he has not despised or disdained*
> *   the suffering of the afflicted one;*
> *he has not hidden his face from him*
> *   but has listened to his cry for help.*
> *From you comes the theme of my praise in the great*
> *   assembly; before those who fear you will I fulfill*
> *   my vows.*
> *The poor will eat and be satisfied;*
> *   they who seek the Lord will praise him—*
> *   may your hearts live forever!*
> *All the ends of the earth*
> *   will remember and turn to the Lord,*
> *and all the families of the nations*
> *   will bow down before him,*
> *for dominion belongs to the Lord*
> *   and he rules over the nations.*
> *(Psalm 22:24–28)*

As he dies Jesus commends his spirit into God's hands, declaring, "It is finished." Jesus in the grave awaits his vindication by his heavenly Father. And God either raised him from the dead or Christians, as Saint Paul says, can only be considered pitiable (1 Corinthians 15:14–19).

By his own election, Jesus also made his vindication dependent on his followers and those who would come after them. The world's final judgment as to the character of his death—as a martyrdom, or as the execution of a religious troublemaker—awaits not only the empty tomb and the resurrection appearances, but also the continuing realization of Jesus' life through his Body, the church. He entrusted his self-understanding as the Christ to his followers, charging them to go throughout the world declaring the good news of God's love. Those who faithfully accept this commission, from the saints of old to those today, enflesh Jesus' life anew and make manifest the living Christ.

Conclusion

From South Carolina to Mexico City to the California coast to Thailand to Rome and Iran I've been privileged to encounter extraordinary people who lend their hands to the work of Jesus. Christ does seem to shape their lives in a way that makes Christ's own presence visible.

Who is the living Christ? *He is the God who is for us.* In Christ we see the God who declared his creation good and delighted in talking with man and woman in Eden. He is the Son of Man: the one who champions our humanity. He embraces us in love and initiates a universal campaign to transform hearts and minds, in order that our hearts' desire for freedom may be realized.

He sustains us and keeps us company on our individual paths, knowing from personal experience the loneliness of life and its many hardships. He teaches us to pray so that beyond every visible circumstance and condition we have access to the Father—the one who alone is capable of weaving every dark thread into a divine comedy. The teachings and actions of Jesus enlighten our minds through diagnosing the essence of the human condition, its challenges, pitfalls, and opportunities. This diagnosis is also a prophetic realization of the only possible remedy, the coming of the kingdom of God.

The living Christ continues to verify the reality of God's kingdom through healing our diseases, both for the sake of healing's inherent good and also as a sign of his power to forgive sin's mortal wound. We can be free of any evil force that alienates us from God because Jesus conquered evil, disease, and even death. He was willing to submit his authority to do so to the final test: martyrdom. Those who join him today in this ultimate wager testify that mortality has been conquered by immortality.

In Christ we are a new creation. Because of Jesus' life and continuing presence through his followers the world is inhabited by a counterforce to its savagery and destruction. In Christ we find what we love and what we want past all wanting: unending life.

If "I in them and you in me" encapsulates Jesus' own theology of the church, Jesus must be the sum and substance of any true gathering of his followers. Jesus must be available in our neighborhood, around the block, within our home, within reach of my own prayers. The nature of drama demands the extraordinary, and so the stories told here make use of extreme situations. There's something wrong with the merely extraordinary, however, something inadequate to Jesus' own prayer. A true living Christ must be local, at hand, just where, in fact, Jesus claimed the kingdom of God to be.

To sum up, then, I thought I'd go visit a local group of believers, to see if I could spy Jesus playing the same roles in their lives as I had in far-flung locales. Was he to be found in a local congregation as wayfarer, healer, liberator?

I had known of Saint George Orthodox Christian Cathedral in Wichita, Kansas, for years through friendships with its members. The people I knew made me suspect that Jesus' prayer was being answered among them. What I found when I visited during Holy Week of 2001 was more than I could believe, as people say. If the reader protests that his local church bears little resemblance to such an alive

congregation, I wouldn't be surprised. I realize how anemic many local churches can be. Saint George still shows what's possible when
Christ's followers live out their faith.

On April 14, 2001, lightning illumines the night with a momentar-
ily blinding power and the tree-bending northeast wind brings
heavy onslaughts of rain, as the first parishioners of Saint George
Orthodox Christian Cathedral arrive in their cars, SUVs, and mini-
vans for the Easter Vigil. The church's monumental dome and sand-
brick façade, lit by strategically placed garden spot lamps, promise a
honeycomb welcoming into the light-filled interior that's glimpsed
through first- and second-story Palladian windows.

The county is under a tornado watch until midnight—red blots
of storm activity are showing up on Wichita's local TV stations'
Doppler radar. There are reports of baseball-size hail not too far
away and sightings of wall clouds; the local meteorologists are paying close attention to hook echoes off the back of storms that signal
twisters. The first undaunted parishioners to arrive—choir members
who will rehearse for an hour before the three-hour service begins—
run for the doors, hunching low as if fighting the downdrafts of a
rising helicopter, and take the rain on hastily raised umbrellas or
their backs.

Among these are Warren and Chris Farha. Chris leads the choir,
having over twenty years turned a gaggle of Midwesterners into the
renewed voice of Byzantium, with its quarter-tone Arabian ecstasies.
She's also an executive at Latour Food Services, one of the many
companies founded by the Lebanese émigré community that built
Saint George. The Lebanese community's twelve hundred or so
members, although a tiny fraction of Wichita's booming three hundred thousand plus, still provide much of the city's merchandising
base.

Chris and Warren grew up hearing *"Nushkur Allah"* (Thank
God) or *"Insh'Allah"* (God willing) at the end of nearly every statement by their pious relatives. Warren's grandfather Namen was
among the first of the immigrants who, beginning in 1895, left the

small valley of Marjayoun in south Lebanon to establish the Wichita Lebanese community.

The Lebanese who founded Saint George came to the United States, as much as the Pilgrim fathers, for religious freedom, although their life in Orthodoxy after nineteen centuries—ever since the followers of Christ were first called Christians in Antioch—was so integral to their identity that they thought in terms of the freedom to be themselves. In the last decade of the nineteenth century, the Ottoman Turks were conscripting Christian youth and placing them in the front lines of their constant skirmishes with the Kurds and Armenians, epitomizing twelve hundred years of religious persecution and economic deprivation, and spurring massive emigration to America. Their faith accompanied the Lebanese emigrants in their wayfaring, and they established a church in Wichita in 1918, several years before they had a resident priest.

Warren Farha's life shows how the community continues to nurture people in finding their way. A tall, leanly built man, with dark, now silver-threaded hair, Warren looks like a Semitic Galahad. His sheltering presence brings many people into his life, often those with wild and troubled pasts—perhaps because he's known his own troubles.

In 1987 he was a married man with two children working in the family carpet and building supply business when his first wife, Barbara Pinkham, was involved in a devastating car accident. For two months she lay in the hospital in a coma or semiconsciousness. During that time, Father Basil Essey (now Bishop Basil) came to be the pastor of Saint George. Father Basil insisted that his reception committee take him directly from the airport to Barbara's hospital room, to pray for her and comfort Warren.

Soon Warren needed his family and his church community more than ever as Barbara passed away. For the next year Warren's sister Lori helped him take care of his two children, Rachel and Nathan. His community saw him through the "twilight life" of his grief and helped him reemerge with new hope. It encouraged him to undertake his longtime vocational dream, which resulted in the founding of Eighth Day Books—surely the most idealistic (and one of the best) bookstores in America. It's a place where the reader can find everything from a complete set of *Writings of the Early Church Fathers* to hard-to-find works by Orthodox writers like Alexander Schmemann and Vladimir Lossky and Catholic theologians such as Louis Bouyer and Hans Urs von Balthasar. As Warren's grief abated and the bookstore took shape, he began dating his childhood friend Christy Cohlmia. They were married in 1988 and three years later had a child together, Timothy.

As the earth continues to rumble and shake with thunder from the night's storm, inside Saint George the sanctuary lies in the twilight of the iconostasis's votive candles. The icon's gold backgrounds glimmer as Jesus, his mother, the archangels Michael and Gabriel, Saints George, John the Baptist, Constantine, and Helena wait. To the left of the iconostasis's royal doors, their curtain drawn, rests the ceremonial bier and *epitaphion*—a linen shroud with Christ's buried body depicted on it—that the community processed with last night, on Good Friday, around the outside of the church.

Still at home, a member of the congregation—I'll call her Lucy—thinks about pausing before the family altar with its icons of Mary as Theotokos (the God-bearer) and Saint John Damascene, to whom she has a particular devotion. She feels invited to prayer, almost guiltily tempted. Lucy has the gift of tears. In church or while praying at her family altar she begins weeping, not for her own sins or even with any particular feeling of sorrow or guilt. The tears simply come, unbidden, and they are profuse. She went to her pastor, Father Paul O'Callaghan, to ask whether what she was experiencing might be neurotic or somehow disturbed. Father Paul told her about the legacy of such a gift in Orthodox spirituality. Her tears were evidence that her life and prayers were being accepted as repentance not for her own sake but for the church and the world—a gift the monks on Mount Athos spend a lifetime praying for.

Father Paul is still at home himself. Holy Week for an Orthodox priest is a marathon, with *five or six hours* of services daily and often more. Nor do Orthodox celebrations have much respect for the need to sleep. The Vigil will end about 3 A.M. this night, and Father Paul will return at 1 P.M. on Sunday for a two-hour Vespers. So Father Paul doesn't practice any particular devotions in preparation for the Vigil. He spends time with his children, talks with his wife, Jeannie. In the past, Easter joy has sprung up within him with an overpowering force. In other years he has felt, after celebrating the Vigil, nothing so much as "We've gotten through it." Like everyone else, he's following the developing storms via a local TV station's Doppler radar screen. He's also worried about the outdoor procession, a reminder of the baptismal procession by catechumens (converts) of the ancient church, which is his favorite part of the Easter Vigil. After the Easter fire is kindled and the celebrants pass the light of their own candles to everyone in the congregation, the people process out the doors and around the church. Will they be able to go outside tonight?

Father Paul loves the moment when, arriving back at the church's doors, the chief celebrant—tonight, Bishop Basil—knocks on the doors and goes through a dialogue three times with a person inside who plays the devil. "Lift up your heads, O ye gates," the bishop calls, quoting Psalm 24, "and be lifted up, ancient doors, that the king of glory may come in."

From inside the person playing the devil replies, "Who is the king of glory?"

"The Lord strong and mighty: the Lord mighty in battle," the bishop answers.

Twice again the bishop knocks, twice more the devil questions Christ's authority. For that moment the church is—symbolically—both an empty tomb and a harrowed hell. Satan is about to receive the message that his power over the world has been broken. In Orthodox icons of the resurrection, Christ stands on the broken gates of hell, with keys and locks scattered about, showing that he has exploded the mechanism of death. The liturgy captures this cosmic explosion of death with its own pandemonium—the bells ringing, the bishop proclaiming Christ's resurrection, and the choir singing, all at the same time. Father Paul loves this moment in the liturgy, when liturgical order breaks apart with the fullness of the mystery. So he checks the TV station again, hoping the worst is headed to their south.

Nina and Ralph Farha begin heading for the cathedral, having lived in Wichita so long that they take severe weather in stride. In 1975, Nina suffered an aneurysm that threatened to take her life. Fifty of Saint George's most pious women knelt in the chapel praying for her as she underwent surgery—many of them so old that they had to have help getting down on their knees and back up. Nina suffered postoperative complications, excess bleeding that again threatened to take her life. Again, the women of the church prayed, and to the surprise of her neurosurgeon Nina recovered. Ralph is convinced his wife's recovery was a miracle, as are many others within the church.

Before the Divine Liturgy (the Orthodox equivalent of the Western Mass) Father Paul stands before a side altar for the *kairon*, or beginning prayers, after which he performs the *prothesis*, the preparation of the Eucharistic bread. Father Paul cuts a cube of bread from the loaf to be consecrated, which is called the Lamb. The cube stands for Christ, the "Bread of life . . . which came down from heaven." Father Paul recites verses from the prophecy of Isaiah: "He was led as a lamb to the slaughter . . ."

While Father Paul continues this ceremony, Father Anthony Scott arrives and quietly stands with him. He thinks how good it is to be back at Saint George. He was the pastor from 1977 to 1987, when the church turned a decisive corner. As a former Southern Baptist, evangelism is part and parcel of Father Anthony's soul. When he came to be the pastor of Saint George, the community was in conflict and inward looking. Father Anthony challenged the community to be more than an ethnic parish. He asked them to give up the liberal use of Arabic in their celebrations and open their church to the greater community. Many feared losing the extended-family dimension of Saint George. Father Anthony suggested that the community's strength would not be diminished; it would grow through its extension to others. So the last major elements of the Divine

Liturgy sung in Arabic were dropped. The community also embraced the Eucharistic renewal taking place throughout American Orthodoxy, leaving behind the fearful or perfunctory piety that limited communion to a once-a-year event. Saint George quickly became a place spiritual seekers sought out.

As the church begins to fill up, a family arrives that's been in the United States only this past year. The ceremonial Good Friday bier before the iconostasis cannot help but evoke powerful memories for them. They are from Aleppo, one of the world's most ancient Christian cities, located in today's Syria. While relations between Christians and Muslims in Syria are generally less tense than in other parts of the Middle East, violence against Christians still breaks out there. Last year, while this family participated in the Good Friday procession around their church, they were attacked by a knife-wielding mob. They have to remind themselves that they are here now, safe.

The community of Saint George continues to provide shelter to those escaping persecution, as the founders of the community once did. Arabic Christians are pouring out of the Middle East. The threat of martyrdom exists as a very recent experience within this community's midst.

When David and Debbi Elkouri enter the sanctuary, they are presented with bulletins and unlit candles with plastic cuplike wax catchers. They stop to reverence the icons in the narthex, crossing themselves and bending low, before proceeding to their places in the choir. As they wait for the service to begin, Debbi is thinking of the last arrangements for tomorrow's community party. (Every year, the Elkouris invite the entire parish over to their house after Easter Vespers.) David already has the barbecue fueled and ready to fire. Debbi hopes the catering crew will arrive as early as possible to set up the bar. Maybe they can help her with the tablecloths and field the dishes others will be contributing. The nervousness will get her out of bed even after such a late night.

She begins to feel as much as hear the gathering crowd around her, and beyond this, the church's repose. The moments just before a Divine Liturgy may be her favorite time at Saint George. Her scattered thoughts start falling into place and grow quiet.

Debbi once took her Orthodox upbringing for granted, even felt alienated from it in the midst of her non-Lebanese friends. How could she bring them to a church service that was half in Arabic? Then her children were born and David and she found themselves explaining what life was about and how to behave, while trying to forgive each other for the slights and inattentions and small betrayals that marriage entails. Saint George with his dragon quickly became not such a fanciful story. They were happy now to acknowledge that life's battle was beyond their own strength and to draw on God's.

The Orthros, or Matins, of Easter begins with Bishop Basil calling, "Blessed is our God, always, now and ever, and to the ages of ages."

Very late now, still at home and at least twenty minutes away, Theresa Wells struggles to dress her small children. Her five year-old, Tristan, has revived from being almost asleep in front of the television set. He is now wide awake and running around in his underwear. The pressure of dressing for church always causes him to go manic. He throws his body around so much that he'll sometimes knock his own head against the wall—which occasions tears and more tears and many protests against the proposed wardrobe. Theresa lets him have his way for the moment while trying to dress her three-year-old, Aidan, who has wombed himself in his blanket so snuggly that she feels guilty for tugging him into church clothes. The pre–Easter Vigil service of Matins at Saint George will go on forever, she knows. There's no real rush, although she wishes that for once she could show up early to a Divine Liturgy, her kids would behave, and she could stand and pray with others with no thoughts but God. What a luxury that would be!

How will she look? Half crazed, haunted, persecuted (falsely)? She's going to put some lipstick on tonight. She's going to spend five minutes doing her eyes, which she almost never does, if only Tristan will ... "Tristan! Please, Tristan, you are going to hurt yourself again!"

Theresa is a compactly built, athletic woman, with plenty of backbone, a nice natural spring to her dark hair, and cutting-torch eyes. She grew up in Grand Rapids, Michigan, where her father worked at a foundry. During her high school years and later on at Michigan State, she threw herself one long party, although she did manage a good degree in landscape architecture.

As a wild child in Grand Rapids she was evangelized by that city's many Reformed Christian teenagers.

"You mean I just say that I believe this stuff and then I'm in, like a club?" Theresa asked.

That was essentially it, yes.

She found the exclusiveness of this approach appalling.

She learned to sail on Lake Michigan and after college she headed for Key West, where she worked on charters for several years. On the verge of receiving her captain's license, she visited her parents in Grand Rapids and saw a young man in a bookstore. She came home and told her parents that she had found the man she was going to marry, although they hadn't exactly met yet.

Her future husband, whom I'll call Ben, turned out to be a graduate student in theology at conservative Calvin College. He was looking for ways to loosen up; she, something to believe in. They courted and married before resolving their searches.

They moved to Wichita, where Ben began working at Eighth Day Books. After several weeks, Warren Farha mentioned that they might visit Saint George.

Theresa's first attendance at Divine Liturgy struck her so powerfully that she still cannot describe all that she experienced. She understood almost nothing of the complicated liturgy. She does not remember the sermon. Yet, despite being virtually without a church background, she received an overwhelming impression of having arrived home.

She went to see Father Paul, somewhat truculently, asking that he prove the truth of Christianity. "Go ahead," she said, "I think I'm ready to listen now."

"I cannot prove it to you," he said. "The truth the church proclaims testifies to God's mystery, which is always greater than what the human mind can grasp."

Everyone in Grand Rapids had tried to prove it to her. Father Paul's approach opened up Christianity not as a club to be joined but as a reality to be entered into and lived.

She went home to read everything she could about Christianity and the Orthodox Church. She was soon confirmed in her new faith.

A couple of years later, though, the long-unresolved differences between Ben and Theresa resulted in a painful divorce. (Ben shares custody of the children and remains a loving parent.)

Theresa's thoughts ran along the lines of Teresa of Avila's, who, on the verge of drowning, prayed to God, "If you treat your friends this way, no wonder you have so few."

The people of Saint George rallied around Theresa, though. They helped her find a better job in a software business, where she now works with Father Paul's wife, Jeannie. They supplied her with baby-sitting and meal-preparation breaks. More than anything, their constant friendship gave her faith in a better future. She has never experienced any sense of condemnation, not for her wild past, not for her difficult present.

As Bishop Basil told me, "They say blood is thicker than water but not the waters of baptism. Not with these people."

Miraculously, once Aidan is dressed, Tristan appears with most of his clothes on, although his shirt is inside out and backward and his shoes are on the wrong feet. He's become pliable, though, and in another fifteen minutes all three are driving toward Saint George.

Although the rain has abated, the lightning-filled skies at midnight compel Bishop Basil to cancel the procession around the outside of the church. Nevertheless the opening invitation that precedes the procession is still offered by the bishop from the altar steps: "Come and receive the light from the Light that is never overtaken by night. Come glorify Christ, risen from the dead." The one lit candle of the bishop soon passes its light to others, spreading a sea of flickering lights through the darkened church.

The bishop then reads from Mark 16, describing how Mary Magdalene, Mary the mother of James, and Salome come to anoint Jesus' corpse. They wonder who will roll away the stone, but on arrival find the tomb open. An angel declares to them, "You seek Jesus of Nazareth who was crucified? He is risen! He is not here."

Then the cathedral bells ring and ring, and the choir sings the announcement: "Christ is risen from the dead, trampling down death by death, and upon those in the tombs bestowing life."

The bishop, wearing a bejeweled miter, crosses to the right in front of the iconostasis to his *cathedra*, his chair. He declares the good news, "Christ is risen!" and the people answer, "Indeed he is risen!"

"Christ is risen!" the bishop fairly shouts.

"Indeed he is risen!"

A divine pandemonium is breaking out, as the bells continue to toll, the choir sings, and the bishop and the people proclaim the resurrection.

The bishop calls out again in English, "Christ is risen!"

Then in Greek, *"Christos anesti!"*

And Arabic, *"Al Maseeh qam!"*

The people answer back, "Indeed he is risen!" *"Alithos anesti!"* *"Haqan qam!"* There is nothing restrained, sedate, or churchy about the bishop's exclamation—he's virtually cheerleading, and the people shout out in reply. "Christ is risen! Indeed he is risen!"

"Christos anesti!"

Acknowledgments

First, thanks to my publisher and editor, Eric Major, who embraced this project and guided it to completion. I benefited throughout the research and writing from his deft editorial direction. Then my ever-present gratitude to my literary agent, Claudia Cross, the best possible business partner and friend.

While the notes make clear specific references, three theological works have most informed my understanding of Jesus: N. T. Wright's *Jesus and the Victory of God,* Romano Guardini's *The Lord,* and Louis Bouyer's *The Church of God.* Interested readers should look to these sources for greater theological depth and insight.

This project found a guiding angel in Father Bernard Massicotte, Cam. O.S.B., of the New Camaldoli Hermitage in Big Sur. Father Bernard helped me contact Barbara Matthias and Father Peter Rookey, and paved the way for me to stay at San Gregorio, the Camaldolese monastery in Rome, where Father Guido Innocenzo Gargano graciously provided lodging in the guest house. (I will never forget singing the morning office in Italian with the monks of San Gregorio and their students from Tanzania!)

Father Bernard also invited me to New Camaldoli in Big Sur so that I could think through the theological issues entailed in this work. Father Isaiah Teichert, the guestmaster at the time, made space for me, even though the usual quarters had been booked months in advance, and took a lively and encouraging interest in this project. During my stay at New Camaldoli, Father Joseph Diemer talked with me about prayer, giving me the benefit of his many years as a contemplative. Father Andrew Colnagni of Incarnation Monastery in Berkeley made all of the above possible through inviting me to live at Incarnation during an earlier period of study. I owe more than I can say to Father Bernard and all his Camaldolese brothers.

Many people associated with the men and women and ministries profiled here helped make this book possible as well. They also made my research visits enjoyable and often great fun. I apologize in advance to those I may be forgetting—I received so much kindness along the way.

The South Carolina story would not have been possible without the cooperation of Harlan Drew, Libby Ballard, Jeff Scott, and the president of Transport For Christ, Scott Weidner.

For help with the Mexico City story, I wish to thank Brother Jim Hrechko, Alexandra Elkisch Sulkowski, the Servite friars of La Divina Providencia, and Juan Carlos Villalón, Miguel Fernandez Garza, and the many others who shared their experiences of healing.

The development of the story in Rome owes much to Father Dan Kassis, Monsignor Salvatore Cordileone, Monsignor Alexandro Cifres, Father Georges Cottier, O.P., and papal biographer George Weigel. Crucial assistance was also supplied by Dave Dillwood and two anonymous angels.

Thanks to Marcia Dickerson for assistance in Thailand. Thanks as well to the current program director at the New Life Center, Karen R. Smith, for an update on the center's work and their contact information.

Bob and Jerrie Castro made my stay in Santa Maria, California, a joy, and Jerrie guided me through the work done to date on Barbara Matthias.

Ebrahim and the late Marie Ghaffari put the resources of Iranian Christians International, Inc., at my disposal and were kind enough to comment on and correct errors in the original text. Marie passed away on Sunday, April 29, 2001, just as this work was being completed. Although I knew her very briefly, I saw what a coura-geous woman she was and how dedicated to helping the persecuted.

Jeff Taylor and Barbara Baker at Compass Direct also provided invaluable research help with the Iran story, and Paul Marshall pointed out its enduring significance. Anyone interested in a broader view of the persecuted church today should consult Paul Marshall's *Their Blood Cries Out* and Nina Shea's *In the Lion's Den*.

My thanks again to Warren and Chris Farha, Father Paul O'Callaghan, Father Anthony Scott, Bishop Basil Essey, and all those, especially Theresa Wells, who told me about their lives within the Saint George Orthodox Christian Cathedral community.

Bill and Emilie Griffin, Patricia Klein, Tim Stafford, and Luci Shaw read the manuscript and helped me with their editorial sug-gestions. It's one of life's greatest gifts to have such astute friends. Thanks as well to Elizabeth Walter for handling so many drafts via e-mail and FedEx and her always helpful spirit. Jane Carr supervised many final details with the manuscript.

To my mother and my late father, I owe the bedrock of what's here. My father always loved to tell stories about heroes of the faith.

Finally and always, my loving thanks and gratitude to my wife, Karen. She's my life.

Notes

Introduction

1. Paul Marshall, *Their Blood Cries Out* (Dallas: Word Publishing, 1997), 8.

2. Augustine, *De Natura et Gratia* 31, in *Catechism of the Catholic Church* (Liguori, Mo.: Liguori Publications: 1994), 484.

3. Thérèse of Lisieux, "Act of Offering," in *Story of a Soul*, trans. John Clarke (Washington, D.C.: ICS, 1981), 277, quoted in *Catechism*, 487.

1. South Carolina

1. Romano Guardini, *The Lord* (Washington, D.C.: Regnery Publishing, 1996); see 242–51.

2. N. T. Wright, *Jesus and the Victory of God*, vol. 2 of *Christian Origins and the Question of God* (Minneapolis: Fortress Press, 1996), 275–78.

3. Guardini, *The Lord*, 263.

2. In Mexico City

1. Holy cards usually have a saint's picture on them and a quotation from the saint or a Bible verse. They have traditionally been used as gifts and remembrances by priests and religious.

2. Heather Parsons, *Man of Miracles* (Dublin: Robert Andrew Press, 1994), 112.

3. On the California Coast

1. Augustine, *Confessions* 9. 10.

2. René Laurentin, *The Way of the Cross in Santa Maria* (Santa Barbara, Calif.: Queenship Publishing Company, 1993), 69.

3. Ibid., 46.

4. See the Resources section, for Father Culver's address.

5. N. T. Wright, *Jesus and the Victory of God,* 451–54.

4. In Thailand

1. "Trafficking in Children," NYTimes.com, May 4, 2001.

2. Kevin Bales, *Disposable People: New Slavery in the Global Economy* (Berkeley: University of California Press, 1999), quoted in *Christianity Today,* October 4, 1999, 26.

3. Patricia Green in Bangkok, Zothan Siami Ralte in northern Thailand, Jackie Pullinger in Hong Kong, Laura Lederer at the John F. Kennedy School of Government at Harvard, and Rich Cizik of the National Association of Evangelicals are prominent Christians in the fight against trafficking in women.

5. In Rome

1. *Tertio Millennio Adveniente* 33, 35.

2. The most comprehensive response to the Church's legacy of anti-Semitism is to be found in the church document *We Remember: The Shoah.* Despite *We Remember,* the specific confession of anti-Semitism on the Day of Pardon, and John Paul II's remarks during his visit to Israel in the spring of 2000, many within the Jewish community believe the church has not gone far enough. A particular sticking point is the role of Pope Pius XII during World War II. His defenders—among them, John Paul II—argue that he did not speak out more forthrightly against the Holocaust in order to save Jews through quiet diplomacy. But many Jewish leaders believe he should have done far more to alert the world to the facts of the Holocaust.

3. There were more serious diplomatic considerations as well, especially relations with the Islamic world. See Chapter 6.

4. The churchmen of the time never anticipated such destructive consequences, of course. After years of persecution, the embrace of Constantine appeared God-given. There were no models of what we know today as pluralism. All states had official religions and others were tolerated only insofar as they did not interfere with the established cult. What else was the church to do?

Because of the breakdown of the old Roman Empire during the Dark Ages, church officials assumed increasing temporal authority. They often ruled far more effectively and with greater justice than secular counterparts.

5. Stanislas F. Belch, *The Contribution of Poland to the Development of the Doctrine of International Law: Paulus Vladimiri, Decretorum Doctor, 1409–1432* (Veritas Foundation: London, 1964), 8.

6. Ibid., 8.

7. Ibid., 9.

8. Norman Houseley, "European Warfare c. 1200–1320," in *Medieval Warfare: A History*, ed. Maurice Keen (New York: Oxford University Press, 1999), 118.

9. This poem by the Austrian poet Peter Suchenwirt commemorates one such scene:

> *Women and children were taken captive;*
> *What a jolly medley could be seen:*
> *Many a woman could be seen,*
> *Two children tied to her body,*
> *One behind and one in front;*
> *On a horse without spurs*
> *Barefoot had they ridden here;*
> *The heathens were made to suffer:*
> *Many were captured and in every case,*
> *Were their hands tied together.*
> *They were led off, all tied up—*
> *Just like hunting dogs.*

See Guy Stair Sainty, "The Teutonic Order of Holy Mary in Jerusalem," http://www.chivalricorders.org/vatican/teutonic.htm.

10. Influenced by their Lithuanian neighbors, the Samogitians officially converted to Christianity in 1413, although pagan religious practice continued among the common people until the beginning of the seventeenth century.

11. George Weigel, *Witness to Hope* (New York: Harper Collins, 1999), 65.

12. Ibid., 72.

13. Ibid., 72.

14. Ibid., 163.

15. According to George Weigel (personal correspondence, October 2, 2000), Murray qualified the applicability of the American model: "He didn't imagine the American constitutional arrangement as a one-size-fits-all template for the universal Church."

16. This review by Wojtyla of Paulus Vladimiri's works in the midst of the council is a fiction—the product of historical guesswork and reconstruction. We do know that Archbishop Wojtyla regularly worked on a variety of writing projects during council sessions. We also know that Paulus Vladimiri could not have been too far from his mind, because on October 20, 1965, about a month after delivering his first intervention of that session, Wojtyla spoke over Vatican Radio to Poland, explaining the council's work on the "Declaration on Religious Liberty."

In this radio speech he used the example of Paulus Vladimiri in order to connect the council's work with Polish traditions of tolerance.

17. "Saevientibus" (1415), in *Works of Paul Wladmiri: A selection*, ed. Ludwik Ehrlich (Warsaw: Instytot Wydawniczy, Pax), 60–61, 9. (The statement on the Jews on page 182 is imported from p. 9 into the statement from pp. 60–61 for context and clarity. The quote on page 183 is taken from p. 9.)

18. George Hunston Williams, *The Mind of John Paul II* (New York: Seabury Press, 1981), 177.

19. Ibid., 177.

20. *Vatican Council II: The Conciliar and Post-Conciliar Documents*, ed. Austin Flannery, O.P. (Collegeville, Ind.: Liturgical Press), 1992, vol. 1, 800, 806–7.

21. Ibid., 809.

22. *Incarnationis Mysterium* 11.

23. Personal interview with Monsignor Alexandro Cifres, April 13, 2000.

6. In Iran

1. Paul Marshall, *The Blood Cries Out* (Dallas: Word Publishing, 1997), 4.

2. *Keyhan*, January 22, 1992, in *Final Report on the Situation of Human Rights in the Islamic Republic of Iran by the Special Representative of the Commission on Human Rights, Mr. Reynaldo Galindo Pohl, Pursuant to Commission Resolution 1992/67 of 4 March 1992,* 44.

3. Chris Hedges, "Iran Wages Fierce Campaign Against Its Christian Minority," *New York Times,* August 1, 1994, A1, A5.

4. "Islam Against the Church," report of the Task Force on Terrorism and Unconventional Warfare, House Republican Research Committee, Chairman Bill McCollum, January 19, 1994, 3.

5. Ibid., 7.

6. This was especially appropriate, of course, as the Vatican's "Fundamental Agreement" with Israel had raised Islamic-Christian tensions worldwide. The Vatican had always considered the Christian communities in the Middle East the cornerstone of its policy there—perhaps the major reason its recognition of Israel came so late.

7. "Iranian Pastor Missing, Feared Tortured or Dead," Press Release, Iranian Christians International, January 26, 1994, 2. See also Barbara Baker, "Condemned Pastor Mehdi Dibaj Released After 10 Years in Prison," *News Network International,* January 21, 1994, 4.

8. "Iran: Picking Up the Pieces," *News Network International,* July 26, 1994, 5.

9. Christian Solidarity International Report, February 2, 1994, 2.

10. As reported from Iranian Christians International, Inc., February 8, 1994.

11. "Body of Protestant Leader Mehdi Dibaj Found in Tehran," *News Network International,* July 5, 1994, 1.

12. "Profile: Symbol of Faith Under Fire: Mehdi Dibaj (1934–1994)," *News Network International,* July 26, 1994, 9.

13. Ibid.

14. "Government Denies New Crackdown on Christians," *News Network International,* July 26, 1994, 6. Some anonymous sources claim that the mole may have been the relative of a man whose name appeared on the list, while others portray the mole's leak as part of the terrorist campaign.

15. Iran: "Picking Up the Pieces," 5.

16. "Government Denies New Crackdown on Christians," 6.

17. These remarks comprise the gist of Dibaj's *Prison Experience* tape recorded in the final months of his life and available (in Farsi) from Iranian Christians International, Inc.

18. These remarks combine a report of Mikaelian's last sermon to Abe Ghaffari, as related in my personal interview with him on December 14, 2000, with the gist of a tape, *Our Identity in Christ* (in Farsi), available from Iranian Christians International.

19. "Government Denies News Crackdown on Christians," 4.

20. "Protests Mount over Religious Persecution in Iran," *News Network International,* July 6, 1994, 1–2.

21. "Government Denies New Crackdown on Christians," 5.

22. Names taken ironically from the first twelve imams of Islam.

23. "Khatami's Cautious Broom," *Economist,* February 1, 2001.

24. "Iranians Amazed Ministry Admits Slaying Dissidents," Associated Press, in *Turkish Daily News,* January 7, 1999, A1, A7.

25. "Iran's Killing Machine," *Economist,* December 7, 2001.

Resources

Those who would like to know more about the ministries depicted here and their parent organizations may contact the following.

South Carolina
Chaplain Ted Keller
P.O. Box 90003
Columbia, SC 29290
(803) 691-4444
www.chaplainted.org
e-mail: ted@chaplainted.org

Transport For Christ, International
P.O. Box 303
Denver, PA 17517-0303
(717) 721-9800
ministry@transportforchrist.org

North American Mission Board, SBC
4200 North Point Parkway
Apharetta, GA 30022-4176
(770) 410-6000

The California Coast

To pray with Barbara Matthias, write to
Father Richard Culver
Our Lady Queen of the World
3155 Winterbrook Drive
Baypoint, CA 94565

Rome

More information about the Day of Pardon may be found at the Vatican's Web
site: www.vatican.va/jubilee_2000/jubilevents/events_day_pardon_en.htm.

Thailand

Karen R. Smith, Program Director
New Life Center Foundation
P.O. Box 29, Chiang Mai, 50000
Thailand
Phone: (053) 263-010
Outside Thailand: (66-53) 263-010
Fax: (053) 263-011
e-mail: newlife@pobox.com
www.newlifethailand.org

International Ministries ABC-USA
P.O. Box 851
Valley Forge, PA 19482
(610) 768-2000
(800) ABC-3USA
jose.gonzalez@abc-usa.org

Mexico City

Father Peter Rookey, O.S.M.
International Compassion Ministry
Room 203
20180 Governors Highway
Olympia Fields, IL 60461-1067
(708) 748-6279
www.smcenter.org/requests.htm

Iran
Ebrahim Ghaffari
Iranian Christians International, Inc.
P.O. Box 25607
Colorado Springs, CO 80936
(719) 596-0010
ICIInc@compuserve.com
www.farsinet.com/ici/

Harold Fickett may be reached at hfickett@excite.com.